THE DUPLEX NATURE OF INDIGENEITY

THE DUPLEX NATURE OF INDIGENEITY

Navigating Identity in the Ahuehuepan Diaspora

FRANS J. SCHRYER

UNIVERSITY PRESS OF COLORADO
Denver

© 2025 by University Press of Colorado

Published by University Press of Colorado
1580 North Logan Street, Suite 660
PMB 39883
Denver, Colorado 80203-1942

All rights reserved

 The University Press of Colorado is a proud member of Association of University Presses.

The University Press of Colorado is a cooperative publishing enterprise supported, in part, by Adams State University, Colorado State University, Fort Lewis College, Metropolitan State University of Denver, University of Alaska Fairbanks, University of Colorado, University of Denver, University of Northern Colorado, University of Wyoming, Utah State University, and Western Colorado University.

ISBN: 978-1-64642-660-7 (hardcover)
ISBN: 978-1-64642-661-4 (paperback)
ISBN: 978-1-64642-662-1 (ebook)
https://doi.org/10.5876/9781646426621

Library of Congress Cataloging-in-Publication Data

Names: Schryer, Frans J., author.
Title: The duplex nature of indigeneity : navigating identity in the Ahuehuepan diaspora / Frans J. Schryer.
Description: Denver : University Press of Colorado, [2024] | Includes bibliographical references and index.
Identifiers: LCCN 2024012367 (print) | LCCN 2024012368 (ebook) | ISBN 9781646426607 (hardcover) | ISBN 9781646426614 (paperback) | ISBN 9781646426621 (ebook)
Subjects: LCSH: Indians of Mexico—Mexico—Ahuehuepan—Ethnic identity. | Indians of Mexico—United States—Ethnic identity. | Indians of Mexico—Mexico—Ahuehuepan—Migrations. | Indians of Mexico—Mexico—Ahuehuepan—Social conditions. | Foreign workers, Mexican—United States—Social conditions. | Noncitizens—United States—Social conditions. | Ethnology—Research—Mexico—Ahuehuepan. | Social mobility—Mexico—Ahuehuepan—Case studies. | Globalization—Mexico—Ahuehuepan—Case studies. | Transnationalism—Case studies. | Ahuehuepan (Mexico)—History. | Guerrero (Mexico : State)—History.
Classification: LCC F1286 .S37 2024 (print) | LCC F1286 (ebook) | DDC 972/.730046872—dc23/eng/20240403
LC record available at https://lccn.loc.gov/2024012367
LC ebook record available at https://lccn.loc.gov/2024012368

This book will be made open access within three years of publication thanks to Path to Open, a program developed in partnership between JSTOR, the American Council of Learned Societies (ACLS), University of Michigan Press, and The University of North Carolina Press to bring about equitable access and impact for the entire scholarly community, including authors, researchers, libraries, and university presses around the world. Learn more at https://about.jstor.org/path-to-open/.

This work is licensed under CC BY-NC-ND 4.0.

Contents

List of Figures and Tables — vii

Preface — ix

Introduction: Toward an Alternative Approach: Between Capricious Saints and the Almighty Dollar — 3

PART ONE: PLACES

1. *Mi Pueblo Bonito*: Memories and Impressions — 19
2. The Alto Balsas Region and Its Towns — 23

PART TWO: THE BROADER CONTEXT

3. Indigeneity, *Mestizaje*, Class, and Racism — 31
4. Mexican Migration — 45

PART THREE: THE HISTORY OF AHUEHUEPAN

5. Historical Background — 51

6. The Pueblo of Ahuehuepan (1923–1985) — 59

7. The Pueblo of Ahuehuepan (1985–2021) — 70

Part Four: Life in Ahuehuepan

8. Daily Life, Standards of Living, and Schooling — 79

9. Getting Ahead and Hardships — 87

10. Family Dynamics, Marriage, Names, and *Compadres* — 93

11. Kinship Clusters and *Riikos* — 102

12. Governance and the Civil-Religious Hierarchy — 109

13. Land Use and the Changing Landscape — 119

14. The Religious Field, Cosmology, and Folklore — 127

Part Five: Going beyond Ahuehuepan

15. Zooming Out to the Rest of Mexico — 137

16. Crossing the Border to Earn Dollars — 148

17. Children of Indigenous Migrants — 155

18. Transborder Families — 160

19. Patterns of Geographical and Social Mobility — 167

20. Different Perspectives on Transnationalism — 173

Conclusions and Final Remarks — 176
Appendix — 179
References — 183
Acknowledgments — 193
Index — 195

Figures and Tables

FIGURES

2.1. The Alto Balsas and surrounding area	24
2.2. Destination of migrants	27
10.1. Sibling exchange	98
11.1. Intermarriage among *riikos*	105
12.1. The town of Ahuehuepan—barrios and town features	115
13.1. Land boundaries and Corral Común	122

TABLES

11.1. Family clusters with *riiko* ancestors	107
19.1. Layers and social mobility over time	169

Preface

This book, the culmination of a long-term research project, examines how global changes are played out on both sides of the US-Mexico border. The center of attention is people connected to Ahuehuepan,[1] a town representative of a dozen indigenous communities in the state of Guerrero. The stories of its migrants, in many respects like those of other migrants, more closely reflect those of the 20 percent of Mexico's population known as Indígenas, including those in the Alto Balsas region.[2] I tried to strike the right balance in my study between broad coverage and in-depth treatment, using a combination of techniques.

The intended audience is scholars specializing in the international migration of indigenous people from Mexico and Central America. At the same time, my book is geared to researchers with a broader interest in theory and ethnographic methods. It should also be of relevance to graduate and upper-level undergraduate university students. In many respects its genre resembles that of a traditional monograph while incorporating such features of ethnographic fieldwork as multi-sited fieldwork. In other ways, this book deviates from other monographs.

Ethnographic research rarely goes as planned. In 2004 I started my fieldwork in the Alto Balsas on the topic of how people make a living, with side trips to the state capital. It soon dawned on me that many of the locked-up houses I saw do not belong to vendors who travel to other parts of Mexico but rather to people living

1 This town has the same name as another one belonging to the *municipio* of Iguala.
2 Research on the Alto Balsas includes García Ortega and Celestino (2015) and Kammler (2010).

in the US. Entire families do not come back for many years. I was confronted with this fact when I saw two boys eating cornflakes and speaking English. Their parents had just returned to Mexico so that their children could meet their grandparents. In February 2007, I combined a visit to Mexico with a side trip to Morelia, Michoacán, to interview Francisco Iglesias, a retired lawyer from San Juan Tetelcingo who spent much of his life in Mexico City, where he occupied important political posts. Later that spring, I made my first trip to Houston, Texas, to meet people from Mexico. During a leave in the fall of 2008, my time was divided between archival work, interviews with government officials, and more fieldwork. I met with other researchers. In March 2010, I spent time in both Houston and Guerrero. Only then, with a good sense of the broader context, including the failed attempt to build a hydroelectric dam in Telelcingo, did I decide to concentrate on the impact of globalization on people associated with Ahuehuepan.[3]

In this book, I acknowledge the voices of my research participants in two ways: through in-text quotations, with corresponding footnotes, and with excerpts of what people said, following subheadings for a person's name or a description of who they are. Both strategies give credit for their insights and to acknowledge that they are the source of information. The text is as close as possible to what people told me in their own words. Unfortunately, it is not possible to mention all the people with whom I interacted; nonetheless, what they told me, including questions to my answers, is the source of much of what I present.

THE AUTHOR'S BACKGROUND AND POSITIONALITY

My background and prior experience in Mexico shaped the way I conducted my research. I would not have been able to get information unless I could win people's trust, especially in the case of undocumented migrants. They would not have invited me to stay in their homes if I did not know their parents or other relatives in Mexico, with whom I got along well because I had lived in Mexico before. In speaking to professionals, I mentioned that I am related to the late professor of Roman law at the UNAM (National Autonomous University of Mexico), Guillermo Floris Margadant, who once gave classes to most of them. A well-known professor originally from the Netherlands, with whom I spoke in one of my earlier trips to Mexico, he happens to be my mother's cousin.

I got to know Mexico in the seventies as one of a group of students who boarded a bus in Toronto, Canada. It took us three days to reach Mexico City before heading

---

3 In an earlier research project using a case study in the state of Hidalgo, Mexico, I reinterpreted the Mexican Revolution (see Schryer 1980).

off to a remote part of the Huasteca, where we boarded with families. That is when I perfected my Spanish. The parents of the Mexican students who were our counterparts, some quite well-off, thought that it was not safe for us to go to remote rural areas, "to live with those people." Canadian and American students from our group based in Mexico City were lucky that they were not killed during the 1968 massacre of protesting students in Tlatelolco. Those experiences were a revelation. We started off as naive, misguided do-gooders who thought our presence would improve people's lives. We soon realized that would never be the case. The students who were radicalized became politically involved at home, while others later ended up working for NGOs or government agencies specializing in international development. I decided to go back to Mexico for several reasons.

The low cost of living in Mexico enabled me to do fieldwork as part of the graduate program at McGill University, Montreal. For my MA, I did a study of local-level politics in Pisaflores, Hidalgo, in 1972. A priest with whom I had many conversations told me he did not consider me to be an anthropologist, because I did not study "Indians." He suggested that I do research for my doctorate in nearby Huejutla, at that time rife with land invasions. My fieldwork in that predominantly indigenous region shaped my grasp of imperialism, political oppression, and the relationship between class and ethnicity. It is where I learned the Nahuatl that I needed to communicate. Little did I expect that that I would end up going back to Mexico, this time to Guerrero to examine a movement to cancel plans for the construction of a hydroelectric dam in the Alto Balsas, a region where people also speak Nahuatl. I soon learned that its inhabitants did not have a regional identity as I was led to believe. When I became aware that most people had migrated to the US, I changed the focus of my research to the impact of globalization on one of the towns, including its migrants. From the beginning, I took part in village activities, but it was not a good idea to ask about politics and other sensitive topics until people got to know me better.

In my research, I was interested in doing an in-depth examination of people from rural Mexico, in part because I am myself an immigrant, born and brought up in the Netherlands. My parents ended up living in a small town in rural Ontario, Canada, where I finished my elementary schooling. I was thus already acquainted with, and had experienced, the cultural assimilation and changing identities that are part of international migration. However, I had to take my positionality as an outsider into account, plus to think about the implications of my research in Mexico. In this book, the theories and methods used in my earlier studies were expanded, culminating in an approach that treats the perspective of an outside researcher and that of insiders as complementary (see the introduction).

ETHICS AND REPRESENTATION

My research presented ethical dilemmas. Research funders require investigators to give proposals to show how their work meets the guidelines for research on human subjects. Modeled on medical studies and psychological experiments, the protocol of asking people to sign consent forms is not well suited for open-ended questions, collaborative research, or archival work. An ethnographer is in a quandary; if we had to ask people to sign a consent form before talking to them, participant observation would be impossible (Hellman 2008, 233). Nevertheless, when doing interviews with schoolteachers and other professionals, I did obtain written consent. Most of the other people with whom I interacted received a document outlining the nature of my research and how they could contact me. I signed that and left a copy. I explained in Nahuatl to people who do not know Spanish who I am and what I do.

Another ethical issue was anonymity. Anthropologists typically use fictitious names for individual people, but they rarely disguise places. In contrast, historians handle names mentioned in the archives, as well as those of people still alive. I use a mixed strategy that strikes a balance between the anonymity expected in the academy and meeting the wishes of people who would like researchers to tell their stories. I present real names for all places and anyone who is no longer alive in 2022,[4] as well as for people who are in the public domain. I assume that the people I got to know would want to be acknowledged as the source of facts and insights. In that regard, I follow the example of the French researcher Aline Hémond (2003), who reveals the identity of artists of a town where she did her fieldwork. The American economist Tyler Cowan (2005) likewise uses the names of the people he interviewed in his book on Nahua artists. To keep what I write as genuine as possible, real names appear when presenting well-known facts about where people went and what occupation they had; yet I disguise the names of undocumented migrants, plus names supplied by other people, by assigning pseudonyms drawn from local surnames that disappeared decades ago. The names of those individuals are shown in italics.

INSTITUTIONAL AFFILIATION

To do research in Mexico, one must have an affiliation with an institution of higher learning. Prior to my first trip, I went to the Colegio de México for a letter of introduction. For a longer stay in 2008, I used a document from the Institute of Social Research (IIS) of Mexico's National University (UNAM). During the last stage

---

[4] I name most individuals by their paternal surname, unless more than one person has the same two surnames (paternal and maternal), in which case I add their maternal surname.

of my research in 2016, I set up a connection to BUAP (Benemérita Universidad Autónoma de Puebla). Their introductory letter made it possible to find documents in Iguala, but it did not help me in Xalitla, where I wanted to consult records about elementary school students in an office that had not been open for three months. It turns out that there were two district supervisors—one belonging to the ruling party, and another to a dissenting faction with its own union—but the one in charge gave me access.

SPELLING CONVENTIONS

In most of the literature, the word *Indian* is capitalized while mestizo is not. In this book, I capitalize both *Indian* and Mestizo as well as the Spanish words *Indígena(s)* whether referring to individual people or specific groups. I do not capitalize mestizo, *indigenous* and *indigeneity* (or its Spanish equivalent, *indigenismo*), or the term *indigenista*, when those words refer to communities or towns, government programs, or languages in general.

When it comes to the spelling of surnames that are shared by individuals who are not related, I use numbers (e.g., Villalba1 vs. Villalba2) to distinguish different unrelated families.

ORGANIZATION OF THE BOOK

This book, with five parts, consists of twenty chapters, not counting this preface, the introduction, a conclusion, and an appendix. The introduction outlines the theory and methods used in my case study as well as the logistics and trajectory of my research. I define four key terms used throughout the book (duplexity, field, layers, and clusters). One can visualize the organizational structure of the rest of the book in terms of a lens that zooms in and out to reveal how social forces at different times and at various levels shaped people's lives, going back and forth between Ahuehuepan and other locations.

Part 1 has two chapters. Chapter 1 gives a more detailed introduction to the town through impressions and memories, while chapter 2 is an overview of the Alto Balsas and its towns. Part 2 ("The Broader Context") includes a review of the relevant literature: chapter 3 presents an overview of indigeneity, racism, class, and *mestizaje*, and chapter 4 summarizes the research on Mexican migration. Part 3, with three chapters, covers the region's history going back to the arrival of people prior to the Spanish conquest. Part 4, which switches gears, consists of seven chapters that delve into diverse aspects of life, from daily routines to cosmology. Starting in part 5, with six chapters, I go beyond the local level to encompass the region, then the rest of the North American continent, including children of migrants on both sides of the border plus patterns of geographic and social mobility: first through multigenerational case studies (chapter 18), then the presentation of the findings of my census (chapter 19). The last chapter before the conclusion covers transnationalism. An appendix offers detailed information on the technical aspects of my census.

THE DUPLEX NATURE OF INDIGENEITY

Introduction

Toward an Alternative Approach

Between Capricious Saints and the Almighty Dollar

International migration and mass movements go back to before recorded history. The pace of people's relocation accelerated with the faster transport of goods, new forms of communication, and altered patterns of migration. A telling case is the outcome of the people's movement within the North American continent. Millions of migrants, many undocumented, have both Mexican- and American-born offspring, including the thousands of children born in the US whose parents have been deported or moved back voluntarily. These developments are changing the face of both countries. Mexico now has speakers of indigenous languages who are US citizens, while more Spanish than English is spoken in parts of the US. The diaspora of Mexico's population is altering identities and transforming traditional practices on both sides of the border.

The Duplex Nature of Indigeneity serves as a springboard for generalizing about transnationalism and the impact of globalization on the Alto Balsas region, focusing on Ahuehuepan and the places where its inhabitants have gone. Some people associated with that town speak English and Spanish but have not been to Mexico, while others, born in the US but who live in Mexico, speak Nahuatl and Spanish but know little about US history. Those born in Mexico include children of migrants who speak only Nahuatl. My book shows how the diaspora of the region's population, changes in livelihoods, new identities, and the transformation of worldview are interconnected. Continental economic integration has transformed people's lives.

A DUPLEXITY PROGRAM: AN ALTERNATIVE APPROACH

Writing this book involved rethinking my methodological framework, going beyond earlier analytical distinctions. To make sense of my research findings, I looked to various scholars for inspirations. In the 1970s, I drew on the neo-Marxist historicist school, well suited for analyzing a violent conflict over land in the Huasteca, a region known for the polarization between Spanish-speaking rancheros and a Nahuatl-speaking, landless population (Schryer 1990). I went beyond a Marxist approach in my research in the Alto Balsas, whose class and ethnic dynamics are quite different than the Huasteca; none of its towns experienced open class conflict. For my recent research on postwar Dutch immigrants in Canada (see Schryer 1998), I relied more on Pierre Bourdieu (1984, 1985, 1991), whose concepts of social field and cultural capital are particularly useful. Robert Murphy (1971) continues to be a source of inspiration; his central thesis, shaped by the insights of Georg Simmel, is that social life consists of an interplay of what people do, what they believe, and the reasons they give for their behavior.

While reading material not related to Mexico, I came across the work of Robert Nadeau and Menas Kafatos (2003) and of Karen Barad (2007), all of whom advocate the extension of the concept of complementarity, as defined by physicist Niels Bohr (1937), to other disciplines. Nadeau and Kafatos (2003) argue that Bohr's version of that concept overcomes Descartes's stark division between body and mind. Their position is consistent with a realist perspective such as that of Archer (1995), who sees the mental world and its products as emergent phenomena rooted in a material reality. Gaston Bachelard uses a similar approach, "applied rationalism" (see Tiles 1984, 29, 217). Anthropologists influenced by the writings of Bohr, as interpreted by Barad and others, talk about "quantum anthropology" (Kirby 2011; Trnka and Lorencová 2016) and "quantum ethnography" (Elizabeth Vann 1994–1995, 71, 80). I drew on all those scholars in developing a duplexity model in writing this book.

The term *duplexity*, used by Edward LiPuma in an article challenging Pierre Bourdieu's claim to have overcome the objective/subjective dichotomy (1993, 30), refers to communication between two points in both directions simultaneously. In an earlier article where I referred to broad-based groups as duplex entities (Schryer 2001), I proposed the term as a guide for research. My version of duplexity is a multi-method approach going beyond other holistic perspectives. It is not just a matter of triangulation, where qualitative methods enrich the findings from a quantitative study. Duplexity calls for the use of diverse techniques of data collection and conceptualizations, including the perspectives of Ahuehuepan's inhabitants and migrants, to give readers a fuller understanding of a social reality whose nature is complementary: "Complementarity entails two features: mutual exclusivity and mutual necessity. For two variables to be complementary they must be both simultaneously necessary and mutually exclusive" (Barad 2011, 444).

In physics, complementarity refers to disparate theoretical constructs and their images—particle versus wave, position versus momentum—to refer to the duality of matter at the subatomic level. A duplexity program, a social science equivalent of Bohr's notion of complementarity, is not an attempt to replicate physics, nor is it a form of reductionism. Rather, it examines social life through binary oppositions that capture the nature of diverse sides of people's lives.[1] In some ways, my approach resembles that of Jonathan Amith, who highlights the pointlessness of following one research trajectory while ignoring others; in pursuing any line of inquiry, one will, in the end, "face structures and issues that initially appeared to be located on the other side of seemingly impermeable boundaries" (2005, 26–27). In *The Möbius Strip*, which deals with the spatial dimensions of human interactions in Guerrero during the colonial era, Amith uses that trope as a way of mediating between agency and structural constraints although he is aware of the difficulty of using such oppositions. Yet, Amith avoids binary oppositions. My program also resembles that of Fox and Rivera-Salgado. Their method, which brings together vertical and horizontal integration, combining what Marx called infrastructure and superstructure, incorporates diverse dimensions of a multilevel process, from local to national (2004, 28); yet they too are leery of opposites associated with one-sided methodologies. Duplexity is different in its embrace of oppositions that could be labeled *dichotomies* or *dualisms*, such as microscopic/macroscopic, continuity/discontinuity, idealism/materialism, subjective/objective, animate/inanimate. However, I do not treat such dichotomies as separate domains.

The emic/etic distinction is particularly useful. The emic perspective is defined by the way the findings of researchers are endorsed; validation requires the assent or agreement of the people under study. However, that perspective still consists of the presentation of what people say based on questions designed by the researcher. An etic approach is confirmed if it is accepted by the research community. Many think that an etic approach is a better explanation, while other scholars would consider using only one method, whether emic or etic, to be problematic. A researcher using a strictly etic perspective might focus on how indigenous professionals occupy a higher-class position within the group to which they belong, and the extent to which they speak the same language as the people represented, ignoring or downplaying the fact that they are aware of such class differences. Scholars mainly using an emic perspective, who might say little about the class status of those professionals, would

---

[1] Not every binary opposition is complementary, such as when curators in the heritage field contrast indigenous traditions and modernity (see Shlossberg 2018).

focus on the subjective or ideational side of how indigenous professionals portray themselves in terms of their role in fighting for the interests of those whom they represent. My position is that using only one approach is not enough for tackling sociocultural phenomena. The combination of emic and etic research plus other contrasting perspectives is the only way of generating the inconsistent conclusions required to reveal the complementary nature of sociocultural life. That is the central, but not the sole, justification for using an alternate approach.

Going beyond Emic and Etic Perspectives

My duplexity approach goes beyond prior combinations of emic and etic perspectives by including voices that are tangential and even contrary to the perspectives of outsiders. For example, most people in Ahuehuepan believe that their economic success is the result of the support they receive from the saints, but only if one gives offerings to those saints. Margarita Gómez of Ahuehuepan was convinced that would also apply to me: "You need to pray to the saints and give them offerings. That is the only way your study will succeed."

Her perspective, like the belief of other people about what contributes to success, goes contrary to my own, yet I do not discount the role that belief plays as a source of people's motivation and perseverance. Another example of discrepancies in perspective between those of researchers and the people they study is the extent to which people in rural Mexico still grow maize, as shown in the first part of chapter 13.

A duplexity program requires researchers to treat all social groups in the same manner and as having the same worth. From the time of Franz Boas, a scholar who respected the perspectives of non-Western people, anthropologists have debunked the idea that some groups of people are inferior. Like Boas, they reject the concept of race while recognizing the continuation of racism; nevertheless, even well-meaning researchers have not gone far enough to shed paternalism and sexism, nor have we done enough in highlighting the colonialist nature of much of Western scholarship. Critical scholars have introduced the term *racialized groups* as a better, nonprejudicial, way of characterizing the people about whom they write. However, in so doing, they tend to paint all forms of discrimination (blatantly racist, subtle, or unrecognized) with one brushstroke, overlooking the progressive side of earlier research inspired by Boaz. In contrast, a duplexity approach acknowledges the positive contributions made by scholars with diverse perspectives even if, and sometimes precisely because, they are inconsistent.

A duplexity approach invalidates one-sided perspectives, whether they be scholarly, journalistic, or commonly held notions: a focus on the macro level while ignoring or downplaying the role of individual action, or vice versa; portrayals that either romanticize or examine the deficiencies of indigenous communities; and stark contrasts between indigenous and nonindigenous. Instead, it makes use of such binary opposites to explore the complementary nature of social life. By so doing, I destabilize, while iteratively cross-cutting, specific binaries the way this is done in quantum physics as pointed out by Barad (see Juelskjaer and Swennesen 2012, 3). Duplexity as a methodology recognizes that a traditional worldview that emphasizes cooperation and equality is not incompatible with a drive to get ahead, as demonstrated in chapters 13 and 14. The aim is to be comprehensive while avoiding overgeneralizations, distortions, and misrepresentations.

THE USE OF NEOLOGISM

For the rest of the book, I avoid using such terms as *culture, classes, groups*, and *institutions* that may conflate opposing perspectives or may be misunderstood. For example, the concept of culture, central to anthropology, does not have a single meaning. For some researchers, it signifies a way of life; for others culture refers to systems of meaning, to be distinguished from the ways people interact. Other scholars refer to groups as cultures. To minimize such ambiguities, I employ neologisms to refer to those interconnected components of social life. I do not dismiss but rather build on the insights of scholars who use culture or class as their key concepts. My alternative approach envisions social life as a multidimensional social space that consists of a set of complex interconnections among fields, layers, and clusters, each of which can be examined from a duplexity perspective.

Fields

Field, a term from Bourdieu, refers to what people do. Social fields can be thought of as games, each with its own reward structure and unwritten rules (Bourdieu and Wacquant 1992, 70, 98–99; Jenkins 1992, 70). Researchers using his approach examine fields in terms of the distribution of power (or capital) specific to each of them: economic (resources, including their corresponding currency), social capital (connections), and cultural capital (knowledge obtained in and outside the classroom) (Bourdieu 1985, 724–25). Tara Diana Wilson and Alba Gámez (2010) examined the level of success of beach vendors in terms of the relative distribution of those capitals. They found that family social capital (number of relatives) outweighs human capital (formal schooling and other forms of education and talents) as determinants of revenue (449).

People from Ahuehuepan operate in diverse fields, each with its own logic. In agriculture, a person must take part in various stages of cultivation for at least two years to know how to grow maize. It can be learned by most, although using a plow requires greater skill. Once learned, the main way of evaluating performance is by the amount of effort exerted, taking knowledge of plants and soil conditions into account. The main form of inequality is the ownership of more plow animals and the use of hired hands. In contrast, not everyone has the same aptitude to learn the skills needed for distinct phases of craft production, such as creating original designs versus filling in the outlines drawn by others. It takes years for an artisan to perfect the skills to sell their products or win awards. Moreover, social fields overlap, as when artisans create posters for a movement to oppose the building of a dam (see chapter 14), illustrating the connections between the craft industry and the political realm. At the same time, each field has its own dynamics; thus Henry Kammler treats religion as a field with more autonomy in his study of the entry of new denominations in towns close to Ahuehuepan (2010, 65).

Layers

Layers and layering refer to society's vertical divisions. One could talk about social stratification or hierarchy. Social layering is multifaceted, including economic, educational, and gender-based hierarchies. Economic layering has been examined from diverse perspectives, from Marx's class analysis to Kingsley Davis and Wilbert Moore's functionalist theory. Researchers whose primary focus is class in a Weberian or Marxist sense continue to distinguish between social classes and minorities, recognizing, yet downplaying, forms of inequality based on gender, sexual orientation, manual versus nonmanual labor, age, level of formal schooling, and phenotype. In today's world, ownership and the control of economic capital is the dominant source of social inequality, although we need to also look at other forms of layering, such as those based on the raw power of international drug gangs and the far-reaching control of the military and police complex in countries with weak states. Such diverse axes of layering often intersect, and their relative import and interconnections vary. To what extent they coincide or constitute parallel forms of social inequality is an empirical question (Knauft 1996, 321).

Mexico has long been layered along racial and ethnic lines; people who don't speak Spanish are known as *indios*, synonymous with being poor and ignorant; yet the standard of living and average income of indigenous people in the Alto Balsas is higher than those in nearby Spanish-speaking towns. Furthermore, social layering at the local level belies the romantic image of an indigenous community. Scholars and journalists alike portray such communities as homogenous and "classless." Yet despite an emphasis on unity and on how "everyone is poor," people in Ahuehuepan use the word *riiko* (a Spanish loan word) to categorize forty-eight individuals with a higher standard of living and more property. Their families lived in big houses with all the amenities. The *riikos*, also known as *ganaderos* (cattle ranchers), rented out mules and donkeys, up to twenty at a time. People with few resources worked as hired hands for those better-off families: *gañanes* used the teams of oxen of their employers to plow the land; *molenderas* were employed for the endless task of making tortillas. For every man a *riiko* hired for plowing, they needed a *molendera*, who toiled in the fields in addition to preparing food. A man once told me; "if a *riiko* used three *yuntas* (yokes) he would need three gañanes and three *molenderas*."

Given the duplex nature of social layering, the examination of its symbolic side is bound to generate findings different from an investigation of its material side. The representational dimension of different types of layering (each with its own status distinctions) versus the differences in power and access to resources are complementary. It does not make sense to talk about the relationships between these facets of layering in terms of reciprocal causation or as a lag effect; their intertwined dimensions are characterized by discrepancies and inconsistencies.

Clusters

Clusters are collections of people, including informal associations, cliques, and clubs. They are described in terms of how their members identify as well as how strangers label them. Their dynamics differ according to size, from small families to large aggregations recognized by common language, occupation, or citizenship. My definition of a cluster is "a set of individuals who share one or more common attributes, and who are directly or indirectly interconnected through social interaction" (Schryer 2001, 706). People belonging to a large cluster may share few attributes, although they are more likely to meet with one another than with members of other clusters. Alternatively, people who share traits may interact with only a handful of those who belong to the cluster with which they identify. Yet identity, social interaction, and common attributes are present in some combination.

Clusters are not mutually exclusive, yet even with overlapping memberships people may downplay one or more of their identities. At the same time, clusters are portrayed as mutually exclusive. The writing of academics may contribute as much to their existence as the pronouncements of its representatives. This is as true for those based on occupation as it is for clusters grounded in ethnicity or religion. The salience of any form of clustering is predicated on the success of downplaying alternate memberships. Moreover, their objective components are rarely consistent with their subjective constituents.

Each town in the Alto Balsas is associated with a cluster whose members identify with a geographical location. In turn there are subclusters such as Ahuehuepan's four neighborhoods, called barrios, each with its own name (chapter 12). One can further zoom in on households, including those with members in the US. The members of dispersed households concurrently belong to broad-based clusters such as Nahuas, Cristianos, Roman Catholics, Americans, and Jehovah's Witnesses. In the case of large clusters, people may share an image of how a typical member looks and acts that differs from the attributes detected by outsiders (external identity). An outside observer is more likely to detect internal diversity and discrepancies between a cluster's material and symbolic sides. In Mexico, *indígena* and mestizo, treated as mutually exclusive, are associated with the adoption or denial of one of those identities. Most people in the region are seen or see themselves as *Indígenas*, but others may argue that these same people may change their identities or use alternative ones, including that of Mestizo, depending on context and material interests.

Researchers sometimes merge subjective and objective data, examining clusters in terms of mutually reinforcing variables yet also recognizing that external and internal identities vary independently. Such diverse perspectives are bound to generate incompatible accounts. Cluster labels are ambiguous, as in the case of the term *artesanos* (people who make crafts). Most artisans are vendors who sell what they make plus what they buy. However, former artisans sometimes sell only what they buy. Wholesalers who sell crafts may have never learned to make what they sell. Yet they are still referred to as artesanos. Such ambiguity is as relevant for the perpetuation of clusters as it is for their transformation.

PUTTING IT ALL TOGETHER

Fields, layers, and clusters are interconnected. Field refers to the ways people conduct their lives and how they make a living, while layers define their socioeconomic positions within fields. Whether individuals occupy similar positions across fields varies. It is challenging to examine the connections between clusters and layers, particularly when that task is compounded by conceptual confusion; the terms *group* (cluster) and *class* (a form of layering) are often used interchangeably. Scholars employ the expression *groups and classes* or *ethnic groups and classes*, thereby conflating clusters and layers. Each is subject to extensive research, but the analysis of their interconnections is prone to simplification, especially when it comes to conflict. Marxists see conflict between ethnic or religious clusters as either an expression of, or an obstacle to, class struggles. Others hold that ethnic cleavage is more salient than economic class divisions. That position, articulated by Glazer and Moynihan (1975), has resulted in the bifurcation of the study of social economics versus other forms of layering. Pierre Bourdieu has a broader definition since he talks about "the social classes (but also the sex and age classes)" (1984, 483; 1991, 233). Yet layering is not synonymous with clustering. Mestizos and *Indígenas* are perceived as distinct classes (i.e., layers). However, they are often put into a single class (layer) when activists and scholars use the expression *Campesinos y Indígenas*.

The internalization of cluster labels makes it less likely that its members will become aware of discrepancies between objective and subjective dimensions. Even researchers may see a homology between them, especially in daily life, where most people tend to overlook internal diversity and inequality. A sense of homogeneity inherent in cultural cognition gets reinforced through symbols such as flags or clothing. Mobilization against social inequality within clusters is predicated on the emergence of alternate identities. Marx would say that a class-in-itself (an objective category) becomes a class-for-itself (people becoming aware of their subordination). Gerardo Otero (1999, chapter 1) uses the expression *political class formation*. I conceptualize political mobilization along class lines as the emergence of a new cluster associated with a new identity. However, successful mobilization that results in a reconfiguration of clusters may generate new forms of layering, as with the mobilization of Mayan-speaking people in Chiapas during the 1950s. The outcome was the emergence of a regional elite, including former teachers who became money lenders and wholesalers. This process of differentiation within a cluster was obfuscated when Mayan leaders converted a label based on ethnicity into a new hegemonic vision. Their appeals to communalism and solidarity echoed those of anthropologists working for a national institution (see Rus 1994).

Most clusters are associated with various fields. In Ahuehuepan, barrio clusters are relevant to what anthropologists call the cargo system, which can be considered a social field that is both religious and political. Kinship-based clusters, such as households or people connected through ties of *compadrazgo* (a form of fictitious kinship), are relevant to daily interactions in a variety of fields, including commerce and agriculture. Clusters and fields are interlinked, yet membership in a cluster may not have the same currency in each field. Broad-based clusters have a reputation and a position in society, but reputation and economic differentiation vary independently. The same cluster may be dominant in one field yet inferior or subordinate in another. Inhabitants of the Alto Balsas, known for its craft production, are seen as prosperous. Even poor artisans and beach vendors may be seen in that way by outsiders. The way they are perceived and experienced, as opposed to the distribution of material wealth within and between clusters, is complementary.

The duplexity approach provides readers with a better understanding of social transformations associated with globalization that involve the reconfiguration of clusters and layers that, in turn, are linked to the emergence of new fields and altered connections among existing fields. Some fields, particularly the craft industry and schooling, appeared during an earlier phase of globalization when Mexico had a different political system. The transformation of layering goes back even further to a time when globalization had a less dramatic and less direct impact at the local level, as we will see later.

In looking at social change, one cannot separate livelihoods and cosmology. A blend of pre-Hispanic precepts and Roman Catholicism enabled people to cope with the vagaries of subsistence farming subject to extreme heat and unpredictable rainfall (this is where the capricious saints come in). Their worldview, including the belief that maize plants are central to life, served people well when they supplemented growing corn with seasonal wage labor and craft production. Those ways of making a living no longer offer a secure income, resulting in a dependence on remittances[2] (see also Sandstrom and Sandstrom 2022b, 326). People who cultivate maize need those dollars (hence the "almighty dollar" referenced in the title of this introduction). In the Mixtec town of San Jeronimo, relatives in California subsidize the cost of working the land (Kearney 1996, 21). People brought up and raised in that town and in other parts of Mexico have been absorbed into a postindustrial world with new forms of inequality and different worldviews. While some look for novel ways of making sense of it all, most draw on long-standing rituals and beliefs for coping with life's tribulations.

DATA COLLECTION AND CREATING AN ETHNOHISTORICAL CENSUS

Research on how migration transforms people's lives requires longitudinal and multi-sited research. Rather than spending a year in one place, I spread my fieldwork over a decade. Conversations were the source of more than half of the information. Another source of data was social media, enabling me to contact more people who know me from photos and comments posted on Facebook. Further ethnographic work, interviews, a household survey, trips with guides, and weekly phone calls produced added data on social interactions at the global and local levels, all of which was incorporated into an ethnohistorical census, to which I make many references in this book. Surveys and census data are particularly worthwhile for the study of a community whose members are absent at different times. The examination of the connections between household traits, various forms of migration, and cultural responses to migration helped me to codify what people told me.

My census has information on anyone with a connection to Ahuehuepan, including 394 people not born there. While a quintessential quantitative technique, it incorporates what I learned from oral histories and written sources, including archives: the 2003 population census; the Registro Agrario (Office of Land Reform Records), with information on a 1969 agrarian census; records in the civil registry;

---

[2] Money sent by migrants to their home community or to relatives.

documents about schools in Xalitla and Iguala; and copies of applications for credit in the Rural Development Office in Tepecoacuilco.

My census distinguishes five periods or cohorts: prior to the outbreak of the Mexican Revolution (1830–1910); the Revolution and its aftermath (1911–1940); the Mexican Miracle and Craft Boom (1941–1975); a period of economic crisis (1976–1995); and the NAFTA (North American Free Trade Agreement) era (1996–2021). The number of people in each period, from 421 up to 3062, is consistent with expected population growth. In each case, I included anyone who died as a child, plus anyone else when they reached maturation, that is, fourteen, the earliest age for marriage. Those who lived beyond the end of each period do not appear in later cohorts; most will have finished their schooling or started working before the end of their assigned period. My census also includes information about those straddling two or more cohorts. The 3,341 people who make up half the population lived during one period. The rest straddled two periods (1,941 or 28.9%); three (1,336 or 20.2%); and four or more for those who lived to an old age (25 or 4%).

Not all traits apply to everyone; it does not make much sense to include ownership of vehicles before there were highways, just as growing maize does not apply to those who never lived in rural Mexico. I could have created separate data sets, but putting all data together supplied more flexibility, such as the possibility of combining cohorts. Comparisons of relationships between variables reveal long- and short-term trends (chapter 20). By the time I was ready to write up the results, I had the names of 6,715 people, 78 percent of whom were alive in 2021.

TRAJECTORY AND LOGISTICS OF RESEARCH

Fieldwork in Ahuehuepan started on Monday, June 23, 2003, the day I arrived at a house where a room was available. On my second day, I saw the arrival of policemen, who came to transfer a man to jail. I did not find out what led up to that incident until ten years later; it takes a long time to gain people's trust. Returning in the summer of 2004, I began linguistic work to improve my Nahuatl. It was a challenge to find people to help me with transcriptions. The men I employed soon quit; they did not need extra income since they earned enough money as vendors. Others had to fulfill public duties that did not leave enough time to work for an anthropologist. Finally, I found someone short of the cash he needed to buy more merchandise.

Apart from transcriptions, I created kinship diagrams and genealogies that I showed to people to check for accuracy. I also spent a lot of my time in the field doing participant-observation. A friend of the family with whom I stayed asked me to be a sponsor, as *padrino*, for his son's graduation; someone else suggested a suitable gift—a pair of pants and a shirt—that I bought in Iguala, a city where people from the region go to do their weekly shopping. Research grants do not cover such expenses, nor do they cover the costs of reciprocity that go with being a member of a community. The money I spent was more than what I could have afforded when I was a graduate student.

I lived with the same family for my first two stays in Ahuehuepan but found another place during my third trip, because there was not enough room when returning relatives came back. While living with another family, I spent a day helping them haul water and collect the dried stalks from an earlier harvest. I covered the costs related to my lodging; initially people did not want to accept payment, but I explained that my university reimburses me. I got to know other households, where I only visited, including that of Basilio Gómez, who became my *compadre*, a relationship explained toward the end of chapter 10.

Between the fall of 2006 and the spring of 2010, I got to know more people, including Toribio Pascual. I had heard about that teacher during my second trip and arranged to stay in his house in the fall of 2008. I attended the festivities associated with the San Lucas celebrations, in which I followed a procession, carrying a pumpkin. However, it was too soon to ask about politics; I waited until people volunteered to tell me what they knew. In March of 2010, while staying in the house of Genaro Aliano, I started my household survey of Ahuehuepan. Half the population does not live there year-round, not counting families that have not been back for decades, so it did not make any sense to go from door to door. I had almost given up on the idea of doing that survey, when someone showed me the forms filled in for the 2005 population census. The next source of information was other people, particularly the late Margarita Gómez Marcos, Basilio's sister. She and members of that family helped me in the compilation of a list of households. Margarita was my Nahuatl teacher and research assistant for over a decade.

On January 23, 2011, I flew directly to Mexico for my first stay in Ahuehuepan as my exclusive focus, staying in the house of Daniel Cardoso and Juana Salvador, whose name will appear often in this book. We had conversations about Mexico's system of education and health care. In October of that year, I made my first trip to the Sacramento area to meet people from Ahuehuepan. During my next trip to Mexico in January 2013, I lived with the Cardoso-Salvador family again, as I did for following trips. In 2014, what started off as a household survey was expanded into a census of every person, adding people with a connection to the town, including teachers. What seemed like an endless task continued for several years. During my third stay with the Cardoso-Salvador family, my research entered a new stage when I ventured into the town's territory. I took readings with a GPS tracker, employing guides. Between 2013 and 2017, ten men went with me, for a total of forty-one trips.

In the fall of 2013, I spent time in Los Angeles to visit a textile factory and went to San, where I interviewed a man from Ahuehuepan who used to be a craft vendor. I met other family members. They told me I was welcome to come back any time. When I took up their offer the following year, I became worried when I could not reach anyone, so I checked into a motel, not sure what to do. When I found someone at home the next day, I found out that the man who had earlier invited me to stay with them had not received my calls because his cell phone was not working. That incident illustrates that fieldwork involves setbacks. In between those visits, I spent three weeks in Ahuehuepan, where I attended a wedding. I did not go to Mexico in 2015, although I made my third visit to Houston on my way back from a trip to Ames, Iowa. In the winter of 2016, I twice went to Mexico, each time staying for close to a month. For a three-week stay in Ahuehuepan that fall I had to take an insecure political situation into account. This time, instead of staying overnight in Iguala, Juana and her husband came to pick me up at its bus terminal.

I was always on the lookout for documents. Initially I thought there were no written records in Ahuehuepan, yet during my fourth visit, in 2007, I found a notebook with the names of authorities and post holders going back to 1987. Not until 2016 did I gain access to documents related to one of their major festivals, but I was not able to find one of four notebooks. Nine months later, I got permission to look at it in the house of a man for whom I had created a family genealogy, illustrating the crucial role of reciprocity in anthropological fieldwork. For the rest of my stay, I went back and forth between Ahuehuepan, Xalitla, Tepecoacuilco, and Iguala to consult documents. December 8, 2016, was my last day in Mexico, although I continued to stay connected through social media and phone calls until the end of 2021.

Writing Field Notes

The common denominator in the ways I recorded what I learned was the writing of field notes, which has been covered in the literature (see Emerson, Fretz, and Shaw 2011; Sanjek 1999). I used a steno pad for interviews, transferring my handwritten notes to a laptop. The best time to do so was first thing in the morning while waiting for breakfast. To record people's stories, I used the first person, writing in the language used. Back in Canada, I continued typing notes on what I learned in each interview and what I remembered in retrospect. My text files, including transcriptions of tape recordings, were imported into NVivo, designed for handling qualitative data. During my trips with guides, I was constantly jotting down notes. My calculation of how much time I spent writing notes when in the field is 40 percent of the time I was awake.

Limitations

My research, spread out over a decade, lasted longer than earlier projects. Once I felt I had enough information, I stopped doing fieldwork and phone interviews. More could have been done. I missed the chance to talk to several older people during the early stages before they got sick and died. I would have liked to have gone to more places. I was unable to find out more about the first expansion of land owned in common as an *ejido* after the cancelation of a trip to Mexico City where more complete records related to the land reform are kept, nor did I have the extra time to interview more people from Tampico or other places where internal migrants live. In the US, I did not visit several cities, including Atlanta, Chicago, and Seattle, although I got in touch with at least one person in each place through Facebook. Towards the end of my last trip, I could not accept a last-minute invitation to go with someone to Huitzuco where records of the state school are kept.

Part One
Places

I

Mi Pueblo Bonito

Memories and Impressions

Dogs barking, people on donkeys,
    Intolerable heat, maize drying in the sun.
Ignacio paints amates by candlelight.
    Faustina, his mother, will sell them in Taxco.
Ignacio's father is going back to Houston,
    Leaving behind his precious Toyota.
"Won't be back for another five years!"
    Faustina's transplanting her chili plants.
Girls enter the plaza clustered together,
    Blue rebozos draping over shoulders.
The cadence of Nahuatl voices,
    Oblivious to the politician giving a speech in Spanish.
Men with cowboy hats smoking cheap cigarettes.
    They ignore a young man—drunk, lying on the ground.
Smoldering copal fills the church with fragrance.
    "When will the priest arrive?"
Using their camcorder, Ignacio's sisters
    Record the village festival.
Old women dancing, encircling a man (a dancing, angry bull),
    Ensnaring him with white ribbons.

At twilight, elaborate fireworks,
    Boys laughing, dodging a shower of cinders,
Their heads covered with cardboard sheets—
    Ear-splitting music from the village band.
El extranjero climbs the ladder to his room:
    Concrete blocks, a single bulb hanging from the ceiling—
Gazing through an open window
    Between work and reflection:
A couple ascending a dark path—
    Mountains, figures, blurring.

Frans J. Schryer

FIRST IMPRESSIONS

I saw Ahuehuepan for the first time in June 2002. A man from Xalitla who offered to introduce me to one of Ahuehuepan's former *comisarios* (commissars) suggested we catch a ride from a passing truck. It took more than half an hour as it wound its way along a pot-holed road. We got off in front of a house on the outskirts, but no one was home. I did not know that we could have reached the town's center on foot in less than twenty minutes; the man who came with me was afraid we would not be able to catch a ride back, so we climbed aboard a vehicle that was just leaving. During my second trip in the company of a teacher from Ahuelicán, I got to know the plaza where the church and school are found. I met more people as we looked for a family who could put me up. Two days later I arrived on my own. After three stays, I still did not have a good sense of the lay of the land, given the bewildering array of mountains and ravines.

First impressions were shaped by chance encounters. Visiting homes and going to the *cancha* (for playing basketball) and the graveyard (*campo santo*) resulted in a more rounded yet still incomplete picture. After more stays, my impressions became more varied. Favorable ones include the haunting sound of women singing; tasty posole served during fiestas; carefree children riding on donkeys; the smell of copal (a type of resin) and flowers; open discussions during meetings; the lush vegetation during the rainy season and pleasant temperatures from September until the end of January. I was impressed with the large houses with parabolic antennas. I did not like the loud music blaring from ghetto blasters; pigs eating human feces; and four months of stifling, unbearable heat. There is a dearth of bathroom facilities, so many people use the open air, which is inconvenient for older people and visitors. During the dry season, the landscape resembles a desert. Waste is dumped in ravines, and raw sewage spills into the streets. It was frustrating finding my way to people's houses. Streets, which turn into narrow paths ending up at the bottom of a ravine, or someone's cornfield halfway up a hillside, do not have signs. Is Ahuehuepan the best place in the world or a place with deficiencies? That question does not make sense, nor does the truth lie somewhere in between. Contrasting impressions are equally important.

Young people in the US, with warm memories of growing up and going to school, once helped their parents in the cornfields. They are familiar with the hillsides, gullies, and streams where they fetched water and transplanted chili plants. Each place has a name: Lamasapotitlan, Itsahchiampoyo, Tepeeyekapitstle. In casual conversations, I heard the phrase *mi pueblo bonito* (my beautiful town). I was told how visitors are welcome, that strangers are invited to eat during their annual fiesta. Hospitality is extended throughout the year. Living with one family, I noticed that men from a neighboring town were allowed to sleep in their house even though they were not their workers. Ahuehuepan is not the only town known for its generosity and lavish parties. People in Tepecoacuilco told me how much they appreciate the fiestas hosted by "the towns down by the river," with live music, rodeos (*jaripeos*), and fireworks. Their inhabitants have a sense of loyalty to their hometowns. Couples in the US go home for their wedding and to have their children baptized. When attending parties in Ahuehuepan, I was surrounded by young men asking me, "Do you like our town?" They could not understand why I had attended only one Quinto Viernes celebration. The cycle of fiestas is foremost in their minds; it is what they miss when away. Children of migrants have a romantic image of the place where their parents grew up. One boy told me he loved his first visit, that he could not wait to return. Alfonso made his first visit in 2014 to attend the wedding of a half-brother. When I asked what it was like to see his grandparents' village, he said, "it's like a dream." Only teenagers visiting during other times of the year complain that there is not enough to do.

Not everyone has happy memories. Older people, including those with cattle, told me how they once suffered hardships. They say that life has become better, how they are now happy and well-off. Young people might not agree. Rebecca, who used to come home while attending school, did not appreciate the sexist comments made about her when jogging. She disliked the attitudes of older men. Her feelings are not unlike those of her mother, who remembers the day she came home after completing her studies. Rather than being proud that his daughter was employed as a teacher, her father told her a woman's place is in the kitchen. One day a woman I had not met before made sarcastic comments during a shared taxi ride. As we drove into town, she said, "Look at my pueblo bonito, our good Catholic town. Men do not take mistresses, they do not have children out of wedlock, they never hit their wives." She vented to a stranger because she had recently discovered her husband had been unfaithful. However, her attitude is ambivalent; she liked aspects of living in Ahuehuepan, including close ties with her cousins and siblings.

Feelings of belonging differ for people brought up in neighboring towns. *Inocencio* never felt at home in Ahuehuepan even after he became one of its citizens:

> An outsider like me cannot give his opinion. When I was secretary in the *comisaría*, I said it would be safer to rent a bus to bring the authorities to a feast. But they did not take me seriously; instead, they transported people in an open cattle truck. Just outside of town it rolled down an embankment. It was a terrible accident.

Inocencio is not the first person to marry in. José Delgado from Ahuelicán, who decades earlier got access to his wife's land, did not feel excluded.

IMPRESSION OF OUTSIDERS AND COMPARISONS

An older man in Xalitla.

"I remember how people in Ahuehuepan used to be poor, wearing homespun cotton clothes. Today many families have big houses, even bigger than those in Xalitla. Before, they spoke only Nahuatl, but now they are more vigilant; they have woken up."

One cannot leave out the viewpoint of visitors with favorable impressions. A former school inspector commented on the town's progress when he came for a visit during the 1970s. He called Ahuehuepan "the new Taxco." Other outsiders were not as positive. A teacher who arrived in the early 1950s abandoned his post when no household was willing to provide him with meals. He thought Ahuehuepan was the most backward town he had ever seen. I have heard both positive and negative comments from doctors who have lived there. One man and his wife, both doctors, liked the town and its atmosphere.

People make invidious comparisons. Each person insists that his or her town is the best. They point out that only people from their own community use the correct form of Nahuatl; they poke fun of how other people talk. Ahuehuepan's inhabitants told me how they are united, in contrast to Ahuelicán and Tetelcingo, both rife with conflict over religion. In contrast, I heard negative views from people in other towns. Women from Ameyaltepec compared their clean streets with Ahuehuepan's roaming pigs. While staying in Ahuelicán, I was told that Ahuehuepan was full of thieves and murderers.

Contrasting impressions plus diverse and even contradictory views are expected from a duplexity perspective. However, what a researcher learns after only a few stays only scratches the surface. I first had to spend more time in the region.

2

The Alto Balsas Region and Its Towns

My study of migrants in various localities and circumstances must be placed within a broader context. Ahuehuepan is one of a dozen towns in the region whose name was coined during a movement in the 1990s to stop the building of a dam. Its political leaders used the name Consejo (advisory body) de Pueblos Nahuas del Alto Balsas (CPNAB), which academics employ as I do in this book.

Situated in the northern part of Guerrero, the region's climate is dry, with a rainy season starting in June and ending in September (see figure 2.1). It gets windy in February. Temperatures fluctuate between 32 and 38 degrees Celsius, rarely going below 21. The predominant flora are acacia shrubs, cactus, since cacti bear fruit and other fruit-bearing plants, including guamuchil and gourds (*guajes*). The leaves of the *yepakihle* tree, along with *wahkihle* and *kokokihle* (plants), are part of a daily diet when in season. Wild animals include coyotes, skunks, armadillos, iguanas, and snakes. Several of my guides brought along a slingshot to kill small birds such as pigeons and swallows. The vulture figures prominently in folktales. Domesticated plants consist of maize, beans, squash, and sesame seeds.

Researchers should examine each town on its own terms. The ones closest to Ahuehuepan are Xalitla, Ahuelicán, and Ameyaltepec. Others well known in the literature include San Juan Tetelcingo and San Agustín Oapan. By the end of three centuries of Spanish rule, all those towns had forms of land ownership and customs associated with the closed corporate peasant community (CCPC) and with its civil-religious hierarchy, terms coined by Eric Wolf (1957). This meant that in

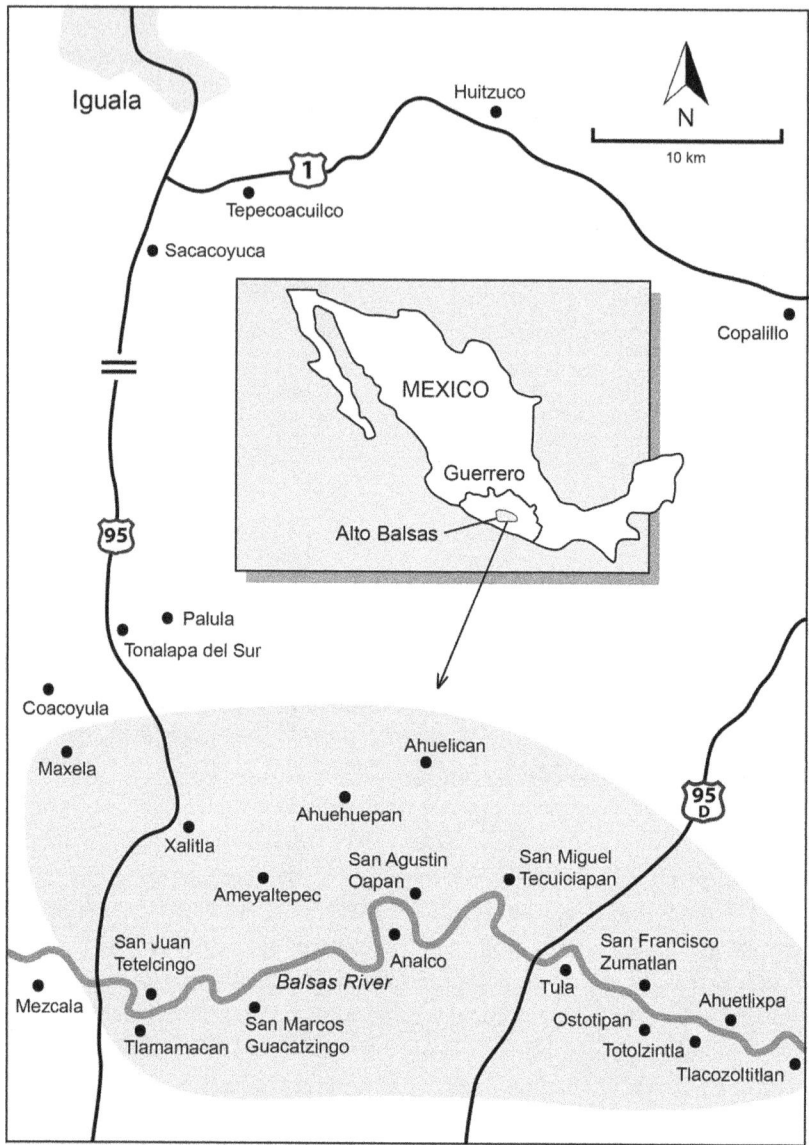

Figure 2.1. The Alto Balsas and surrounding area.

terms of their social structure the towns of the region differ from places in other parts of Mexico, as noted by a young man whose parents moved to another part of Mexico and then returned to Ahuehuepan when he was still going to school: "I had to learn the customs and traditions of Ahuehuepan, which were different from those in Puerto Penasco."

The Mexican Revolution, which ended in 1917, disrupted ways of life, while the expansion of a national state presented new challenges. During the last decade of the twentieth century, the region experienced change at a fast pace. Once farmers, almost half its population became workers in American cities. Those in Guerrero include teachers and health care workers, bricklayers, and former migrants, most of whom grow maize for subsistence. New forms of making a living and novel destinations have transformed patterns of social mobility, identities, and language use.

DIFFERENCES IN WEALTH AND LEVELS OF POLITICAL INFLUENCE

Research on the impact of globalization must take social inequality into account, as shown by the following quotations:

Esteban Gómez (in Ahuehuepan; born in 1937).
"The *riikos*, who once lived in adobe houses with tile roofs, owned cattle. One had five teams of oxen. They remunerated their *peones* with maize. Another *riiko* owned three houses. That man, who had more than twenty mules, owned land close to the river."

A teacher in Tepecoacuilco.
"Some craft vendors in Ameyaltepec have lots of money. I once saw one of them in his air-conditioned vehicle passing someone on a donkey. People with money, who think it is nothing to spend five thousand pesos for a trip to Taxco, consider me to be poor."

A woman who lives in Ahuehuepan (born in 1971).
"My friend married a man who made many trips as a vendor. He had a post in Cuernavaca, which is where they met. He became rich and owns a store in Tlaxcala. That man has three vehicles (*camionetas*), but he does not own a house in Ahuehuepan."

At the turn of the century, seven families in Ahuehuepan derived their income from profits made as wholesalers rather than from renting out plow animals. At that time no one needed to work in the US. In contrast, today most people, including the offspring of rich parents, derive their income from migrant work or as street vendors. This change in the way of earning money has enabled many to build bigger houses. Even members from less-well-off families earn more than rich people's descendants, who have not been able to keep, much less augment, their capital. Social inequality took other forms once young people became teachers or health workers; yet most other people have opted to emigrate.

In terms of political influence, some of those elected or appointed to government posts at the municipal level or higher can influence public affairs. The only one in Ahuehuepan able to do so to a limited extent is Toribio Pascual; he has close connections with authorities in Tepecoacuilco, the administrative center of the *municipio* where he occupied an administrative post. Cleotilde Alcaraz, also from Ahuehuepan, does not, even though he had a seat in the municipal *ayuntamiento* (town hall); he mostly spends his time in another part of Mexico. People who have occupied administrative positions at the state level consist of a half dozen men from Xalitla and someone from San Agustín Ostotipan. The only one who assumed influential posts at the federal level, including during the period of Luis Echeverría, is Francisco Iglesias Mendoza. He had much to say in what happened in his hometown of Tetelcinco after he went to Mexico City, although he did not openly support the movement to stop the construction of the dam in 1991.

AHUEHUEPAN AND ITS MIGRANTS

Ahuehuepan, whose church is surrounded by a plaza, is nestled between the Aakoontepeek mountain to the south and a hill to the north (Tlapitsahkotsiin). Footpaths take people into two ravines: Aawitstitlan ends up in Xalitla's terrain in the west; in the east, the Aapankoyootl ravine traverses that of Ahuelicán. North of the highway to Xalitla, a mule trail turns into a three-prong fork with side trails ending up at the top of Tepeeyekapitstle (1,080 meters above sea level) to the left or in Tepeeyewahle (1,100 meters above sea level) to the right. Alternatively, one can descend into a ravine to reach a tributary of the Tepecoacuilco River. A complex topography of mountains, depressions, and streams presents challenges during the rainy season.

Ahuehuepan is not just a geographical location with its own form of governance; it is an identity for a broad range of people, especially for those who have spent their entire lives there as did everyone prior to the middle of the twentieth century. The same applies to those going back and forth as vendors and by working in the service sector in the US; yet others who identify with Ahuehuepan to a lesser extent only know the town from brief visits or watching videos.

The exodus of the town's inhabitants first took the form of migration to other parts of Guerrero and to Morelos where they worked as day laborers and servants. During an economic boom following the Second World War, those migrants became artisans who painted amates (pictures on bark paper) and carved masks sold in Taxco, Acapulco, and Mexico City. They next ventured to more distant locations, first Tampico, then further to Puerto Peñasco, close to Arizona, where several were recruited to work as farmhands in the US. Starting in the 1970s, people

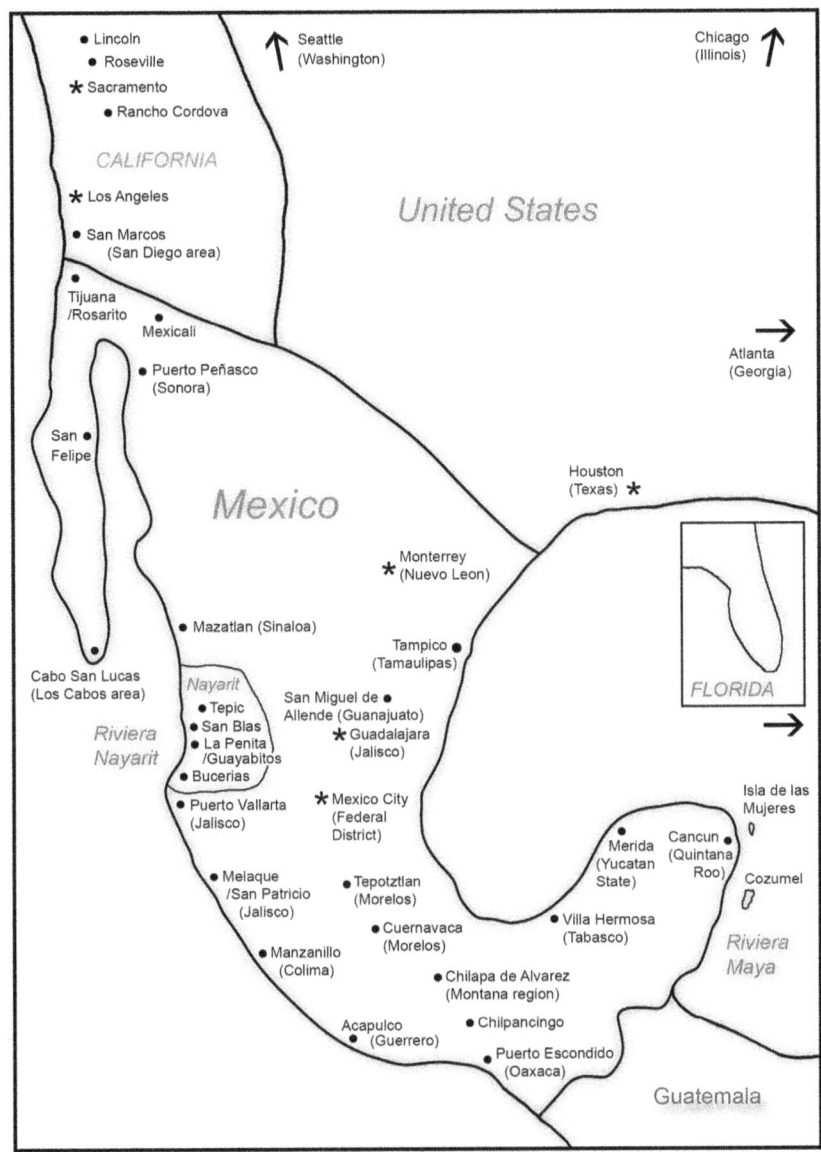

Figure 2.2. Destination of migrants.

crossed the border without documents to work in several cities. In towns such as Ahuelicán, they started leaving ten years earlier, while those in other towns much later, with Ahuehuepan in between. Not until the mid-1990s did people from the whole region start migrating en masse.

Emigration to other parts of Mexico and to the US each has its own dynamic. Internal migrants used to take their children home during holidays. Eventually they rarely returned for visits, yet those people made sure that the population census listed their children as members of their parents' hometowns. Their offspring learn Spanish in schools in other parts of Mexico. In contrast, most external migrants learned their Spanish by attending a school for Indigenous students (*escuela bilingue*). Like internal migrants, they now see themselves more as Mexicans. On the other hand, the identity of young people whose parents brought them to the US as toddlers is foremost that of being "American,"[1] although legally they are undocumented migrants who lack US citizenship. Like their US-born siblings, they speak to each other in English; in contrast, children whose parents took them to Mexico at an early age do not, nor are they acquainted with the history of the US. It is not uncommon for the child of a migrant studying in an elementary school in the US to have a nephew in Mexico speaking more Nahuatl than Spanish (see figure 2.2).

---

1 Technically Canadians and Latin Americans are also Americans.

Part Two
The Broader Context

3

Indigeneity, *Mestizaje*, Class, and Racism

Indigeneity refers to a form of identity as well as being a label for places and people. This chapter begins with the way that this and other terms are defined, followed by the connections between racism and *mestizaje*, including the history of the relationships between ethnicity and class. The next section covers the advent of Indigenous intellectuals plus the appearance of multiculturalism in Mexico. It ends with a discussion of contrasting perspectives on indigeneity of scholars doing research in rural Mexico.

DEFINITIONS AND THE BROADER CONTEXT

Indígena and the terms *indigenista* (indigenist) and *indigenismo* (indianism) have various connotations. The most common usage of the first term is as part of an opposition of *Indígena* versus Mestizo, where the latter refers to the Mexicans whose native language is Spanish, while the former is associated with people whose native language is usually an indigenous (Amerindian) one. Used by itself, *Indígena* is sometimes equated with *jornalero* (day laborer), a broader meaning that does not necessarily include language (see Knight 1990, 74). Negative connotations equate being *Indígena* with ignorance (Velasco Ortiz 2002, 253). The institution, PRONASOL, defines *Indígena* as "the poorest of the poor" (Martínez Novo 2006, chapters 2 and 3). Most academics and journalists who talk about "*campesinos* and *indígenas*" assume that Indígenas are poor and exploited. They reversed the emphasis when they started to write "*indígenas y campesinos*" to emphasize ethnicity more than class status. On the other hand, for indigenous politicians, the term is a source of pride. Marisol de la Cadena (2008, 345) points out that neither Indígena nor Mestizo is an "easily discernable entity," that in some situations individuals formerly classified as mestizos may claim an indigenous identity. Alan Knight (1990, 74) shows that, depending on the criteria, "an individual may seem to be Mestizo (or Ladino) to fellow-Indians but remains Indian in Mestizo eyes." Similarly, an "Indian" in El Salvador might pass for a Mestizo in Guatemala.

Few people would dispute that the people who speak Nahuatl at home are indigenous. It is not so easy to thus characterize their US-born offspring. Like most indigenous people in Mexico, they do not identify as Indígenas. While a handful of people in Ahuehuepan use that term to refer to themselves, they may not be aware of how it and related words are used in a broader context. They certainly do not refer to themselves as *indios*, which has pejorative meanings.[1] The expressions referring to indigenous people are not the same everywhere. Discourse around their meaning and the related notion of autochthony is complex and highly politicized (Pelican 2009, 52). The word has several meanings: being the original inhabitants of a specific region, close attachment to a territory, and the survival of customary institutions. Administrators further define indigeneity according to language when different from an official national one. A UN-commissioned report also includes identity. José Martínez Cobo adds that each country should produce its own definition (1986, 5); yet African governments argue that the term does not apply to them (Pelican 2009, 53). Even states with institutions for indigenous people do not employ it in the same way.

Francesca Merlan (2009, 305) distinguishes between criteria-based and relational definitions. The former focuses on specific traits, while the latter puts more emphasis on relations between indigenous groups and their "others," such as those who have settled, occupied, or colonized the area associated with them. Sidsel Saugestad (2004, 43) produced three criteria to characterize the structural position of an indigenous group: nondominance (i.e., being subordinate to a state over which it has no control), cultural distinctiveness (i.e., being different), and self-ascription. In his report on human rights and indigenous peoples, Rodolfo Stavenhagen (2007) proposed a wording close to the relational definition, with an emphasis on the importance of recognizing autonomy, self-management, and participation, but even that definition is open to criticism.

Some argue that the terms *indigeneity* and *indigenous* are unclear, especially when seen as synonymous with *tribal* (Béteille 1998). Adam Kuper (2003), whose

---

[1] At one point, they referred to themselves as *maasewaalmeh*, as do speakers in the Huasteca.

comments on the problematic nature of the concept of native people triggered off debate (see Pelican 2009, 53), argues that that it fosters the notion of essentialism. Alan Barnard (2006, 7–9) agrees that indigenousness is not a useful concept, that it is futile to find a single definition; yet he acknowledges that it can serve as a useful legal construct. Identification with an indigenous label may enable people to gain access to resources and recognition of their rights. Barnard proposes to refine the term "according to local requirements for the achievement of legitimate political goals" (7–9). The cancelation of the Tetelcingo dam in the Alto Balsas is an example of how an indigenous organization can achieve such goals. Its leaders appealed to the declarations of the UN on the rights of indigenous people. The involvement of their spokespeople in the international arena illustrates the emergence of a global form of indigeneity in the late 1960s (Brysk 2000, 26). The main home of that form of indigeneity, implying a commonality among people who, in their totality, are contrasted with "others," is within the UN system (Merlan 2009, 303).

The understanding of race and indigenous identity in the US is quite different from and clashes with what they mean in Mexico. Maria Eugenia Cotera and Maria Josefina Saldaña-Portillo (2015) point out that in the American context, Mexicans could not be Indians and Indians could not be Mexicans. Nor does the word Indian have the same meanings as the word *indio*. In her book about racialized violence against native, Mexican-origin peoples in the US-Mexico borderland, Saldana Portillo (2016, 8) argues that the two words are untranslatable and incommensurable, meaning different things in the respective contours of the US's and Mexico's "racial geography" (17–23). Christina Leza makes the same observation in her book on indigenous identities on the US-Mexico border (2019, 135–49). In the introduction to a special issue of *Cultural Studies*, Carmen Martínez Novo and Paval Shlossberg (2018) portray ongoing discrimination against indigenous people in terms of "lasting and resurgent racism." Other scholars, including Ana Alonso ([2007] 2020, 191), Inés Duran (2018, 6, 9), and Emiko Saldívar (2018, 483) also consider Latin America to have racial inequality (Martínez Novo 2006, 5).

Racism and Mestizaje

Racism is a tabooed subject in Mexico, where people prefer to call it discrimination, even when it is in part based on physical appearance and descent. Charles Wagley (1994) considers Mexico's racism to be part of a continuum, with an emphasis on cultural factors, especially language, as opposed to the form of racism that is part of a dichotomy (white versus non-white) based solely on ancestry. Paula López Caballero sees Mexican racism not so much as a cult to a superior race as a blind faith in the existence of an inferior race (2017, introduction). She points out the irony of the combination of an emphasis on a glorious Aztec past with the assumed inferiority of current indigenous people. Furthermore, one cannot overlook the racism directed against people from China (Knight 1990, 116–18), recent refugees from Central America, or prejudice against people of African descent (Martínez Novo and Shlossberg 2018, 355).

A discussion about racism must include *mestizaje*. A rough equivalent is "racial mixture," although the Spanish word also refers to the result of miscegenation within indigenous groups (Poole 2020, 221). In Mexico many people consider Mestizos to be better than *Indígenas* due to racism against indigenous peoples. José Vasconcelos Calderón (1948) coined the term "cosmic race" to justify the adoption of mestizo as a group identity. He was in favor of the assimilation of indigenous people. According to Poole (2020, 189–90) such a "we-they" position is reflected in spaces like museums, whose exhibitions manifest an implicit contrast between the ethnoracial category of Mestizos portrayed as the nation's center versus *Indígenas*, whose social position is relegated to the periphery. Maylei Blackwell, who uses the expression "racial discourse of *mestizaje*" (2012, 71), illustrates ethnic-racial inequality by showing that 30 percent of Mixtec and Triqui workers earn less than their mestizo counterparts. She refers to the "entrenched anti-Indian hatred enacted by Mestizos and Ladinos" (Blackwell 2017, 127).

The Mexican state, whose vision of *mestizaje* is a single nation without racist views, condemns discrimination. This position presents a dilemma. Deborah Poole's insights can shed light on the problematic nature of that vision, whose aim is to achieve a single national identity based on the eradication of indigenous identities while at the same time celebrating the greatness of an indigenous nation in the past: "The hegemonic status of *mestizaje* as a political project depends on the inherent impossibility of *mestizaje* given that it consists of a process of racial and cultural mixing that can never be brought to conclusion" (Poole 2020, 203).

The Relationship between Ethnicity and Social Inequality

Discussion of racism and *mestizaje* must take class dynamics into account. While native people are more likely to be poor farmers, the relationship between ethnicity and class is not straightforward. Indigenous communities may have significant inequalities. Moreover, the average income and quality of housing of indigenous people in some regions might be higher than those of other regions. For example, most households in Ahuehuepan are better off than those in a completely Spanish-speaking town in the state of Hidalgo, where I did fieldwork in the 1970s. People in both places started working in the US in the 1980s, but migrants in Pisaflores do not have the large houses of their counterparts in Guerrero.

There can be significant inequalities among native people. A minority of indigenous men (*Hñähñu*, once labeled as Otomi) in the valley of Mezquital in Hidalgo are wealthy caciques (strong bosses) who dominate the rest of that region's population as shown by Knight (1990, 95, 137). Such forms of intra-ethnic inequality influence people's identities. In my study of the Huejutla region in Hidalgo, I found out that most outsiders portrayed Nahua caciques as mestizos, thus equating class and ethnicity. At the same time, landless Spanish-speaking peasants presented themselves as indigenous, at least to outsiders, to obtain political support (Schryer 1990).

COMPARISONS

Given the diversity of regions whose inhabitants are predominantly Mestizos versus Indígenas, it is difficult to compare regions in terms of the levels and types of inequality between ethnic clusters. Based on my experience of living in three regions, I know that Huejutla, Hidalgo, has blatant inter-ethnic inequalities and social conflict, while the region of Iguala, Guerrero, has less. It would not make much sense to include the Sierra de Jacala, to which Pisaflores belongs, in such a comparison, because that region has few indigenous communities. It is even more difficult to do a comparison of cultural differences, apart from language use and cluster identity, since mestizo and indigenous rural communities share religious beliefs and practices, forms of governance, and customs.

Scholars must consider any cultural comparisons and the dynamics of intra- and inter-ethnic inequalities from a broader historical perspective.

THE HISTORY OF ETHNICITY, RACE, AND CLASS IN MEXICO

At the time of the conquest, the dominant pre-Hispanic state was the Aztec empire. Its central city, Tenochtitlan (today Mexico City), surpassed Madrid and other European urban centers in size and amenities. The Aztecs had earlier taken over what remained the Mayans, although they did not control the Tarascan Empire, whose Purépecha rulers had dominion over another multiethnic Mexican region. Given the superior technology (guns and horses) of the Spaniards, an early alliance with the Aztecs' enemies, plus the decimation of people exposed to new diseases, the conquerors soon had almost total control. Miscegenation resulted in a mixed population. Initially the Spanish imposed a scheme of racial categories (*sistema de castas*) consisting whites (Spaniards), mestizos, and "indios." That system, designed to control all aspects of people's lives, was not workable. A simpler form of caste inequalities continued until its abolition. The main *castas* were whites (Spanish), mestizos, and *indios*. People labeled as *negros* and *mulatos* (with some Spanish blood) occupied the lowest position.

The recognition of rights to land for indigenous towns (*repúblicas de indios*) gave rise to two forms of colonial control, with Mestizos subject to the *república de españoles* (Cotera and Saldaña-Portillo 2015, 555). The system as whole "was necessarily fluid, with families changing *casta* from one generation to another (556)." The system, which started to erode during the eighteenth century, continued to exist, if not legally, for much longer (Knight 1990, 72, 78). It does make sense to talk about a gradual transition from a colonial model based on a casta system to a class-based society. The two coexisted, with the balance gradually tipping from caste to class, a slow process far from complete at the end of the Revolution. Class counted for more, but ethnic status was far from irrelevant (Knight 1990, 31). New forms of discrimination continue up to today. Roger Bartra (1974, 479) argues that even modern capitalist entrepreneurs "see Indians more as an inferior caste than as a class." At the same time, a new category (*indígena*) appeared.

Mestizos versus *Indígenas*

The term *mestizo* has a long history, going back to when it was one of the colonial castas. Their numbers grew exponentially over time, with new implications for that term. As the offspring of Spaniards and Indigenous persons, they originally had "fewer rights and privileges than both Spanish and Indigenous people." Nevertheless, their racial mixture was valued and documented as an example of Christian unity (Cotera and Saldaña-Portillo 2015, 555). As the number of acculturated native Americans grew and with ongoing miscegenation during three centuries of colonial rule, academics and functionaries alike started using the term *mestizo* to refer to anyone of mixed descent, even if the Spanish part was minimal. Estimates of percentages from diverse sources and for various times vary greatly; the most conservative figures would be anywhere from 20 to 25 percent for the period after Independence, when creoles (people descended from Spaniards) constituted anywhere from 8 to 20 percent after Independence. Creoles whose lifestyle and thinking were primarily European (including French), and who owned the plantations and mines, looked down upon the rest of the population, whom they saw as a single "uncivilized" mass.

This situation changed at the time of the Mexican Revolution, when those in power started to consider Mestizos as the true Mexicans, based on the ideas expounded by Gamio and Vasconcelos, writers influenced by Andrés Molina Enríquez (Knight 1990, 84–85). In *Los grandes problemas nacionales*, Molina Enríquez (2016) argued that the Mestizos, whom he called "Indo-Mestizos," were the most capable of bringing about the modernization of the country. Some

Mexican scholars referred to them as the "bronze race." In 1930 the Mexican census no longer included the category *mestizo*—only *indígena*. Yet people throughout Mexico started to use the group label *mestizo*. Anthropologists like Robert Redfield (1930) and Eyler Simpson (1937), whose case studies date from the 1920s and early 1930s, used the label *folk people*. The people they described were bilingual and more integrated into the national economy and politics, yet authors classified them as "Indian" (in terms of dress, religion, "cargos," and *compadrazgo*) (Knight 1990, 98). By 1970 they saw them as Mestizos, although most people living in rural areas still did not see themselves in that way. Nor did the 8 percent of people classified as "Indians," using a narrow definition (Knight 1990, 98). By 2008 Mestizos probably constituted well over 50 percent. According to various sources, the estimates of their numbers by 2020 vary from 60 to 80 percent. At that time, outsiders considered people living in the Alto Balsas to be *Indígenas*.

Use of the Word *Indígena*

A woman from Oapan living in California.
"My grandchildren don't want to talk *Mexicano*. They say it is the language of Indígenas, that they are not Indígenas, that they are Americans."[2]

A man born in Ahuehuepan, living in California.
"People who live here are not aware that there are Indígenas in their midst. My neighbor told his children that people who speak Nahuatl were killed a long time ago and that Indígenas live far away. I had to prove there are Indígenas in Sacramento who speak Nahuatl and that I am one of them."

An anthropologist born in Xalitla.
"People from Maxela are Indígenas to some extent. That town is part of the Alto Balsas. Its agriculture and system of governance are the same as those of Nahuatl-speaking towns."

A young man born in Iguala, living in Mexico City.
"México is racist, especially toward Indígenas; some people don't want to sit in a bus beside an Indígena."

A government worker from Xalitla working in the state capital.
"My parents did not want to speak to us in Nahuatl. They no longer considered themselves to be Indígenas, nor did people in nearby Tonalapa del Sur, where people once spoke Nahuatl."

---

2 All quotations in this section are my translations of what people told me in Spanish.

A young lawyer of indigenous descent in the Mezquital Valley (cited in Bartra 1974, 468).
"Discrimination? No, not here—not here! The Mestizo treats the Indígena well—besides, the latter no longer puts up with it."

Scholars and government officials used *indígena* and words such as *indianidad* before the people to which they refer started to identify with those labels (see Fox and Salgado 2004, 12). Before that, most people in remote regions identified with their home communities and such terms as *masewaahle* (country people) that do not correspond to the categories of outsiders. Such lack of correspondence is a sign of the complementary nature of this phenomenon. With the expansion of government programs and increasing contact with anthropologists, people throughout Mexico also started to refer to themselves as *Indígenas* and with more specific labels such as *Nahuas* and *Mixtecs*. Scholars, including academics of indigenous descent, espoused the closely related term *indigeneity*. Those designations go back to the Mexican Revolution. That decade-long event coincided with the presence of the International School of American Archaeology and Ethnology in Mexico City, founded by Boas (García Valencia 1995, 223). It was the precursor of the School of Anthropology and History associated with the National Institute of Anthropology and History (INAH), which dates to 1937. Their founders coined the label *Indígenas* to refer to the descendants of Mexico's original inhabitants. Mexican painters and photographers also adopted the term *indigeneity* (indianidad), including those living in Milpa Alta, where some people (about 5 percent) speak Nahuatl (see Escalona 2019).

Milpa Alta is home to many artists and people working in the government bureaucracy. It was the home of Isabel Ramírez Castañeda, the first woman archeologist of Mexico, who died in 1943. Luz Jiménez González, a linguistic informant who served as a model for painters and photographers (Escalona 2019, 826), also lived there. The professionals helped to run an institution with programs to help and to integrate Indígenas into a single, Spanish-speaking nation. People born in Milpa Alta, with a degree of autonomy, took advantage of those programs as a way of protecting their access to communally owned land. They found it helpful to emphasize their Aztec ancestry. People in literary, university, and artistic circles now consider that region to be an indigenous enclave and even a "nucleus of resistance" (López Caballero 2017, introduction). At the same time, indigenous people from other parts of Mexico who moved to Milpa Alta presented competing claims to public resources such as access to swimming pools and eligibility for government jobs. Ironically, instead of continuing to emphasize their indigenous status, members of long-standing, well-established families in Milpa Alta adopted a new identity as *originarios* (the original inhabitants) as part of a new distinction of *originario* versus *indígena* (López Caballero 2010). It was a way of dismissing the demands of those indigenous newcomers who were eligible for the support of federal programs. Paula López Caballero (2017) portrayed these diverse sides of indigeneity, taken in their totality, as a "regimen of otherness (*alternidad*)." I consider such diversity as a form of complementarity.

The diversity of experiences and identities of indigenous people has various manifestations, as in the case of Mezcala, a town on the shores of Lake Chapala, Jalisco. Its inhabitants lost their language (Cora) a long time ago; nevertheless, they started to identify as Coras as well as *Indígenas* even though the state government does not recognize them as such. Once mainly dependent on fishing and agriculture, its inhabitants now work in assembly plants (*maquiladoras*) in nearby Guadalajara, and in a developing tourism sector. Mezcala also has migrants in California, with clubs in both countries. In her study, Inés Duran Matute examines the complex dynamics of ethnic identity retention in that community. She concludes that "identities should be understood as ambiguous, contradictory, convoluted, dynamic, in permanent tension between fluidity and fixedness, between past and present, location and dispersion" (Duran Matute 2018, 196). Christina Leza (2019, 149, chapter 6) also noted such complexity in the case of the identity construction and representation for US-Mexico border peoples.

It took a long time for a pan–Native American identity to appear. While Native Americans took part in the War of Independence and the Mexican Revolution, the primary loyalty of indigenous peoples at that time was to their own communities, to what had been *república de indios* (see also Knight 1990, 75). A large number supported the cause of agrarian reform and took part in struggles for land in the early twentieth century, not as *Indígenas* but as *campesinos* and *agraristas*. Even the indigenista Gamio had to concede that "it is not the Indians who made the Revolution; nevertheless, its deepest roots grew and continue to grow in the Indian race" (cited in Knight 1990, 77). With some exceptions, the identity of indígena was imposed from outside.

INDIGENISMO

Until recently Mexico's government had an institution, the National Indigenist Institute (INI) with programs that oversaw economic development, education, and land reform. Its philosophy, *indigenismo*, has a precedent under the emperor Maximilian of Austria, who saw himself as the "protector of the Indians." He wanted to undo the liberal land reforms designed to dismantle the communal lands of indigenous communities. After the Revolution, Mexico adopted a different kind of indigenismo as a way of integrating its indigenous population by "mestizo-izing" them (Knight 1990, 86). Manuel Gamio (1883–1960), intellectual leader of a program of indigenismo that spread to other Latin American countries, made it clear that Indigenous people have the same aptitudes as whites and Mestizos, but that their poverty and subordinate position holds them back. However, his attitude was paternalistic (Reynoso 2013, 350–51). Gamio held that Indígenas represent a lower stage of cultural evolution (Friedlander [1975] 2006, 195; Negrín Da Silva 2012, 145). As minister of public education in the Secretariat of Public Education (SEP) he set up the first national anthropological institutions in the country and was an advocate for the social causes of the Mexican Indigenous populations (Gutiérrez Chong 2015) as part of an effort to eradicate illiteracy and create national citizens (Marak 2009). Indigenismo also took the form of mural art as a way of promoting Mexican nationalism (Brading 1988, 87). Exhibitions of "Indian" arts, crafts, dance, and music became important components in the creation of a sense of nationhood (Shlossberg 2018, 428). However, the Mexican state envisioned the disappearance of both indigenous languages and a separate identity. Its elite was able to do so without repercussions because, unlike in Andean countries of South America, there was no threat of a caste war. The participation of the indigenous population in the Revolution and in agrarian struggles was anonymous since they did not struggle in the name of indigenous people. It became manageable to deal with Mexico's "Indian problem" because the number of indigenous people was declining (Knight 1990, 28).

From the start, indigenismo's programs were transformed, each phase associated with the involvement of anthropologists and other scholars. Moisés Sáenz (1888–1941), an educator and student of John Dewey in the US, started reforms with an emphasis on rural areas. However, while responsible for expanding schooling, he was not as successful in incorporating elements of indigenous culture in the process of turning indigenous people into members of a national society (Palacios 1988). Indigenismo did not change much under Lázaro Cárdenas, Mexico's president from 1934 to 1940, although his programs had an impact on indigenous communities. He set up the Department of Indigenous Affairs (DAI), replaced by the National Indigenist Institute (INI) in 1948. The number of schools increased; students received instruction from teachers who could communicate with them in their own language (Dietz 2009). The programs under his direction were run by coordinating centers such as the Tzeltal-Tzoltzil Center in Chiapas. However, when giving a speech at an international conference in 1940, Cárdenas said that the goal of his programs was to "Mexicanize the Indian" (Riding 1984, 202). The fifth such center was set up in 1963 in Tlapa de Comonfort, Guerrero. No such center was set up in the Alto Balsas, although its population received benefits from its programs.

Luís Echeverría's presidency (1970 to 1976) included a revival of agrarianism (Schryer 1990, 194). His regime also oversaw the expansion of coordinating centers

(CCI), starting with the Plan Huicot for the Wixárika (Huichol) region responsible for land reform, bilingual education, and support for agriculture. Such programs continued during Mexico's second oil boom. During that phase of indigenismo, its programs were not immune to criticism. In *México Profundo* ([1996] 1987) Guillermo Bonfil Batalla criticized the notion of a unified mestizo society. Instead, he called for a vision of a pluricultural state. A proponent of self-determination, he was one of the anthropologists who signed the Barbados Declaration at a symposium in 1971. His ideas promoted a participatory form of indigenismo (Muñoz 2010). However, they held contradictory positions on how to deal with indigenous people on their own terms, recognizing the vital importance of their cultures yet turning them into Mexicans to create a modern nation with a homogenous culture (Overmeyer-Velásquez 2010, 63). The next anthropologist to develop the philosophy of indigenismo, Gonzalo Aguirre Beltrán, author of *Regiones de Refugio* ([1967] 1991), placed more emphasis on problems associated with the social structure of regions characterized by caste-like relations between members of a Ladino (Spanish-speaking) elite and indigenous communities. He argued that the colonial nature of such regions stands in the way of modernization and national integration.

Around 2004, conferences of scholars interested in hemispheric approaches became a part in the ongoing creation of a sense of nationhood (Delgado and Childs 2012). In 2008 the University of Minnesota hosted a symposium bringing together scholars to bridge the gap between how those in the English-speaking, as opposed to the Spanish- and Portuguese-speaking, academy would start seeing themselves as indigenous (Castellanos Domínguez and Johnson 2017, xiii–xiv, 15). It became clear that there is a gamut of indigeneities: First nations in the US and Canada; people of Mexican descent in the US who identify as indigenous; Canadian Métis; and people in Latin America who keep their indigenous languages or cultural practices. Their discussions brought areas of dispute and misunderstanding into the open, especially the terminology surrounding Mexico's indigenous people versus that in the US. With a few exceptions, migrants from the Alto Balsas living in the US had little contact with, nor did they know much about, people of Mexican descent who emigrated earlier.

The Advent of Indigenous Intellectuals in Mexico

By the early 1990s, indigenous students in Mexico were continuing their schooling beyond high school to become teachers, accountants, and health care workers. When I arrived in Ahuehuepan, there were three such professionals—three men and two women. Other towns such as Xalitla and Telelcingo have more professionals, including those working in their home regions. Marcelino Díaz de Jesús, an economist, exemplifies the emergence of such native professionals. He does not speak Nahuatl, nor does he spend much of his time in the Alto Balsas; yet he dresses up in traditional clothing at international conferences. Other professionals who speak on behalf of Indigenous people are associated with university programs whose names include words such as "indigeneity" and "critical indigeneity." I refer to them as a specialized cluster. No one in Ahuehuepan is a member, but professionals from Ahuehuepan might become part of that cluster in the future. Their indigeneity is the opposite of early *indigenismo*, which tried to change an indigenous way of life.

Indigenous professionals, including those who do not speak a native language, dislike the paternalistic nature of development programs, and they have challenged the assumptions of *indigenismo*. They want a say in such programs and make demands for real sovereignty. Scholars refer to them as indigenous intellectuals (see Saldívar 2018, 443), many of whom take on leadership roles in transnational organizations (Velasco Ortiz 2002, chapter 5). Also known as *gestores* or *promotores culturales*, they have met with resistance from mestizo landowners (Saldívar 2018, 443–48). Their response to government initiatives takes many forms, involving negotiations among themselves (de la Cadena [2007] 2020, 30).

Indigenous spokesmen (few women participate) are diverse in place of origin, level of education, and occupational background: college professors, broadcasters (of bilingual radio programs), legal advisors, and traveling salesmen (Velasco Ortiz 2002, 163–66). Instead of indigenismo, they coined the term *indianismo* (Friedlander [1975] 2006, 203). Some are intermediaries between government officials and indigenous peasants (Saldívar 2018, 433). Mexico's political elite reserved seats for them in the national assemblies (as *diputados*). Ideologies which situate indigenous people as "primitive" and obstacles to Mexican progress persist despite the selective "multicultural" representations of indigeneity in Mexican political spaces.

PLURICULTURALISMO

A new government policy on ethnic diversity, *pluriculturalismo*, glosses over social inequalities by treating each culture, including those associated with Mestizos and Indígenas, as a unique independent entity. According to Francesca Merlan (2009, 311) its emergence is not a surprise, given that it is congruent with neoliberal economic policies, as shown by Rebecca Overmeyer-Vasquez (2010, 16–17, 88) and Charles Hale (2006). Some scholars argue that multiculturalism and neoliberalism have not ended inequalities. Instead, they reinforce racial inequalities dating back to colonial times, at the same time declaring an end of racism (see de la Cadena [2007] 2020, 9; 2008, 347). Cadena uses the concept "state racism," distinguishing an old and a new version. Those associated with the former want to transform Indians into Mestizos through formal schooling and medicine, while the latter "adds the will to improve life through an exacerbated rhetoric of economic growth" while reclassifying land to the detriment of indigenous communities. Carmen Martinez Novo (2006) and Maylei Blackwell (2012) present a similar analysis in a special issue of a journal, edited by Carmen Martínez Novo and Paval Shlossberg (2018), a publication going beyond existing critiques of neoliberal multiculturalism.

In her study in Jalisco, Inés Duran Matute (2018, 9) argues that multiculturalism is the continuation of *mestizaje* and *neoindigenismo*, both of which are a "means of securing racism and domination against indigenous people." Deborah Poole (2020, 204, 225–26), who examined a demonstration in Oaxaca, presents the same argument. Emiko Saldívar (2018, 438) points out that neither interculturalism nor multiculturalism has eradicated racial privileges, although he does not exclude the possibility of real change. In his conclusion, he writes: "Overall, multiculturalism, interculturalism and the politics of recognition, pushed by the demands of indigenous people, have opened important spaces where indigenous voices can resonate and where maybe *Mestizos* can become intercultural interlocutors." He ends with the warning that this will not happen "if issues of racism are not addressed."

CONTRASTING PERSPECTIVES IN ACADEMIA

The term *indigeneity* has been applied to individuals, social clusters, and communities. Some scholars wonder if it is useful for social scientists to continue studying communities on the assumption that they are indigenous or "Indian." Scott Cook is critical of the approach that assumes people associated with towns labeled as indigenous are "outside of, or peripheral to, the capitalist nation-state matrix of typical citizens" (1993, 304). They further argue that neither economic nor social characteristics are useful for classifying indigenous communities, showing that participation in the fiesta cycle and involvement in craft production cut across the Mestizo versus *Indígena* dichotomy (Cook and Joo 1995, 45–46). He advocates a new paradigm, arguing that anthropologists should not continue to assume that a given population is Indian. Instead, he proposes the opposite: "It is empirically more correct to assume a priori that any given population is *Mestizo* and Mexican" Cook (1993, 330). I prefer a modified version of one of his recommendations: anthropologists working in Mexican towns or villages should assume that their populations reside in class- and ethnicity-differentiated communities in some stage of openness. I took out Cook's words "are Mexican citizens" because people living in Mexican communities may be American citizens. In any case, a duplexity perspective embraces as well as accounts for such contrasting perspectives (330).

Cook's position—like that of Friedlander ([1975] 2006, 68), who found a "profound sense of inferiority" and little evidence of customs identified as Indian (79–94)—is diametrically opposed to that of Catharine Good Eshelman. She portrays Ameyaltepec in the Alto Balsas as a vibrant indigenous community with an economy based on reciprocity (1988, 221–22). Their inhabitants, proud of their language, have only reluctantly accepted government-appointed teachers. They have certainly not been subject to the impact of what Cook and Joo (1995, 34) call Mexico's ubiquitous "bourgeois Mestizo hegemony." Such opposite perspectives are not right or wrong per se; they are equally relevant for a complete understanding of a complex social reality.

This chapter, which started with definitions of Indigenous people, also talks about Mestizos. However, it does not make sense to fix a precise line for dividing up what is really a continuum with indigenous and nonindigenous polar ends, whether dealing with individuals or communities. Ahuehuepan comes closer to one end of that continuum, but other towns in the Alto Balsas fall closer to a fuzzy middle. The broader phenomenon of indigeneity is more complex and not easy to untangle. Indigeneity, like the use of the labels *indígena* and *indigenista*, is characterized by ambiguity, discrepancies, and contradictions. Each can be examined from different, even inconsistent, perspectives. People's portrayal of themselves, their group identity, and any beliefs and ideals they share constitute their subjective and ideational side, which may contradict the perspective of outside observers. A comprehensive explanation, requiring the use of diverse perspectives, can be achieved by treating them as duplex entities. The next chapter will first cover the literature on international migration from Mexico to the US, including the migration of indigenous people, including Nahuas.

4

Mexican Migration

The movement of people back and forth across the border goes back a long time, given that the American Southwest was part of Mexico until 1848. After that date, people and goods crossed the line that now separates two countries, although few stayed on the US side until refugees moved north during the Mexican Revolution. In the twenties, more people left when recruiters started arriving in Mexico's central states, which ended when the US closed its borders during the depression. The US economy again needed Mexicans in the 1940s and 1950s when the Bracero Program supplied work for farm laborers. When that ended in 1965, Mexicans were again given permits to work on farms, but those who sought jobs in US cities did so without documents. The flow of undocumented workers did not abate until another crackdown on migrants (Schryer 2014, 19–21).

Initially migrants from central Mexico did not distinguish between the US and northern Mexico; they were just "going north." More people joined them after the collapse of the peso in 1982. A further decline in wages and the number of jobs resulted in more migration. In 1986 the American Congress created an amnesty for undocumented workers, making 2.3 million of them eligible to be legalized. The number of illegal border crossings dropped, but that lasted less than a decade; by 1990 illegal crossings exceeded those of the pre-amnesty era. The outcome was a de facto guest worker program. International migration continued after the 1994 free trade agreement that was supposed to slow it down. However, the American government made it more difficult for undocumented migrants to cross the border.

Until then it had been easy to do so when migration from Mexico consisted of a "revolving door" system, with people who were sent back reentering after two or three days. By the turn of the century, migration picked up again. The number of border crossings did not abate until after the terrorist attack of the Twin Towers in New York in 2001. After that attack, tourism to Mexico declined, resulting in fewer sales. The demand for crafts, which shrank, did not provide a livelihood for all but the most experienced vendors with established clients. Tourism ground to a halt with the outbreak of the coronavirus epidemic in 2019; yet people continue to go to the US to look for jobs. The gap in wages and living standards between the two countries is too big not to.

The ongoing and often rapidly growing influx of Mexican workers to the US is bound to result in contradictory perspectives. Given the wage gap between the US and Mexico (around one to ten), wages considered adequate and even generous from a migrant's perspective are considered inadequate by those born in the US. For migrants, the ability to have enough money left over to send home remittances seems miraculous. The same could be said for all migrant workers in the US, with its diverse mix of newcomers from different countries. Mexicans are more noticeable because their numbers run into the millions rather than thousands, which gives them a competitive advantage. They already have a reputation as a reliable labor force. In her study of bussers in restaurants in Chicago, Gomberg-Muñoz (2011) noticed that Mexicans exerted pressure on coworkers to live up to their reputation as hard workers. However, they are not homogenous; migrants come from different regions and do not all speak the same first language.

THE MIGRATION OF INDIGENOUS PEOPLE

The presence of Mexican indigenous people in the US is not a new phenomenon, although Americans, including those of Mexican descent, may not be aware that there are migrants who speak a language other than Spanish. Not all ethnicities are proportionally represented; Nahuas, one of the two largest ethnolinguistic groups, did not cross the border in large numbers (Fox and Rivera-Salgado 2004, 5), which is surprising given they make up a tenth of the linguistically defined ethnicities in Mexico (3). They are not mentioned a lot in the literature, although there is an allusion to some Nahuas from Tlaxcala involved in a strike of *braceros* in California in the late 1950s (2). The literature has more information on Mixtecs, Zapotecs, Triques, Purépechas, Chatinos, and Mayans, who were among the eighteen ethnicities who sent representatives to a conference in California at the turn of the twenty-first century. In terms of regions of destination, migrants went to Oregon, Illinois, Florida, and New York, as well as to Baja California in northern Mexico.

They originated in Michoacán, Puebla, Hidalgo, Yucatan, Chiapas, and Oaxaca, but few from Guerrero.

Studies on indigenous migrants have dealt with people from small towns who ended up working in agriculture, domestic jobs, and the service sector in mostly rural, though sometimes urban, settings. Few got jobs in manufacturing. Lynn Stephen (2007), who did fieldwork in Oaxaca, conducted a study of Mixtecs who spent time in Baja California before they moved to California and Oregon. She focused on gender inequality and the creation of a binational indigenous organization. Adrianna Cruz Manjarrez (2013) introduced the term *transnational social space* to conceptualize the close connections between migrants and towns of origin, taking generational differences into account. Felipe López and David Runsten (2004), who compared Mixtec and Zapotec communities in Oaxaca's central valley, guessed why people from the former ended up working in dead-end agricultural jobs in the US after first spending time in other places in Mexico while the latter went straight to LA to work in restaurants. The reasons that they cite do not apply to the Alto Balsas. In the case of Ahuehuepan, international migration was initially to American rural destinations, while after 1994 it was primarily to urban centers. Most have crossed the border without documents; yet their presence and how they are viewed are equally diverse.

Part Three
The History of Ahuehuepan

Women whose family names were never recorded and children who died prematurely left faint traces in the archives and in people's memories.

5

Historical Background

A historical approach based on different perspectives is a crucial part of a broad, holistic analysis informed by duplexity; yet it is a challenge to write the history of a town that is not an administrative center. Ahuehuepan first appears in an 1881 map. Civil registry records start in 1930, with death certificates going back to 1845 and the earliest handwritten document to 1905. I also relied on secondary sources. Amith's writings (1995; 2005) show the intertwined histories of the Alto Balsas and the valley of Iguala. Ian Jacobs's book (2004) enabled me to place local history in the context of state politics, and the writings of other scholars were the source of more information. For the recent past, I relied on documents and peoples' memories, which made it possible to include the perspectives of local people.

For three centuries, everyone grew the maize they needed for survival; however, people's livelihoods hung in a precarious balance. An inhospitable environment meant that outsiders did not encroach on their land. At the same time, the fact that only one crop can be cultivated each year made them dependent on crafts and commerce to generate extra income. Maintaining that balance became more difficult when the main choice was migration to the US.

THE PRE-HISPANIC ERA AND THE SPANISH CONQUEST

A Nahuatl-speaking population has occupied the region since the middle of the twelfth century. Archaeological evidence for earlier settlements shows signs of

Olmec influence going back to 1500 BCE. Their ethnic affiliation and language are unknown (Paradis 1995, 120). Based on ceramic styles, it is classified as part of the Mezcala region, with sites close to Ahuelicán, San Juan Tetelcingo, and Ahuehuepan. Mezcala lost its cultural independence with the arrival of the Coixca, one of the Nahuatl-speaking clusters that entered Mesoamerica from the north. They in turn lost their sovereignty when they were conquered by the Meshicas (Aztecs). The province of Tepecoacuilco, dating back to the sixteenth century in a period of Aztec rule, corresponds to the current *municipio* with that name. It had three subdistricts, including San Agustín Oapan, a collection point for tribute (Amith 1995, 210). The conquerors kept those administrative divisions when they set up *encomiendas* for the collection of the tribute. Centers like Oapan became *cabeceras* (administrative centers) with jurisdiction over subordinate towns (*sujetos*). They were "Indian Republics" with limited autonomy, separate from "Republics of Spaniards" (Levaggi 2001). Their inhabitants did not have a broad ethnic identity, although they were aware of their Spanish overlords.

THE COLONIAL ERA

Throughout the seventeenth century, the Spaniards imposed nucleated settlements to ease conversion to Christianity, while epidemics caused population decline. The survivors were relocated through *congregaciones*, culminating in the disappearance of most indigenous towns in the more fertile parts of Tepecoacuilco. Spanish farmers and ranchers gained access to that land though grants called *mercedes*. A further attempt at relocation in the Alto Balsas failed. The people of Oapan's *sujetos*, including Tetelcingo, returned to their homes (Amith 1995, 133–35). The marginal nature of their terrain and lack of minerals made it unattractive to outsiders. The Spanish Crown recognized the land rights of Indigenous subjects through *títulos primordiales*. However, during three centuries of colonial rule the region was not isolated from the rest of the world; its towns were a vital link in an emerging global economy. Mule trails crossing the river Balsas were the only way to transport goods from the Philippines and the Andean countries destined for Europe. Galleons arrived in Acapulco to be unloaded, then the cargo was put on mules. The passage of pack animals and people on rafts made from interwoven reeds was the way men fulfilled labor obligations as their tribute (Good Eshelman 1988, 216). The Nahua dignitaries of towns along the river's banks became merchants (Aline Hémond 2003, 59, 61). Dry weather, making only one harvest possible, accounts for more permanent forms of migration to the Iguala valley.

Initially most of the Iguala valley was leased to two cattle producers, until one of its landowners ended his lease in the 1750s so that he could use his land for agriculture (Amith 1995, 135). By the mid-1760s, maize-farming displaced cattle. Unlike other parts of Mexico, the owners of those landed estates did not become directly involved in production with the use of day laborers; instead, they rented out land to tenants. That is how farmers from Oapan moved to a hacienda surrounding the abandoned town of Palula early in the seventeenth century. Its internal organization and terrain, including some that today belongs to Ahuehuepan, did not change over two hundred years. The tenants in Palula reconstructed the social and political structures of their town of origin. They were joined by people from San Marcos Oacacingo, Ameyaltepec, and Ahuelicán. At the turn of the eighteenth century, with no more room in Palula, migrants sought opportunities in new hamlets. That is how families from Ameyaltepec ended up in what became Xalitla and Maxela. Amith uses these examples of mobility alongside more flexible and open social boundaries to call the closed corporate community model into question (Amith 2005, 355, 381). Yet open communities like Palula became more closed towards the end of the colonial period (429). Around that time there was no settlement in Ahuehuepan, although inhabitants of San Juan Tetelcingo were growing maize in that part of their communal land.

The *cuadrilla* of Ahuehuepan was settled later. The earliest that people started going there would be around the end of the eighteenth century, when Tetelcingo became involved in a dispute with Ahuelicán, which is subordinate to Oapan. The conflict started in 1710 when a land grant favored Oapan. It is possible that people from Tetelcingo went to what is now Ahuehuepan sometime after 1716 when land granted to Oapan was restored to Tetelcingo. They are more likely to have gone there between 1797 and 1809, when Ahuelicán was abandoned after a resumption of conflict between Oapan and Tetelcingo (see also Amith 2005, 1014).

FROM INDEPENDENCE TO REVOLUTION

The War of Independence (1810 to 1821), which transformed the Viceroyalty of New Spain into the Empire, then Republic, of Mexico, did not have much impact on the region; nor were its inhabitants affected by infighting between Conservatives and Liberals or the interlude of foreign intervention by the French (1864–1867). In 1852 the state of Mexico was carved up to create Guerrero, whose districts and municipalities stayed the same. In that year, some families were living in Ahuehuepan. None of the documentation mentions the two other significant places where families dwelled. According to oral history, a cluster of houses just east of Ahuehuepan was called Chaantilowayan ("where people used to live"). That former settlement, where one can see the remains of house posts, is contiguous with Kopaxokoihtik, on the border with Ahuelicán. Atlalko was three-quarters of an hour on foot farther north. People from those three places moved to Ahuehuepan around the time of the Revolution.

The legal change with the biggest impact was the privatization of the land of communities and religious corporations, which coincided with the transfer of ownership of the hacienda of Palula. Its administrators, the Gómez family, were thwarted in their attempt to gain full control when an outsider, Colonel Juan Montúfar, registered it in his name in the 1860s.[1] The impact of disentailment of land on indigenous communities, whose legal status was that of corporations with rights over land (*terrenos de común repartimiento*), was uneven. While the remaining towns in the Iguala valley lost their land, those in the hilly region expanded their land base, and the allocation of parcels continued as before. Ahuehuepan is a good example of both trends.

Disentailment intensified the dispute between Oapan and San Juan Tetelcingo. In 1861 Ahuehuepan received its share of Tetelcingo's land through an informal arrangement (Jacobs [1982] 2004, 56) even though Oapan claimed it. The conflict was resolved in 1881 when the land was divided in half. On one map, Ahuehuepan appears to the left of a line showing the new border. It continued to belong to Tetelcingo and had its own chapel (see also Amith 1995, 141).

The Porfiriato

Victor Tomás (an older man born and raised in Ahuehuepan).

"One man, who had land that bordered on the communal land of San Juan, sold some of that land to others but kept some for himself. I bought two parcels when I was young."

In 1877 Porfirio Díaz assumed power at the national level at a time of intense infighting among rival caudillos (Jacobs [1982] 2004, chapter 20). The next three decades saw the consolidation of a centralized state. Díaz's regime promoted foreign investment, the surveying of public land, mining, and export-orientated agriculture. Further economic development transformed Mexico; its impact on the northern part of Guerrero became noticeable after a railway reached the district of Hidalgo in 1899. Its immediate consequence was the decline of Tepecoacuilco, hitherto a crucial commercial center (Jacobs [1982] 2004, 37).

In 1888 renters in Palula, who continued to make payments to its new owners, had to deal with different owners when this now privately owned estate was fragmented into smaller units following a dispute among Montúfar's descendants (Amith 1995,

---

[1] The Gómez family did not lose all control; Febronia Gómez, daughter of Antonio Gómez, married Montúfar after the death of her first husband.

139–40). To the east, in a section of land also with the name Ahuehuepan, tenants handed over a percentage of their harvest to Montúfar's widow, Febronia Gómez. Other sections of the Montúfar estate were auctioned off to pay off legal debts or were sold to Nahua communities (Amith 1995, 140, 200, 384). Some of the estate bordering on Ahuehuepan's communal land was sold to Pedro Santiago Márgaro, a wealthy farmer and rancher from Tetelcingo who bought land in the northern side of a tributary of the river that flows west towards Ahuelicán. It is shown as "Pedro Santiago's land (*propiedad*)" in figure 13.6. That land was cultivated into the second half of the twentieth century; entire families brought their cooking utensils to live in temporary dwellings during the rainy season.

Pedro Santiago did not become the owner of this land on his own; other men supplied money to cover the cost of registration and travel. Although put in his name, those men got their share. From that point on, tenants growing maize in that land paid rent in kind to a handful of their neighbors. The names of the owners, including Pedro Santiago, who died more than seventy years ago, appear in the register of the tax office in Tepecoacuilco, even though many of them are no longer alive! The descendants of those owners paid land taxes, but in 2020 they were in arrears. Such changes in the legal status of land and the movement of people to the Iguala valley must be placed in a broader historical context.

As in other parts of Mexico, the Porfiriato led to the growth of a middle class. Elders in Ameyaltepec reported to Catherine Good Eshelman (1998, 181–82) that their grandparents once lived well. One of her informants recounted that his grandfather owned cattle and mules and that he ate cheese. He was also a merchant whose workers traveled to the coast to obtain salt. These accounts are consistent with what people told me about the prerevolutionary period. Well-off families, who lived in bigger daub-and-wattle houses with three rafters, accounted for less than a quarter of the population. Their houses had thatch roofs, more durable than the palm roofs of poor families. Only rich families could afford to install wooden doors. Those *riikos* were not much different from the "modestly prosperous farmers, typical of the rancheros of northern Guerrero" described by Ian Jacobs ([1982] 2004, 54). They also learned trades; Juan Marcario, Galdino Bernall's son, became a master bricklayer. Yet even poor farmers were well-off compared to the sharecroppers and day laborers in the neighboring state of Morelos.

The case of Pedro Santiago supplies insights into intergenerational mobility. He owned several properties: part of the Aakoontepeek mountain overlooking Ahuehuepan, a section of the former Montúfar estate, and more land in the ambiguous zone, including Kapiires. Pedro did not have male heirs; hence his surname did not survive, nor did his descendants replicate his success. In 2020, 838 people (13.7% of the population) were related to Pedro Santiago, although of the half dozen *riikos*, only Juan Marcario Bernal could trace his descent back to him. This lack of continuity in layering holds true for other families. Of the descendants of people who bought land in the former Montúfar estate, most were no longer "rich" by the third generation.

THE MEXICAN REVOLUTION AND ITS AFTERMATH

Toribio Pascual (a teacher who lives in Ahuehuepan).
"Courageous men who became leaders were attractive to women; it was easy to seduce them. The leaders of the Revolution took whichever girls they wanted, whether they or their parents liked it or not."

The Mexican Revolution (1910 to 1917) ended the rule of Porfirio Díaz. United in their opposition to his rule, the revolutionaries represented people with different grievances. Ten years of civil war followed by political unrest and minor rebellions continued throughout the 1920s. In Guerrero the Revolution was spearheaded by the Figueroas, landowners from Huitzuco. The Revolution's instigator, Francisco Madero, was from Coahuila. Like the landowners in Huitzuco, Madero was in favor of free elections, states' rights, and municipal autonomy that had been eroded. Influenced by liberal educators, and willing to collaborate with reformers, his political movement was predominantly urban and middle-class. It did not take long to topple Díaz, but Madero did not satisfy his more radical supporters; he did not share the vision of Emiliano Zapata, who wanted to restore the lands of indigenous communities, so a rupture was inevitable. In Guerrero, the Figueroas' respect for private property clashed with the ideals of the followers of Zapata; Odilón, a member of the Figueroa clan, did not agree with Pablo Barrera, the Zapatista in Tepecoacuilco. Yet Barrera was a different agrarian than Zapata, since his focus was to incite the tenants to stop paying rent.

During the Revolution, people found themselves in an ambiguous situation. Unlike their counterparts in Morelos, they owned land and engaged in small-scale commerce. The *riikos* resembled the leaders of native communities in Oaxaca, although the latter never answered the call to arms. Between 1910 and 1912, when the Figueroas expanded their control beyond Guerrero, people in Ahuehuepan, left to their own devices, got caught up in the fighting among rival chieftains. In 1913 Rómulo Figueroa fought against Victoriano Huerta on the side of Carranza, together with Zapatista forces, including those headed by Encarnación (Chon) Díaz. The son of a farmer from Mayanalán, Chon had followers in Ahuehuepan, whose tenants sympathized with Pablo Barrera's agrarianism. The ensuing events included a rupture between Carranza versus Zapata and Villa, catapulting the country into three more years of civil war. During that interlude, the Alto Balsas and the valley of Iguala remained firmly under the control of Zapata, who continued to resist Carranza until his assassination in 1919.

The Revolution's impact was disastrous. Government soldiers and revolutionaries alike looted and raped. Every time a new faction assumed power, soldiers on horseback came racing in. They ordered women to deliver tortillas, entering houses to take away cooking utensils and consuming all the chickens, confiscating animals, and entering granaries to haul away remaining maize. Maize became scarce and people lost their cattle. They fled to the hills, in fear of their lives, eating whatever they found. However, they were not only victims but also took part in the Revolution. Chon Díaz in Mayanalán knew that Ahuehuepan was known for the fabrication of *cohetes* (firecrackers). He recruited one of its renowned *cueteros*, Modesto Chino. Working with gunpowder is a dangerous occupation; men who make cohetes, plus their family members, suffered injuries because of explosions while working in their thatched-roof houses, prone to catch fire. During the Revolution, they were exposed to greater danger when they made bombs by mixing gunpowder with chili and ground-up garlic that irritated the horses of government forces. People have told me that Chon Díaz could not have taken Chilpancingo in 1914 were it not for the *bomberos* (bomb makers) of Ahuehuepan.

People took part in the fighting for distinct reasons: economic necessity, a sense of adventure, and prior loyalties. However, they did not always understand the difference between rival revolutionary factions: Obregonistas, Villistas, Carranzistas, and Orozquistas. Santiago Tomás became angry when soldiers fighting for Madero confiscated his oxen. Instead of protesting, he joined the forces of Chon Díaz, who gave him a horse, a rifle, and four rounds of ammunition. Upon coming back for a visit, Santiago brought back clothes and two rounds of cheese for his family. Manuel Salvador, a young man at the start of the Revolution, also joined one of the revolutionary armies, as did Porfirio Muñoz. The two men continued to be friends even though they were on opposite sides. Porfirio Muñoz, a cuetero, was a follower of Chon Díaz, while Manuel Salvador, the son of a *riiko*, ended up as a soldier for Huerta. Members of families that were not well-off, like the Manuels, also fought for opposite sides. However, not everyone was sympathetic to the cause. Juan Mauricio, a rich man, had no use for Zapata.

Who the heroes or villains were depends on with whom you talk. Students accept the official accounts taught in school—that the revolutionaries were engaged in a heroic struggle to defend the poor, that Modesto Chino invited Chon Díaz to help oust an abusive government force. Older people who did not go to school supply different accounts, pointing out that Zapata's forces committed crimes and that Zapata stayed back during the major battles while others took the risks. They debunk the official version of how Chon Díaz looted stores to redistribute clothes to the poor by pointing out that he sold those clothes for his own profit. The local hero, Modesto Chino, was a womanizer who took the wife of a humble peasant, Joselito "Chivo," by force. Joselito killed Modesto in revenge. These competing accounts are all relevant for creating a complete picture.

During the turbulent period during and after the Revolution, people were displaced, which is how members of the Gómez1 family ended up in other towns. Evaristo Gómez moved to Xalitla, where he married a woman whose family left Maxela after that town was burned. He went back but his children moved to San Miguel. Families from other towns, including the Martíns, moved from Maxela to Ahuehuepan. Overall, life continued to be precarious in the five years after the Revolution, with periodic food shortages. Yet a combination of sources shows that limited autonomy, plus participation in commerce, allowed the region's inhabitants, including people in Ahuehuepan, to keep their customs and language.

6

The Pueblo of Ahuehuepan (1923–1985)

Mexico's history from 1923 until today can be divided into four periods: the consolidation of a political system (until 1945); an economic boom, combined with social unrest (1945 to 1975); the decline of the economy (1976 to 1994); and a period of neoliberalism, multiparty democracy, and drug cartels (1995 until today). The corresponding history of Ahuehuepan followed its own rhythm, not always in sync with what was happening at the national level. While Guerrero became one of Mexico's poorest states, the Alto Balsas region was well-off in comparison.

Ahuehuepan became a pueblo in 1923, a date within the memory of people alive when I knew them. Asked about how their lives differ from when they were young, they told the same story time and time again.

Bonifacio Marcos (born in 1940, he spent most of his life in Ahuehuepan).

"We used to suffer a lot [*titlaihyoowiah*]. The money people earned was barely enough to buy *jabontsiin* [a bit of soap]. Women got up early in the morning to get water, and to get the dough ready to make tortillas [*tlapanayaayah*]."

Reynulfo Morales (born in 1945, he became a part-time butcher).

"Since we were poor, I did not attend school for very long. I dropped out because I had to help my mother in our milpa."

Rosa Aldama (born in 1915).

"During the fiestas, men would climb up thatch roofs to prevent them from catching on fire because of sparks. That is how the roof of the *juzgado* once caught on fire.

Several houses were burned. The people who lived in them suffered burns and three women died."

Roberto Ignacio (born in 1951).
"I used to cut sugarcane in a place near Iguala. I was also a *hornero* [in charge of the kiln]. I would burn my fingers taking the hot *panela* [unrefined sugar loaf] out of its mold."

Getting information about what people thought about the relevance of what happened and how it affected their lives was bound to supply a variety of viewpoints and opinions. Asked about how their lives differed from when they were young, many people told me: "We did not wear shoes, only sandals with soles made from used tires. Our hair was full of lice." Yet others put more emphasis on the positive aspects of their lives and how they were better-off than people in other regions. Nevertheless, it became clear that in general people were more prone to get sick. The records of the civil registry show twenty deaths from malaria between 1948 and 1952, the last one in 1973. The main source of death for children was measles. Since then, there have been improvements. Today there are health clinics. Most households are on the electrical grid. Yet in talking to strangers, people say residents of Ahuehuepan are still poor and that there is still a lot of sickness.

THE FORMATION OF A NEW TOWN

When Ahuehuepan became a pueblo, a new national political system had not yet been secured. There was no stable transfer of power before 1931. A tradition of *caudillismo* (rule of warlords) lingered on as long as Plutarco Calles ruled behind the scenes. He instituted the precursor to what became the PRI (Institutional Revolutionary Party), a party that became part of a state bureaucracy. While using traditional methods of control, the ruling elite derived its power through control of labor unions and peasant federations. The only way to achieve political prominence was by working through the political system (Jacobs [1982] 2004, 136–37).

Life was not affected by events of other parts of Mexico, including the Cristero Insurgency of the thirties. During that period, Abelino Martínez, Márgaro Alejo, and Juan Ausencio built up the herds they had before the Revolution. People resumed cottage industries, and the salt trade resumed. Twenty-three men, including Juan Mauricio, Blas Ortiz, Fructoso Morales, and Juan Alejo, made trips to the Pacific coast. The oldest, José Villalba, born in 1879, went there before the Revolution. Flores Martínez made his first trip at age eighteen, and Miguel Alejo Morales joined them as a paid helper at age twelve. The *riikos* sent mule drivers or supplied advances to small-scale merchants, which is how Miguel Alejo could take part in the salt trade. Flores Martínez recalled making a trip with twelve other men. Women prepared toasted maize with sesame seeds for barter and to be eaten during the journey. The trip to the lagoon of Tecomate took a week. On the way back, they sold salt in Tonalapa, Palula, Cuacoyula, and Apipilulco. Only men who bought larger quantities of salt made a profit. Flores found another form of commerce more rewarding. After each harvest, he went to Ixcatla and Mexcalcingo in the nearby Montaña region, to buy pineapples. They sold out quickly in a fair in Quetzala del Progreso. With the completion of a highway connecting Iguala with Acapulco in 1939, the trade in salt was forbidden. Other forms of itinerant trade became more difficult.

The renewed salt trade coincided with the advent of a stable government that used periodic land redistribution as part of its policy (Jacobs [1982] 2004, xx, xxi). This is how Montúfar's land was handed over to his tenants. In Ahuehuepan, Cesario Catalán promoted the granting of an *ejido*, although it took decades for the legalities to be settled. Bonifacio Bárcenas was instrumental in setting it up. Ten years older than Cesario, Bonifacio later became the ejido's secretary. Yet some of that land was distributed to *riikos* such as Emigdio Ausencio, who served as *comisario ejidal* (1930 to 1933).

In 1930 all but a handful of people had learned some Spanish. Suspicious of outside authorities, they were hesitant to bring crimes to their attention. This situation changed after the introduction of formal schooling. In 1933, Agripino (Pino) Ocampo from Tecuescontitlan taught in a one-room school. Twenty-eight students included four married men and two daughters of Graciano Aldama. Miguel Alejo1 learned numbers and how to sign his name, enough to serve as secretary in the *comisaría*. After Ocampo left, no one attended until the mid-1940s, when a state school named Leona Vicario opened its doors.

Like other towns, Ahuehuepan was endogamous but with some intermarriage. Guadalupe Felipe married Marcelino López from Oapan. An outsider, Marcelino did not have land rights, but he gained access to the land where his wife's father worked as a tenant. Legal recognition came about when Lázaro Cárdenas promoted further land reform. However, given a language barrier and little knowledge about what was happening in the rest of Mexico, people did not know that Cárdenas made a stopover in Iguala while campaigning for the national presidency.

Members of better-off families contributed to the town's social life. In 1935, the sons of three *riikos* made their first trip to Mexico City, to buy musical instruments. Juan Marcario Bernal, a trumpet player, was their bandleader. Moisés Mauricio taught children the dance of the *retos*, performed on ritual occasions. They were not the only ones who took part in the town's recreational life; Antonio Muñiz was a poor farmer, as was Silverio Gómez, who played the fiddle. Their love of music illustrates the shared interests that is the basis of a cultural compromise,[1] consisting of a consensus when actors with overlapping interests are interested in the exchange of resources. Women also contributed; Silveria Silviano, who served as a midwife, made the large doll used during carnival celebrations.

THE 1940S AND 1950S

During the 1930s and 1940s, a handful of men dominated politics. The most influential, Manuel Salvador, was *comisario municipal* twice (1933, 1942). Porfirio Muñoz served as *comisario comunal*, as did men who did not take part in the Revolution, including Fructoso Morales (in 1940). During a short-lived period of prosperity, they started building adobe brick houses with tile roofs. Juan Mauricio, who hired bricklayers from Tonalapa, was followed by Fructoso, Manuel Salvador, Galdino Bernal1, Juan Alejo2, and Emigdio Ausencio. By 1955, there were eight such houses, plastered and whitewashed.

At the national level, Cárdenas promoted the development of industry and commercial agriculture as part of a policy of import substitution. Tariffs on imported goods stimulated the growth of Mexican-owned factories (see also Schryer 2014, 17–18). Starting in 1940, manufacturing transformed Mexico into an urbanized country as people converged on its capital city, which became the largest city in the world. The "Mexican Miracle," a period of rapid growth that started during World War II, had its winners and losers. People in Ahuehuepan had to wait for another decade before they saw any benefits. With the end of the salt trade, they became day laborers during the dry season. Men toiled as casual laborers in Mexico City, while women were house cleaners. Other people worked in the sugar plantations of Morelos to earn the money they needed to buy hats and the cotton cloth for making clothes. Still others found jobs in a mine in Huitzuco, orchards in Santa Teresa, and a lumber mill in Iguala. Only *riikos* did not have to do so. A memorable event at the local level was an accident in 1949 during restoration work on the church, resulting in three deaths. The project was not completed until 1959.

During the 1940s, when the *comisario* dipped into his own pocket, it became more difficult for one man to feed out-of-town visitors. In 1943 a decision was made to set up the barrio system to share the costs of the annual Quinto Viernes celebration. That year people who had not yet received help from redistribution got access to more land with an extension of their ejido. Those working on the land once

---

1 Andreas Wimmer (2013, 98–99) uses that concept to avoid the notion of false consciousness while also circumventing the impression that such a compromise is permanent.

owned by Juan Montúfar used a different strategy. Known as private property, it was not eligible for expropriation. Fearing that they might lose legal rights to use it, the tenants sent a representative to see if Febronia Gómez, then elderly, would sell the land. When that did not work out, the tenants took it, knowing that she would not be able to go to Chilpancingo to defend her claim of ownership. Ongoing competition also took the form of a flare-up of a dispute with Oapan about a slice of land called Tekiloomah, in 1950.

The introduction of a publicly funded school in the late forties did not bring formal education to everyone. Isidro Alejo remembers how one teacher, who spoke only Spanish, often lost his temper; he hit students with a rod if they spoke Nahuatl. Isidro thought it was a good thing that his teacher was strict, yet he stopped attending because he preferred working in the fields. None of the teachers over the next two decades had more than a minimal knowledge of Nahuatl, which they picked up when interacting with students. When I asked one of them how it was possible to teach students who spoke only Nahuatl, he said, "It was like magic. We spoke to the children in Spanish and used hand signs, but somehow they adapted. We had contact with them outside the classroom." However, not all students were able to adapt. Roberto Ignacio, who did not learn anything during the two years he went to school, learned Spanish by working in Mexico City. One woman learned little because she had to stay home to look after her sick mother. The next teacher, María Antonieta Hernández from Tepecua, preceded a couple (Juan Antonio Morales and his wife, Dionecia), who taught throughout the 1950s and early 1960s. The school, made of adobe with a tin roof, now had two classrooms plus a house for the teachers.

Conflicts around Education and Religion

Prior to 1960, the clergy did not interfere with people's syncretic beliefs and practices (see Fallaw 2013), and at least one priest even played up to such beliefs. Padre Francisco Guerrero, who portrayed himself as a *caballero* (cavalier) with magical powers, preached in Nahuatl on mountaintops to perform pre-Hispanic rituals to assure rain. Benigno Bravo Valadés, who arrived in the region around that time, considered such practices as idolatry that stood in the way of progress. That priest also was a strong believer in Catholic education. He set up a school in Oapan but faced opposition and moved it to San Miguel. He arranged for boys to continue their education elsewhere. However, while he helped many people, he antagonized others. Bravo used to yell at people. People in Ahuehuepan did not like it when he threw out the garlands used in the church to adorn the saints. The priest used food offerings to feed pigs. When his parishioners lodged a complaint, a *comandante* fetched the priest, tying him up; he was released from the town's jail after paying a fine. Despite setbacks, Father Bravo went ahead to carry out his mission, opening a private school in Ahuehuepan in 1957. This is how the Pascual brothers, Toribio, Gregorio, and Francisco, started their schooling. However, that school pitted people against each other. Those in favor of the priest, the *curistas*, were a minority. After two years, the school was closed. The ensuing bad feelings coincided with an end to the custom of jointly growing maize to defray the costs of religious events.

Trials Tribulations and New Opportunities

During the rest of the 1950s and the early 1960s, life became easier with the introduction of hand-held mills. However, getting water became onerous as rainfall became less predictable. Women got up at 3:00 a.m. to fetch water at a spring that often ran dry. They walked over an hour to get to the river to bathe and wash clothes. Roberto Ignacio had vivid memories of what life was like for men: "We wore home-sewn clothes made from cotton and used sandals (*huaraches*). I did not start using factory-made pants and shirts until after 1957." That year, Roberto's father, Ruben, then thirty years old, worked as part of the Bracero Program for Mexican workers. When Ruben's friends in Xalitla invited him to join them, they gave him a quick lesson about what to say when they got to the border. The second to go was his younger brother Irineo. Juan Enrique worked for two months in Arkansas in 1961. In total, twelve men went to the US under contract until that program ended in 1964. The last one, Juventino Juárez, followed the example of his brother Angel, who used his earnings to build a house made of cement and bricks. Upon returning, they resumed growing maize.

In 1955 the highway from Iguala to Acapulco was paved. However, it was still a chore to reach Xalitla to board a bus. Guadalupe Romero, the owner of a store in Iguala, invited men from Ahuehuepan to build a dirt road using picks and shovels. That road, whose construction continued with government support, reached Ahuehuepan in 1959. It did not have much traffic; only large trucks could climb its steeper sections. Prone to falling rocks, it had to be constantly repaired. Most people went on foot or used donkeys to get to Xalitla.

THE 1960S AND 1970S

A former craft vendor in Ahuehuepan (born in 1968).

"It is not worth your while trying to grow corn. I once sowed thirty-five *cuartillos* but did not eat a single *elote* [fresh ear of corn]. We had a bad drought that year. Even better-off people did not have enough money left over to hire a helper. That is when they realized they could earn more with *artesanía* [the craft business]."

Julia Ignacio (born in 1951).

"Like other women in Ahuehuepan, I made clay *koomahle* [griddles], using cow's dung to fire them. I used to make tortillas and corn dough on a *metate* [a flat stone for grinding grains], but no one does that anymore. Women now use a metal press to make tortillas."

Juana Salvador Morales (a teacher born in the early 1960s).

"Some people learned how to paint even though their parents did not. They learned from a spouse or a relative who already knew. Some, who learned out of necessity because they had to make a living, did so by watching other people."

Margarita Gómez Marcos (Ahuehuepan, 1949–2018).

"For ten years, I made clay figures for necklaces. I sold them to vendors in San Juan, where several buyers would arrange ahead of time to set a day to drop them off. I used to take mine inside of baskets, on donkeys. We left at three in the morning, passed through Ameyaltepec around five, and arrived in San Juan at eight or nine."

The year 1960 marks the start of two decades of prosperity. Guerrero was left behind; but, within that state, the Alto Balsas profited from tourism when American visitors started driving along the new highway to places like Taxco and Acapulco. It did not take long for people to realize they could get money by making crafts to sell. The craft industry has its origin in the 1950s when people from Oapan and Ameyaltepec started painting clay pots and ashtrays for sale. People from those two towns next painted on the same kind of bark paper once used by the Aztecs. Known as *amates*, they were popular. A style known as *historietas*, which depicts traditional houses and events from an idyllic perspective, started in 1969 (Good Eshelman 1988, 31). Other crafts were adopted; people in some towns specialized in carving masks, others in decorating gourds, clay ashtrays, and bowls. Artisans from Ahuehuepan used clay to make necklaces, then began carving wooden fish that were decorated with amate-style designs. What makes the region's craft industry unique is that they sold directly to tourists, with no intermediaries. Men no longer worked as hired hands in neighboring regions. Women no longer worked as maids.

Craft production was gradually transformed. At first, one did not need much money. Paint was made from the dyes of plants. People dug up soil suitable for making clayware. They knew what kind of trees to cut down for carving wood. Start-up costs were covered by loans from relatives and friends. They sold their crafts in places that could be reached by boarding the bus they flagged down. Once they got off in Cuernavaca or in Acapulco, people faced the risk of getting robbed and being harassed by the police. Over time the craft business became more complicated. Artisans started using store-bought acrylic paints, varnish, and electric sanders. As they ventured further afield, vendors brought along family members; their children helped to sell in the street. Income from sales enabled people to eat better and to build better houses. Eventually a minority became full-time vendors who rarely came home. *Riikos*, who had the capital to become wholesalers, bought crafts from people in other towns, setting up bases of operations in cities like Mazatlán.

The craft boom coincided with a better infrastructure and the expansion of public education. The road to Xalitla became more passable after 1969, allowing teachers to commute between Iguala and Ahuehuepan. However, uneven economic growth at the national level triggered social unrest, including guerrilla movements and an uprising ending with the massacre of students in Mexico City in 1968. That year the city hosted the Olympic Games. At the local level, people in Ahuehuepan faced encroachment of land when Ameyaltepec claimed the property of the woman we met earlier. When an engineer for the Land Reform Office came to investigate, he sided with Ahuehuepan. The de facto owners, who had earlier taken control of the land, set up an organization to legalize their possession, appointing a *riiko* as representative. Around that time another *riiko* appropriated land in the ambiguous zone, claiming he had rights as one of the Pedro Santiago's descendants. In the 1960s, a dispute over land between Ahuehuepan and Ahuelicán was peacefully resolved. In that decade, younger men took on important public posts. Bernardo Martínez became *comisario municipal suplente* in 1961 at the age of twenty-one. From then on, the average age for *comisarios* was closer to thirty than to fifty. On the state level, the political status quo was challenged when Genaro Vásquez, inspired by Fidel Castro's uprising in Cuba, created the *cívicos* in 1959. Their candidates for office were not allowed to run for office, triggering off a confrontation with the army in 1962. Vásquez was jailed. After his escape from prison in 1968, he fled disguised as an old man, hiding out in Maxela. On two occasions he passed through Ahuehuepan, where he had sympathizers.

None of the town's teachers stayed long. This situation changed with the arrival of a new principal, Lorenzo Hernández, in 1966. Lorenzo grew up in Xalitla at a time when most parents there no longer spoke Nahuatl to their children, but he picked it up teaching in Oapan. Lorenzo, who lived in Ahuehuepan until his departure in 1983, had four teachers working under his direction, including Isabel Galicia Marcario. Students were intrigued with that teacher who used to travel back and forth on a mule from Ahuelicán. Lorenzo persuaded the town's authorities to tear down their bullring, then close to the center, for a basketball court. The construction crew brought in a bulldozer to level the ground in another location for a new and bigger bullring. During the time he ran the school, a rural support program sent in a five-person team: Alfredo, a veterinarian; his wife, Sara, a nurse who sent off Silveria, the town's midwife, for further training; Alfonso, a carpenter; and two bachelors. Women learned how to inject medicines, and men were taught woodworking and cattle branding. The town got its first kindergarten in 1972 when a woman from the Montaña region promoted the idea at a meeting with parents. Starting in the early 1960s, students studied until grade two, although some entered grade three in Xalitla. Cirilo Pascual used to go there on foot, leaving at 6:30 in the morning. He then studied at a technical school in Sabana Grande, as a member of the first generation there. Other students got further formal schooling in places where they were lodged (*internados*), coming home two or three times a year. Six boys attended San Gabrielito, near Tepecoacuilco, while girls went to Atenango del Río, near Huitzuco. Still other children did not attend school at all.

The 1960s and 1970s saw new developments in religion and secular entertainment. When the second Vatican Council amended the Catholic liturgy, some innovations, such as the replacement of Latin with Spanish, were not controversial. Having the priest face the congregation presented a problem. Nahuas, who had their own way of interpreting the liturgy, considered it scandalous for the priest to "turn his back to the saints." That is the reason people in Ahuelicán joined a breakaway church and paid for the cost of building a chapel. Around that time, the seat of the parish in Oapan was moved to Xalitla. In 1977 carnival (*aawihle*) fell by the wayside. Held during the week before Lent, it is a feast that does not involve the adoration of a saint; it was a time for frivolity, including role reversals. Carnival needed men who knew songs full of double entendre. Its most enthusiastic supporter, Santiago Mendoza, organized activities together with his brother-in-law, Gabino Alcaraz. No one wanted to take over when Santiago was getting too old, even at a time when two other participants died.

The 1970s, peaceful compared to the 1960s, saw changes, including improvement, in physical infrastructure. The erection of hydro poles started in 1970, with the inauguration of the grid three years later. Craft production continued and people from other countries came to visit. However, it became problematic to farm on irregular terrain, prone to drought. Around the middle of that decade, two men started renting land in Zacacoyuca, a town in the Iguala valley, where they used tractors instead of plowing with oxen. Five families went there off and on, while three more arrived in the mid-1980s. Some families went to Cuacoyula. During that decade, younger men held top posts in the *comisaría*. Heleodoro Martínez2, a vendor who sold in San Blas, became *comisario municipal* in 1977 at age thirty-two. His cousin Toribio Pascual, at that time teaching in the Montaña region, served as the *comisaría*'s secretary in 1968 at age twenty-one.

In the 1970s, women went further in their studies. Juana Salvador started school at age ten, in 1972. Her parents had not registered her, so she was an *oyente* (she audited). No one told her that she was not eligible to continue her schooling without a birth certificate. When Juana found out that teachers from the school in Atenango del Río were recruiting students, she was determined to get the required documentation. Her story of what happened in the municipal office illustrates the sexist and racist attitudes prevalent in those days. She told me, "An official did not want to give me the papers I needed, because he thought a woman, especially an indigenous one, should not continue her studies. I could not yet speak particularly good Spanish." Luckily, a man who overheard that conversation showed Juana how to get an extemporary birth certificate. She started at that school in 1979 together with five other girls. Only three finished; the others were homesick and went home. Juana, who went on to become a teacher, worked in the fields when not going to school. She continued to grow corn with the help of her children and her husband, also a teacher, until the early 1990s.

In 1975 Rubén Figueroa was chosen as governor at a time when the PRI was firmly in control. Luís Echeverría, Mexico's president from 1970 to 1976, channeled funds into rural areas. At the municipal level, Oscar Bárcenas, a teacher who wanted to bring about changes, forged patron-client links with indigenous communities. Aware of the rising influence of Toribio Pascual and Santos Bernal, a craft merchant, in Ahuehuepan, Bárcenas maintained their allegiance when he became municipal president in 1981. He collaborated closely with those men in the construction of four new classrooms. However, trade deficits put strains on the economy. A crisis was averted with the discovery of offshore oil, which allowed López Portillo (1976–1982) to continue social spending. One of the last projects during his term was a dam in a ravine near Ahuehuepan. It only lasted for two years, when it was washed away.

In 1978 the *primaria* (six grades of elementary school), part of the state system, closed its doors to be replaced with a bilingual federal school. This transition, which involved fighting, resulted in two years without classes. Many students dropped out, but four boys did their schooling in Xalitla, which requires an hour-long walk. Three quit and only one stayed until graduation. A bilingual school, Vicente Guerrero, opened in 1983, with Toribio as principal. The earlier teachers were replaced with ones from places where people speak Nahuatl: nearby Ahuelicán, Copalillo, and Zitlala. Living in rental accommodations, they taught in Ahuehuepan for more than twenty years.

An Impending Crisis

By 1979, with the craft boom ending, well-established vendors still had a chance to get ahead. Five men, including Pedro Rodríguez Villalba, were known for their dexterity in painting although they never got the capital to become wholesalers. Artisans and vendors found it increasingly difficult to make a good living. The cost of art supplies rose sharply while the prices paid for amates declined. When prices rose again, further inflation wiped out the price increase (Good Eshelman 1988, 32–33). Artisan-vendors were squeezed out and their children were not able to replicate their parents' success, resulting in more migration. Between 1983 and 1987, four consecutive crop failures made life difficult. People bought *maseca* (packaged corn-meal) in a parastatal institution, CONASUPO (National Company for Subsidies for the Population), that supplied basic foods. It often ran out of supplies. Vendors had a serious setback with a major earthquake in 1985. The worst was yet to come.

7

The Pueblo of Ahuehuepan (1985–2021)

This period of the town's history was a seesaw, with many ups and downs, including the start of the mass migration that eventually turned Ahuehuepan into a municipality with features of a ghost town. However, unlike in several other towns, Nahuatl continued to be the language spoken daily, and most people, including its migrants, continued to see themselves as Catholics.

The 1980s, the "the lost decade," saw a drop in oil prices, fiscal debt, and the devaluation of the peso. Investment in infrastructure stopped and people became disenchanted. The biggest problem was a lack of water. In the mid-1980s, people started moving to Colonia El Progreso, near Tonalapa del Sur, where they grew maize on rented land. Fortino Martínez, the first to leave, sold his house to his brother-in-law. They and three other families moved there when they became Jehovah's Witnesses. It is unclear to what extent the Witnesses were run out or if they would have left in any case. A few years later, Juan Catalán moved to Tonalapa solely due to a lack of water. His son Narcisco, who makes *cohetes*, has kept in close contact with his hometown.

Throughout the 1980s, girls left to work as cleaners and babysitters in San Marcos, California, while adults joined those working in Los Angeles, which happened around the time when another source of income disappeared. For a long time, people had sold *ajonjolí* (sesame), which ended when the factory that bought it closed. Given the absence of people, it was difficult to get a good turnout at meetings. The spread of a charismatic movement within the Catholic Church resulted in tensions. Older people were scandalized by prayer meetings with singing and hand clapping.

The political field was transformed. Under PRI rule, other political parties were tolerated until the PRD (Party of the Democratic Revolution) presented a serious challenge. Towards the end of the decade, the economy got worse, making remittances a more important source of income.

Census data on maize and craft production for people in the third and fourth cohort (from 1936 to 1995), supply a good idea of how many people worked the land. The proportion of those who did not grow maize quadrupled (from 9% to 30.5%). In contrast, the number of those engaged in craft production declined slightly, from 25 to 24 percent. Starting in 1970, the 315 people who were artisans outnumbered those who worked the land (122), figures consistent with the fact that internal migrants, less likely to grow corn, have continued painting or carving. The biggest change in the way people worked the land was the termination of a communal fence (see chapter 13).

THE MOVEMENT AGAINST A DAM

In 1990 people discovered that the government planned to build a hydroelectric dam in San Juan Tetelcingo that would have resulted in the relocation of several towns. Professionals from Xalitla and San Miguel set up the Council of Nahua Towns of the Upper Balsas (CPNAB) to oppose the project. Marcelino Díaz de Jesús, an economist, recruited Sabino Estrada, a Nahuatl-speaking leader in Copalillo who had just become that town's *president municipal*. Those leaders mobilized people to protest the building of the dam, organized demonstrations, set up roadblocks, and took part in a march to Mexico City. In Ahuehuepan only Marcelino's supporters took part. The following year, Mexico's president canceled the project in part to present a good image to the rest of the world after the Zapatista uprising in Chiapas (Schryer 2010a, 59–60; 2010b, 102–9). CPNAB downplayed its links with political parties even though Marcelino belonged to the PRD. That party did not get the same support in every town and there were internal divisions. Continuing high inflation was brought under control only after a 1994 free trade agreement for Mexico, the United States, and Canada (NAFTA). However, its implementation was not sufficient to halt international migration.

THE POST-NAFTA ERA

Juana Salvador Morales (teacher).

"After 1995, when almost everyone left, the town's economy changed completely. Recently Mexico's and particularly Guerrero's economy has deteriorated. The cost of everything has gone up and there are no craft sales. Vendors are coming back because the beaches are closed. People from the *montaña* [a nearby mountainous region] are also coming here.

"People who used to make visits around the time of Quinto Viernes also bought things to sell. The last time they returned, their merchandise remained unsold because of the lack of clients due to the spread of the virus [the COVID-19 pandemic]. A truck from Cuernavaca that used to drop off merchandise here has not come here for months, nor have we seen the wholesalers from Temalacatzingo near Copalillo."

Daniel Cardoso Mendez (a teacher from another town who moved to Ahuehuepan).

"There is no longer security now that people have entered houses to steal things like stereos. They are the same delinquents deported from the United States. That is why everyone is more careful about locking up. Houses where no one lives are especially vulnerable."

In 1994, the year that NAFTA was signed, tension between PRD and PRI supporters came to the surface with the creation of the Fondo Regional Indígena. It had a hefty budget, although funds were not disbursed until a decade later. Ahuehuepan's share consisted of four vans that were supposed to be managed as a cooperative; it became the private property of the men who did the paperwork, which is a bone of contention. Life became even more challenging with conflicts over public education. PRD supporters mobilized parents whose children were attending the *primaria* where Toribio was principal, to ask for his transfer. The infighting resulted in the closure of the school in 1995 until a new principal was found. Around that time, people who migrated a decade earlier started returning; they included young people whose dress and tattoos did not conform to local norms, including juvenile delinquents who were labeled as *cholos* by older people in Ahuehuepan who picked up that word with negative connotations from return migrants. In other ways, life became easier with the arrival of a tanker truck for delivering water. It arrived in 1995, but the water system, which brings it up from the river, was not installed until 2004. With the inauguration of a *telesecundaria*, Enrique C. Rebsamen, in 1996, students no longer left town to leave to continue their secondary schooling. However, lack of jobs led to further emigration. Starting in 1995, everyone crossed the border as soon as they finished their schooling.

In 1995 a mosquito-related disease (*chikungunya*) resulted in deaths. Around that time, people stopped painting because they did not see any result. At the national level, increasing dissatisfaction led to the defeat of the ruling party in 2000; the PRI lost its monopoly on power with the election of Vicente Fox, head of the PAN. The introduction of party politics went against the norms of how authorities are chosen, with an emphasis on unity. The introduction of slates of candidates of rival parties opened the wounds of personal enmities, triggering physical alterations. Everyone was scandalized when this rift resulted in the closure of the *comisaría*. Intervention by higher authorities resulted in an agreement that the candidate with the most votes would become the *comisario*, his opponent the *comisario suplente*. That same year, the PRI faction lost one of its leaders, Santos Bernal, who was killed in a drive-by shooting in Mazatlán. Ongoing personality clashes and disagreements led to further divisions among PRD supporters. As conflict abated, party affiliation became less of an issue. The rule of relying on alternating political parties for elections fell by the wayside.

After 2005, when authorities were selected as before, a compromise between opposing factions was restored, although confrontations between rival gangs disturbed the peace. One of the ringleaders, who came back in 1998 after being deported, recruited other former migrants. The other was a member of a gang in California prior to his return. He recruited two brothers from a poor family who had never been to the US. The first gang fell apart in 2008 when its leader was killed in a collision. The other gang turned to criminal acts, robbing the drivers of vehicles making deliveries. At first, everyone thought the robbers were strangers, until they were caught in June 2011 with the fatal shooting of the driver of a truck delivering bottled water. The man responsible ended up in jail in Chilpancingo. From then on, there was little gang activity. With the perpetrators of the worst crimes out of the way, people had less reason to worry. However, they could not ignore political clashes in other parts of Guerrero. Vendors faced new challenges; in 2011 one man lost his vehicle when he was robbed. The next year, someone on his way back to the US was mugged in Tijuana. With violence closer to home, people could not be complacent. The most memorable event is the disappearance of 43 students from the teachers' college of Ayotzinapa in 2014. Buildings in the state capital, including its main archive, were burned by people who protested, resulting in a delay of payments to teachers whose applications for retirement were destroyed. Ahuehuepan did not experience the presence of drug cartels whose members extorted merchants, although there were three kidnappings. A metal gate to prevent vehicles from entering at night was erected. More kidnappings in other parts of Mexico were another incentive for people to leave. After 1995 more international migrants returned to Mexico. One man would have remained longer but left after being involved in a car accident in the US. In Mexico he worked as a bricklayer. Another man, who came back with his wife and children, continued visiting his ranch until he succumbed to an illness. However, they were an exception; more people left than returned, resulting in an overall decline in population. In his 2002 year-end report, a doctor working in the health clinic mentions 1,435 people, a figure lower than the 2,103 people in a 1991 report. These figures do not include those living elsewhere, classified as a floating population. Adding in the migrants, the total number of people in 2020 was 3,000, not including those not born in Ahuehuepan.

After 2015 there were more improvements, including the paving of the road from Xalitla to Ahuelicán, which cut the car trip between Ahuehuepan and Xalitla to ten minutes. At the same time, emigration slowed down due to stricter border controls. Nevertheless, when people could not find good jobs, they had no choice but to leave. One young woman went to California when she could not find a position working for the Red Cross, a job for which she had continued her studies beyond high school. She had just married and given birth to her first child. That couple managed to cross the border, but many more young people did not.

The Decline in Corn Production

Throughout the second decade of the twenty-first century, people continued growing maize, but in decreasing numbers. In 2016 eighty-eight people received a subsidy for the purchase of fertilizers. Since not every person cultivating the land received the subsidy that year, the actual number was higher. According to my census, of the 906 adults in cohort five (1996 to 2021), 46.2 percent never worked the land; 31.8 percent of them learned to grow maize but did so only while living at home; another 15.2 percent did so for several years; and 6.7 percent (61 people) did so for most of their lives but are now too frail to work the land. Adding in the children who did not learn to grow corn (for a total of 1,350), the percentage of those who never grew corn was well over half (57%). I estimate that by 2024 the number of people working on the land will be around fifty.

Recent Developments

Juana Salvador Morales.

"A lot of horses and other animals died in Ahuehuepan in 2018."

I had not yet finished writing this book when the impact of immigration policy under Trump became clear. Flavia, whose baby was born in California, was unable to get back there to join her husband after coming back to Ahuehuepan to deal with a family emergency. After many attempts to return to California, she finally succeeded in 2021. She is now back in California, where she is working in the kitchen of a restaurant. Pablo, a former migrant who created havoc when he came back to Mexico in 2000, had no trouble finding a coyote (human smuggler) to get him across the border. Since then, things have gotten worse, especially in Guerrero. During the previous thirty years, men from a neighboring region had already been working as helpers during the harvest and in the construction of new houses. Starting in 2019, an influx of people, including younger men looking for part-time work, have converged on Ahuehuepan. They are desperate, since there are not enough jobs, not even menial part-time ones.

The most recent development, in 2020, is the outbreak of a global epidemic. By the end of October, a half dozen people were infected, which is less than in other towns; most recovered, but four died, including a young vendor. The economic impact was disastrous: the income of vendors ground to a halt; so, many went back to Ahuehuepan, where they do not need to pay rent. With no cash income, they grow maize to have enough to eat. Like the people already living there, they go to Iguala only when necessary. Some people look for work in restaurants and other dead-end jobs; yet the epidemic was an opportunity for one family to get ahead. A migrant with a decent job in California lent money to his brothers in Ahuehuepan to grow maize to sell to their neighbors at a time of a shortage during the dry season. The brothers, who arranged for a tractor to clear a section of land near the river, were able to harvest a crop early by renting pumps for irrigation. The brothers had no trouble paying off the loan. Unfortunately, the number of people getting sick from COVID increased in the winter of 2021. A climate of insecurity and mistrust of any government is now almost universal.

Juana Salvador Morales.

"As a result of the coronavirus, many stores in Iguala are closed, and men that usually come to deliver merchandise for our stores, mainly beer and soft drinks, no longer show up; I have enough on hand to keep going for a bit longer."

A recounting of Ahuehuepan's history is not sufficient for fully understanding what it is like to live there and how people's lives have been altered by the exodus of the town's inhabitants.

Part Four
Life in Ahuehuepan

8

Daily Life, Standards of Living, and Schooling

Life in Ahuehuepan is characterized by diverse features. It can be peaceful, relaxed, even dreary when you hardly see anyone; at other times, the town is crowded, such as during Quinto Viernes, when people from different towns and those living in other parts of Mexico arrive on horseback or in vehicles. Those in the US fly in. But short visits are not typical of most days, nor is what is eaten on special occasions the same as a normal daily diet. This chapter, the first of seven, looks at various topics, including cost of living, housing, and schooling. An examination of buildings, vehicles, and the ownership of consumer goods supplies insights into wealth differences, while a final section on public life gives added insights into gender. While much of the information in this part of the book was provided by people who told me what it is like to live in Mexico, I also report on what I saw while living in Ahuehuepan.

DAILY ROUTINES AND COSTS OF LIVING

The day starts early, with the sound of *cohetes* (firecrackers) and the announcement of a vendor's arrival. Women sweep the plaza and light fires to boil water for making coffee. The daily staple has not changed much over the years. People prefer locally grown maize. Turning that into cornmeal (*masa*) to make tortillas or tamales is labor-intensive. Alternatively, one can use an electric grinder or pay somebody with a mill. Nowadays the cultivation of maize requires money to buy fertilizer and insecticides, plus to pay someone if not enough able-bodied family members are around to help. The costs are covered by remittances. However, financial aid might not be enough to buy fresh fruit. Women cook on a clay griddle over an open fire although a half dozen houses have gas stoves. Some households have outdoor ovens to make sweet bread to eat with morning coffee. Those with cows make cheese eaten on special occasions, but little milk is consumed. Soft drinks (*refrescos*) are a part of meals, and beer is drunk throughout the day, especially by men. Bottled beverages are bought in stores in people's homes with the expectation that the empties will be returned. People eat better today; they can afford to buy more food, yet they rarely go to a restaurant.

Household Routines and Etiquette

Most household activities are done outdoors; rooms are for sleeping—on a bed, a cot, or a *petate*. During the day, people must scramble. In one house, I saw a boy enter their yard. He bossed around his sister, whose parents were constantly asking her to do something: "Come quickly! Prepare the dough for the tortillas. Turn off the valve; the water tank is overflowing. Your father has just returned. Help take off the saddle." While talking to Margarita, there were interruptions, with dogs barking, someone yelling at kids standing close to the edge of the rooftop of a neighbor's house, and loud music. On one occasion, her brother Esteban, who tried to get the attention of a truck delivering gas, was ignored. Her sister-in-law had to chase it before she returned with a case of Coca-Cola.

Unwritten rules change. The exchange of greetings is the most noticeable. Older people, who complain about lack of respect, remember how everyone used to exchange greetings: *tlaneextihle* (early in the morning), *panoolteh* (after 9:00 a.m.), *tiootlakiilteh* (afternoon), or *kwahle yowahle* (in the evening). Young people no longer greet the elderly that way; instead, they use the Spanish expression *buenos días*. The only nonverbal greeting still prevalent is a bow of the head and a touch of fingertips with a godparent. Such greetings and other norms and customs so far described apply to migrants during home visits.

Houses and *Sitios*

Margarita Gómez Marcos (Ahuehuepan, 1949–2018).

"The best place to get the soil for making adobe bricks [*xaantle*] is Aapankoyotl. An adobe house can still have a zacate roof, but if you want a tile one, you must find a good *albañil* [bricklayer]. Felix Pedro's house that you see below has an old tile roof that has never leaked. Only three men in Ahuehuepan could make them: Wenceslao

Salvador, Fernando Salvador, and Juan M. Bernal. Wenceslao also made stone fences without using cement; he made the one at the bottom of our *sitio* [lot].

"Bernardo Aldama built a good house with a concrete roof in the sitio that belongs to two elderly sisters who lived together in a house with a thatch roof. Bernardo was not related to them, but they gave him permission to build a house with the expectation that he and his wife would look after the sisters when needed."

A man born in Ahuehuepan in 1971 (then moved to California; interviewed in Mexico, 2006).

"Everyone from Ahuehuepan in Lincoln rents. They save money to build a house in Mexico, even if they are not going to live there. I made this great big house. What was I thinking? I should have built a smaller one that could accommodate the whole family. We do not visit Ahuehuepan very often."

Margarita Gómez Marcos (Ahuehuepan, 1949–2018).

"Some people have a proper *panteón* [vault]. Sometimes you can put on a second story if the family already has one. You can also put a small enclosure on top, with a cross, so that you can have flowers and candles on the grave without them getting wet. But that is expensive—seven thousand pesos."

The legal status of urban lots has not changed much. Such lots (sitios) are part of the town's communal land, but houses are private property. Whoever pays for the funeral costs takes over the deceased person's house. Young couples usually move into their own house after having children. The urban zone is periodically expanded to create more sitios, which last happened in 2008. It did not have paved streets, running water, or electricity, but the lots are bigger.

Styles and construction materials have changed over the last eighty years. By the start of the twenty-first century, half the houses were made of *tabiques* (red bricks) and poured concrete. There are no chimneys; kitchens are outdoors or in a separate shed. A house's size and how its walls are finished are indicative of wealth differences. My ethnohistorical census includes data on 1920 houses in Ahuehuepan. The 881 (42.8%) smaller houses are made with inexpensive material. The walls consist of adobe bricks or tabiques, and their roofs are covered with corrugated tar paper, asbestos, or metal sheets (*laminas*). They have earthen floors. The only houses with walls made from daub and wattle (sticks with a mud covering), the norm in the past, are today used as kitchens. The 530 (27.5%) medium-sized houses, which used to have beams and wooden doors, were later made with adobe, with tile roofs. Nowadays such houses are single-story cement structures. The 547 (28.5%) larger than average houses once had at least two wooden roof beams; they are now multi-story structures made from poured concrete. Twenty-five large and luxurious houses

(1.3%) were once characterized by ceramic floors; today they have painted exteriors with all the amenities. Such houses have elaborate arches, an exterior wall with a gate, and a covered tank for storing water. There are also people who own more than one house in Ahuehuepan or elsewhere in Mexico. Of the 2,075 adults who have owned houses, either alone or jointly with a spouse, the vast majority (1,815) owned only one, 143 owned two, and seventeen had three or more. In all cases, ownership passed on to another family member, including the ten cases where someone sold a house to a relative.

Larger but not luxurious houses, such as the three-story one where I lived during my first stay, were built with remittances. My room on the third floor had a window with metal bars overlooking an unpaved yard where beasts of burden were kept. There was a bed, two tables, and a single light bulb. In another room, people bathed by scooping water out of an oil barrel. The back half of the house, partly underground, is used to store the corn cobs from the last harvest.

The two houses of the Gómez family, whom I visited a lot, are typical of the ones whose construction was in part financed by migrants. Their sitio, reached by walking down a path, is situated in a small ravine. One of the houses has adobe walls and a tile roof, while the other has a room with tabique walls, with an extension. Both are surrounded by *corredores* (verandas) with retaining walls made of concrete. On the other side of the ravine, a house built by their paternal grandfather has a clay oven and a car with flat tires that has not been used for over ten years. Its owner, who used to be a vendor, has never been in the US.

Most houses are on the grid, but power shuts down when least expected, so people improvise. When I was visiting one house, a girl pulled out a flashlight when the lights went off. Her mother was about to use an electric mill to grind maize, but she had to wait for an hour for electricity to return. When the circuit in my room shorted out, my landlady changed into blue jeans, returning with pliers to repair a burned-out socket. There is little indoor plumbing; water pumped up from the river reaches houses through pipes exposed above ground. Water is shut off for hours at a time, but not everyone can afford a holding tank for storing water. The main deficiency is that most households do not even have an outhouse or a toilet. Half a dozen houses have showers but no hot water. Only one person has a washing machine.

Each sitio has its history. *Juan Ayala and Maria Luciano*, born in the 1930s, lived in a lot used by other family members going back to the nineteenth century. They had ten children. *Juan* started living there in a small house with a palm roof. It is no longer there, nor are the houses that once belonged to *Juan's* parents. As the family grew, that younger couple built a new house with an asbestos roof. Their six sons would normally have built their own houses in that lot, but the only ones who did so, on opposite ends of the original sitio, are *Mario* and *Felipe*. Around the time of his first marriage, *Mario* built his own house, with a corrugated tar paper roof. He and his wife, who made trips to Puerto Vallarta, had two sons, whom they used to take along. By 1985 those sons built a bigger house for their parents; however, they did not return and have never seen that house. Two other siblings, including the oldest, built houses in another barrio.

When his wife died, *Mario* coped by himself until his parents moved in. *Juan* and *Maria* later left to join *Felipe*, who by that time had his own house. Only one section of the original house survived an earlier expansion of Mario's house. When *Mario* died of cirrhosis of the liver in 1998, his house remained empty. His brother *Felipe* became a vendor who makes trips while his wife stays home. They raised seven children, including four sons. Their oldest son, who became a vendor after spending time in California, married a woman from another town. In 2015 that son, who now lives there, built the first house in the lot considered to be a good house; it has a flat roof made from poured concrete. Another son, who spent part of his life in the US, then built a similar, slightly bigger house. The fifth of *Juan*'s sons, *Filemón*, who lives in a house with an asbestos roof, could not afford to build a better house since he did know how to make crafts, nor did he go to the US. He was never a vendor. Married twice, his children set off on their own. Only one of *Juan*'s sons built a house close to that of his father. By 2021 there were six houses in the original lot.

LOCKED-UP HOUSES

There are houses not used for part of the year or not at all. Migrants used to think they would make return visits. However, if or when they return for good, they will not enjoy their grandchildren, who are not likely to join them. Nevertheless, migrants continue to send home money to build houses. A family member usually makes the arrangements. During a visit in the spring of 2010, I did the first of three tours of 393 locked-up houses. The person who took me around explained that none of the houses are abandoned because their owners will return. During my third trip to Texas, where I stayed with a family, I showed them the photos of such houses taken during my last trip. One of the children asked his father, "Does grandpa live in a ghost town?"

By 2019 there were more unused houses; my census includes information on house occupancy to distinguish between those always closed and houses closed for several years at a time. The resultant numbers were higher for men (111; 102 for both categories) than for women (102 and 83). The difference can be explained by the fact that such houses were built by couples, some of whom separated, while others were owned by people without a partner.

Vehicles and Other Consumer Goods

Most people with big houses have cars. The ownership of vehicles, especially pickup trucks, is more prevalent than ten years ago. In 2016, there were eighty-five roadworthy vehicles in Ahuehuepan, including vans, with families owning up to four. One was registered in a woman's name, and five women drive. By 2021 a total of fifty-four families (but still less than 20 percent), own one or more cars. That number does not include people in other parts of Mexico or migrants in the US. Of those, sixty-two individuals own one or two vehicles. Five own four. In terms of other belongings, not everyone has the kitchen appliances city people take for granted. Half the households have telephones; those without one use a neighbor's phone. The other possibility is a pay phone in someone's house. More than half the households have fridges and televisions. About a third of the population, including teenagers, have cell phones that are used when people are away, given that the town has a poor signal. Eighty-one men own or once owned horses. Today only people who are destitute do not have a donkey or a mule.

SCHOOLING, LIFE EXPECTANCY, AND ALCOHOLISM

Juana Salvador Morales.

"None of my nieces and nephews finished their studies; their parents did not want to spend money. Thirty years ago, the only costs were buying textbooks, but nowadays students need their cell phone and a tablet.

"Many young people do not want to continue their schooling. Some of them, who stay home and 'hang around' [*kikistinemeh*], do not have jobs, unlike their parents, who worked hard to earn the money to support them]. Those young people don't grow maize and do not leave to find a way of making a living.

"Some people, like my brother-in-law, recognize letters of the alphabet and numbers even though they never went to school. They had to be shown a couple of times. Others with the same age learned how to do multiplication with only one year of school."

Not everyone finishes school. Attendance is compulsory, but there are parents who do not send their children. In 2008 I met a young man who did not know how to read and write because his father thought public education was a waste of time. After a parent's death, children usually stop going to school. A quarter of the students drop out. About half of those who complete their *primaria* do not finish the *telesecundaria*, a three-years secondary school where teachers impart classes using televisions programs. They quit when their family emigrates or because they get married. Few students continue studying after *secundaria*.

Lifespan is shorter than in cities because of the low quality of health care and nutrition. The cause of a death reported in 2004—severe malnutrition and chronic bronchitis—illustrates that even people who once had more resources do not live well in their old age. Excessive consumption of beer and soft drinks leads to diabetes, a common cause of early death. Those who require medical attention are as likely to pay a woman who comes from Xalitla to give injections than to go to the local clinic that does not always have a doctor. Treatment requiring an operation is available at the state's expense, but there is no free dental surgery or treatment for cataracts. Pregnant women can go to a free clinic in Xalitla, but they must still pay for a taxi and for something to eat. Most of them give birth at home, while teachers with benefits have their babies in a hospital in Iguala.

Alcoholism is a problem. Even those who are not alcoholics drink to excess, which can result in accidents, especially while driving. Consumption of alcohol, especially during celebrations associated with major life transitions, has been a social norm for a long time. Unlike in some other towns in the region, there is no stigma attached to women drinking during such occasions. In general people drink in moderation during the rest of the year, except for a minority of men. People rarely drink at home because drinking is typically part of a social event. However, due to the introduction of inexpensive beer bought in Iguala, and which is promoted by the owners of the vehicles specializing in its transport, the consumption of that form of alcoholic beverage became more prevalent with men, especially those who have not migrated. An emphasis on drinking *parejo* (in equal amounts) makes it difficult for those who do want to drink in excess to stay longer without drinking, although people (including myself) find ways to make it look like they are drinking more than they want. Those who do not like such peer pressure are resigned to the fact that there is little that can be done to alleviate the situation. A woman sarcastically told me: "One *comisario* arranged for the construction of a retaining wall to prevent those who are drunk from falling from the *comisaría*'s verandah. People thought that was his greatest accomplishment!" I noticed that the only men who stopped drinking for good were those who converted to another religion that had a strict rule about not drinking, which resulted in them cutting off most ties with friends and instead spending more time with other members of that religion. One of his former friends who regretted the loss of contact told me:

> He was my best friend, and I did not want to lose that friendship. I begged him to join me at social events and trips to local stores where people socialize. I told him I respected his decision to join another church and that I would not expect him to drink anything alcoholic and neither would I. We could just talk. But he was not interested.

THE PUBLIC REALM

The cycle of activities associated with worship and governance is marked with cohetes, whose sound is ubiquitous. Village authorities handle part of their cost, while expenses related to recreational facilities, like the *cancha* and the bullring, are shared by the Mexican state. The paving and widening of streets involve monetary contributions and volunteer labor. A government program financed the installation of the water system, but ongoing repairs and upgrades are the responsibility of the town's authorities.

The town's officials occupy a sparsely furnished town hall, with a desk, a side table, two wooden benches, and plastic chairs. It is connected to a smaller room where women prepare food during fiestas. A minor official uses a drum to notify the other authorities that it is time to get together. Meetings start late to allow people to finish eating. In the meantime, other day-to-day business can be conducted. It is hard to figure out when such meetings end. On one occasion, the last item was a discussion about an agreement that the area surrounding the bullring had to be kept clear for parking. An official stood up, proposing that everyone go to look at the area under discussion. Few men got up to go. I went home, not knowing until later that eventually most people at the meeting ended up joining that official.

The town hall is a male domain. In theory it is open to women, but few are comfortable in a male-dominated space where men are smoking, drinking, and joking. During a visit in 2005, I saw how a woman who came to see the *comisario* waited outside until the authorities were ready to see her. This was the second time she had come to lodge a complaint about her husband's disorderly conduct and his failure to support his family. When they sent someone to summon him, he refused to show up. The matter was delayed until the next day; that man refused to show up again. She gave up. Women, expected to attend meetings, must wait patiently to be heard. Occasionally an articulate, strong-willed woman speaks up, sometimes to no avail.

Standards of living are high compared to other parts of Guerrero, although there is local poverty. Nowadays more things are available for sale, but income has shrunk. Experienced bricklayers can make a reasonable living, but only if migrants send remittances to finance house construction. Overall, the town is peaceful, albeit with undercurrents of violence and conflict, with added tribulations, a topic that requires a separate chapter.

9

Getting Ahead and Hardships

This chapter, which covers family and life trajectories, includes the topics of setbacks plus how people cope with stress and help one another. Much of it is based on what people told me. Further insights came from anthropologists who did research in the region.

Victor Tomás (born in 1936; a vendor who also works the land).
"As a boy I worked in Xalitla where I earned ten pesos per day. At age seventeen, I started taking animals to pasture and no longer worked as a *peon*. By the time I was twenty, I worked on my own."

Juana Salvador Morales.
"I told my daughter and her husband that to run a successful store they must always get up on time. You must eat early and stay until eight in the evening or later when necessary.
"People who learn how to paint are constantly getting better and improving their technique; they must get better to find people willing to buy what they make."

Prior to 1970, the only way to advance was with cattle. Their sale was once the main way to get ahead economically. However, animals roaming freely can be lost or stolen. To have security, households must have at least twenty or thirty. Only people with more than sixty were considered as *riikos*. Once the craft industry and jobs as teachers or paramedics offered other ways to get ahead, owning cattle became less important. For several decades, working the land combined with being a vendor was workable, although those gone a lot could not take care of their cattle. After 1994 all young people aspired to work in the US. They do not continue their studies the way they did twenty years ago. They see how well migrants have done. One person commented: "A nurse or a teacher, after years of study, earns less than someone doing yard work in the US. Young people keep trying to cross the border no matter the risks." School dropouts and deported migrants take on jobs as bricklayer's assistants or work on road projects. Other people earn money in craft production with the help of their children. During one visit, I saw a woman and her daughter attaching plastic legs to gourds to make animal figures, dipping their fingers into a bottle cut in half to hold glue. My census shows that 299 such women and 257 men worked on commission; people use the expression *they rent themselves out* (*se alquilan*). However, it is not possible to make progress if you do not sell what you make. For those who cannot leave, the only other option is to set up a store, although that requires start-up capital.

People try to get ahead; however, doing so can lead to envy. Amate painters told Aline Hémond (2004, 39–40) that the economic success of their counterparts in Ameyaltepec is the outcome of a pact with the devil. The suspicion associated with wealth can explain why *riikos* claim to be poor and say that they suffer. Anyone who buys a new car must be careful in case a jealous person inflicts damage. Someone with a fancy watch or who receives a gift from a visitor tries to keep it a secret. A sudden decline in fortune is seen as the result of the intentions of someone who resorts to witchcraft, which in turn could lead to retaliation. The Spanish word *brujería* is used. To some extent this is still the case today.

HARDSHIPS AND COPING WITH STRESS

Juana Salvador Morales (a retired teacher in Ahuehuepan).

"It is unusually cold right now. Many people who lost their homes and belongings do not have the blankets they need. A few people have died."

Daniel Cardoso (a teacher from another town who moved to Ahuehuepan).

"When Jose Delgado's wife was sick, they spent a lot of money to have oxygen tanks delivered to their house. She lived a bit longer. Other people died early because of a lack of medical services or a shortage of funds. A boy next door died because he did not have access to a good clinic."

Margarita Gómez Marcos (a woman, now deceased, who never left Ahuehuepan).

"Juan, a *cuetero*, died when the fireworks he was making exploded. Feliciano lived in a thatch-roof house that burned to the ground; he is alive but has a burn mark on his stomach."

I was told many such stories. One source of grief revolves around urban lots, as in the case of the Atanacio family, where two brothers shared a *sitio*. The younger one died when their father was alive. Francisco, the older brother's son, built his own house on the sitio without leaving enough room for his orphaned nephews. His mother, who could not prevent her son from taking more than his share of the lot, persuaded him to at least set aside a less desirable part. One of Francisco's younger nephews, who went to California, sent money to his older brother, who stayed home to supervise the construction of a twenty-meter house on a steep hillside. When that house was finished, they traded places and that brother left to work in the US. Resentful of how they were excluded when growing up, he got into an argument with his uncle *Francisco* during a trip home. They have not spoken for years.

In the case of another sitio, two brothers each built a house when their father was alive, enclosing their lot with a wall. The oldest son met his wife, a woman from another town, while working as a vendor in Tampico. Through connections with her family, he went to Houston for several years. The other brother, who also worked in the US, became a vendor in La Peñita. Disagreements resulted in the older brother's wife moving back to her hometown, where she and her husband raised their children. They never used the house he built; instead, their parents and two unmarried daughters were living there in 2004. In my ethnohistorical census, twenty-two individuals were caught up in such disputes.

Another source of grief is the loss of loved ones due to accidents, including those that resulted in a child's death, such as when a five-year-old boy fell to the ground after climbing on the bumper of a tanker truck. The driver was not aware of that boy when he drove off. Prior to the introduction of vehicles, people were more likely to perish by falling from a donkey, dropping down a well, the bite of a scorpion, cirrhosis (12 cases), or a fireworks explosion. For the 1,314 people in my survey who passed away prior to 2021, 829 died a natural death, usually at an older age, followed by 348 people who died after a prolonged illness. Other known causes are accidents (56 cases), dying while giving birth (42 women), and homicide (29 men).

Juana Salvador Morales (a retired teacher in Ahuehuepan).

"Miguel, a ten-year old boy, died when several bags that toppled smothered him as if he was buried alive. He had gone with a group of people who dug up soil that they put in large, heavy bags."

Abuse and Violence

The Alto Balsas has its share of intrafamilial violence. Dominique Raby reports that young men in San Agustín consider violence against women as "normal." Women, who have their own interpretation, see men's violent behavior as "expected," yet wrong and against traditional norms (Raby 2012, 170; 2014, 188–89). People told me about men hitting their wives or lovers, at the same time pointing out this was worse in the past. Margarita Gómez recounted: "One man wore out the switches he used to whip his wife. People would hear her cry out in pain, but she never reported the abuse to the authorities. Another woman whose husband struck her with his machete also did not report it."

In some cases, physical abuse follows a long period of setbacks and disappointments. One woman reported:

> I only studied in the primaria. After four years, they started the telesecundaria but that was not for me. Instead, I worked in the fields; after the harvest I would fetch water with my donkey. I also made crafts. The way I grew up was very different than my siblings. My mother did not want me to study; she said that I was the only one who could help her because my brothers were all going to school. Sometimes I felt very bad because I would rather have studied. Afterwards I married in both the church and in the town hall, but my marriage went badly. I had five children, but my husband was violent. I put up with it for seventeen years until I could not take the abuse anymore, so I got separated and I now live alone with my children.

Even when women lodge grievances, they are not likely to get justice. Prior to 1990, a woman rarely left an abusive husband. This is no longer the case; they are now educated and can make their own living. Nowadays a woman will not put up with a man who beats her, yet she is still likely to suffer the consequences of separation. It is easier for a man to have an affair than the other way around. Some men who are deported start living with another woman; this is more difficult for a woman working and taking care of her children. Yet overall, women now speak up and act. One abusive man hit his wife and beat their children every time he came back from the US. She left him and became a migrant herself, taking her children to a city where she would not run into him. Today women are in a better position to defend their rights. *Victoria*, daughter of a vendor in Mazatlán, was married to a man who worked for his father-in-law, who helped the couple buy their own house before they moved to California. After getting deported, the man got involved with another woman; they had a child and started living in a house in Ahuehuepan that belonged to *Victoria*, whose ex-husband went back to working for his former father-in-law. When *Victoria* found out about the situation, she flew back to denounce him in the town hall, saying "it is alright that you traded me in for someone else, but the house in Ahuehuepan is mine, and so is the house in Mazatlán."

Physical violence can take various forms. When a man known for his aggressive behavior cut his uncle with a machete, the perpetrator's relatives no longer put up with him. He left town. A more notorious case is four brothers who terrorized their neighbors. When one of them stabbed Hermilo Isauro, a former *comisario*, over a disagreement, no one dared to report it. Hermilo died from his wounds. When another brother killed a man with a pistol during a return visit, he fled to avoid arrest. Yet another brother, recently deported, recruited young men to intimidate people and vandalize property. They only stopped when he died in a collision. The fourth brother, *Pablo*, who came back in 2000, joined his brothers whenever they confronted anyone with whom they disagreed. They beat up their sister's husband. *Pablo* used veiled threats to become the president of the high school committee, to keep an eye on its teachers. At the same time, he was an accomplice of the younger return migrants recruited by his younger brother, who did not like it when the *comisario suplente* locked them up in the village jail. When he finished his term of office, *Pablo* and his brothers forced the *suplente* to get out of his pickup; they beat him up badly enough that he had to go to the hospital. That man did not lodge a formal complaint. Instead, he waited for the right time to seek his revenge; during a fiesta he pulled out a knife and slashed *Pablo*'s abdomen. This is not the first time that someone took the law into their own hands. Violence usually goes together with excessive use of alcohol. Even when that is not the case, the inability of alcoholics to work causes hardships for other family members. Most disagreements take a less dramatic, nonviolent, form. Boys can be mischievous at the time of a wedding of a woman previously living with another man; they will throw garbage into the place where the couple is sleeping, to remind them she "has already been discarded." Occasionally a marriage is canceled, as in the case when one woman's mother made it quite clear that she and her husband did not approve of their union. The couple had already booked a flight back to Mexico and made all the arrangements for their wedding when she called it off.

Coping with Hardships and Helping One Another

Margarita Gómez Marcos (Ahuehuepan, 1949–2018).

"Three months ago, the daughter of someone I know had a terrible car accident. She is still in the hospital and may not survive. Everyone contributed to pay the twenty thousand pesos in medical costs."

People cope with stress through interactions with saints that enable them to cope with life's misfortunes (see chapter 14). Individuals may have a favorite saint in the church of another town, where they leave a *promesa* consisting of an offering, as part of a petition for something they want. Migrants send money to a relative in Mexico with instructions about where and for which saint to leave it. People also support each other through reciprocal labor, such as when someone puts the final layer of cement on for the roof of a house. A paid bricklayer oversees the work, but everyone else works as a volunteer, mixing the cement and spreading it over a latticework of wooden slats. On one such occasion, it was my job to fill the cracks between the slats with paper to prevent cement from dripping down. When finished the owner invited us to a meal. People likewise use reciprocal labor in their cornfields. They are kind to those who have physical disabilities. I have seen people interact with *Rodrigo*, a mute man; they have figured out how to interpret his hand gestures and return his greetings. Another man, *Victor*, who is mentally challenged, did not attend school. When his father was no longer able to take care of him, people took turns taking him in.

A lack of amenities, combined with a shortage of steady employment, makes migration an attractive alternative to staying home. Young people keep crossing the border no matter how difficult it is. They leave because of a lack of opportunities and increasing violence in other parts of Mexico. Yet the low cost of living and a decent infrastructure in comparison to other regions, plus the availability of social aid, makes living in Ahuehuepan workable. The town is a haven for people who are deported or who fall on tough times, including those who cannot survive the competitive world of selling to tourists. At home they do not have to pay for accommodation. People choose to stay for other reasons; there are enough odd jobs available locally to get by, and one can always earn money producing crafts. Those who have worked long enough as migrants to save up for their retirement live comfortably upon returning. For a complete understanding of people's lives, we must take a closer look at kinship.

10

Family Dynamics, Marriage, Names, and *Compadres*

A household consisting of a nuclear family is the exception. Usually, two or more brothers build houses in the same lot until they run out of space. Households are a convenient starting point for talking about a cycle starting with courtship. In covering that topic, this chapter goes back and forth among what I learned from people, what they report and believe, and what I saw. I will further report on some of the findings of my survey. It ends with a discussion of *compadrazgo*.

Rules around courtship have changed, from strict chaperoning and a long engagement to more flexible norms. Fifty years ago, a young man would make his intentions known through a go-between. A prospective marriage required negotiations, with trips to the house of the woman's parents. A mediator is expected to bring money and gifts, a de facto bride wealth, for the suitor's future father-in-law.[1] A man may first live with his wife's parents, a form of bride service. Sometimes a couple elopes, which means a boy bringing a girl to his parents' house. The Nahua term is *cholowa* (run away), although the Spanish term, *se roba la muchacha* (to steal a girl), is also used. Nowadays couples elope as soon as they finish school. Such a union must still be acknowledged. Someone with the diplomatic skill to placate the girl's parents brings cigarettes, pop, and alcoholic beverages. With international migration, people became more accepting of young couples living together. In 2001 I saw an elopement followed by discussions in the girl's parents' house; it was decided

---

1 A well-known mediator was Bonifacio Bárcenas. The text of his brides' petition (in Nahuatl, Spanish, and English) recorded in 1977, was published in 2008 (see Ramírez and Flores 2008).

that they would live with the boy's father in the US. In 2008 I saw an elopement followed by a civil marriage. Both sets of parents signed the documents. A witness told me: "Parents are in favor of an early marriage, because if a boy promises to marry a girl and then goes off to the States, he might find another girl. If they have a civil ceremony in front of witnesses, they will have a more secure relationship."

Juana Salvador Morales.

"When *Victor Sotelo* died, his wife from Ahuelicán made a living as a vendor. Their oldest daughter took care of her younger siblings in a house in the Aliano patio in Ahuehuepan whenever her mother was away. When the Aliano family discovered that her mother had found another man, those siblings moved to the house of their grandmother in Ahuelicán and later to Mexico City."

COURTSHIP AND MARRIAGE

Margarita Gómez Marcos (Ahuehuepan, 1949–2018).

"In the past, people rarely ran off to live together. A man had to ask for a girl's hand and wait a couple of months. A *wewe* [mediator] sent to the *novia*'s [girlfriend's] house, would remain standing [during the first visit]. On his second visit, they would ask him to sit down and offer a soft drink. Only on the third visit, when and the *novio* and his parents came, would they drink an alcoholic beverage. The young couple sat on small wooden boxes, the adults on chairs.

"When people get married in front of a priest, he has more say than he did in the past. A couple cannot get married in the church without first showing all their documents, including proof that they were baptized as well as confirmed. The priest also requires them to first get a civil marriage license."

Mothers sometimes arrange a marriage, such as when several women paid visits to a couple who were outsiders. They used the expression *nosiwaamon* (daughter-in-law) when referring to the couple's daughter, *Daniela*, with whom I later spoke in Los Angeles. She told me no boy would have agreed to marry her: "They thought I was too outspoken and would call me *tlaweehle* (bad-tempered). However, they all treated me with respect. No boy ever bothered me or made advances. They were afraid of me."

Sometimes mothers had more luck, as in the case of two women who were matchmakers. *Susana Lucas*, a widow living with her only son, was friends with a woman whose husband was well-off. The son started working for them as a hired hand at age twelve. The rich family had five children, all but one of whom were married. The fact that their only unmarried daughter was in her thirties was a problem since women are expected to get married early; a girl who does not have a man by age seventeen is known as *ichpochlamatsiin* (old maid). The two mothers persuaded *Saul*, then fifteen, to marry *Fidelba* as a way of getting ahead. *Susana* and her son paid a visit to the house of that rich family. She left him there to be their son-in-law who would continue working for his father-in-law, an exception to the norm of patrilocal postmarital residence.

There are three types of marriages, including common-law unions. A civil one is separate from a marriage officiated by a priest. The latter is not recognized by a state that considers the children of parents without a civil marriage as illegitimate, and vice versa. Until 1980 most couples were married in front of a priest, followed by a family get-together. A mediator negotiated the amount of flour the groom's family would bring to make bread. Women from the bride's family crushed cacao tablets to prepare a chocolate drink. The parents of Julia Bernal were the first to hold a wedding with a European-style bridal dress and a sit-down banquet. It is called a *boda*, as opposed to "getting married with bread." Before weddings started, only richer families would arrange a civil marriage to legalize the inheritance of property. Around the mid-1990s, most people started having a civil ceremony to get a marriage certificate that may come in handy. One couple went to California when he was seventeen and she was fourteen. When their first baby was born, he would have been arrested for rape if he had not been able to show the papers to prove they were legally married. Such couples return to Mexico for a church wedding only when they have enough money to afford a boda.

Weddings

Margarita Gómez Marcos (Ahuehuepan, 1949–2018).

"Having a boda costs a lot of money. The mass requires paying 300 pesos to the priest. You spend 120 pesos for the fireworks, more for the flowers—fifteen flowerpots [*macetas*] for the church, at fifty pesos a pot—up to 30,000 for a band, another 8,000 for someone to film the proceedings, plus the cost of fifty cases of beer and soft drinks [*refrescos*] at 150 pesos per carton, not counting the additional hundred cases to leave at the house of the girl's parents. If you buy a steer, that is another 10,000."

Obdulia Enrique Calixto (from Ahuehuepan; wife of a teacher also from Ahuehuepan).

"Conjuntos [musical groups] are very expensive. One young man who is about to have his wedding wants the well-known Conjunto de Durango. They charge 15,000 pesos."

A boda consists of a blend of modern and traditional elements. After mass, the wedding party continues to the groom's parents' house for a banquet. Mariachis and the village brass band take turns playing. Next, the couple receives advice from elders on the duties of a husband and of the wife obeying her mother-in-law. At a designated time, they continue to the bride's parents' house, where more refreshments are served. All wedding gifts, including a bed, are presented to the couple, who are subjected to another round of advice-giving. Next the married couple's relatives start the "dance of the bottle," holding bottles of liquor and cartons of beer over their heads. The last stage is another banquet followed by dancing in the *cancha*.

NAMES AND KINSHIP CLUSTERS

Fulgencia Pascual Enriquez (a teacher in Ahuehuepan).

"Many people have two first names, and sometimes we don't know which is the real one. When my grandfather was born, they might have given him the name Ponciano, but he also got the name Domingo because he was born on Sunday [*Domingo*]. Similarly, the name of another man is Lenin Jesus because he was born on the 24th of December."

Unlike other regions with an indigenous word for a family name, Spanish surnames (*apellidos*) are prevalent in the Alto Balsas. Yet people with surnames like Felipe, Pascual, or Toribio, used as first names in other parts of Mexico, could be stigmatized, because such names reveal their ethnic origin; hence some people change their surname, for example from Enrique to Enríquez, "because that sounds more like what it should be." Other names—Muñoz, Calixto—can be found anywhere in Mexico. At one time, most women were not assigned surnames; they were shown in the records only as "Maria." In other cases, it is unclear who someone's biological parents are, such as when an orphan takes on a surname other than the one expected, particularly if he or she lost their mother early. A person gets both surnames of an unwed mother if she did not want her child to get the name of her lover.

Sharing a surname does not always mean that individuals are related. To distinguish between unrelated kinship clusters with the same name, I use numbers (e.g., Villalba1 vs. Villalba2). An examination of three unrelated Martínez clusters illustrates how surnames originate. The Martínez1 family, originally from Maxela, goes back to a man who changed his name from Martín to Martínez. Of his five children, one did not adopt the new surname. The members of the Martínez2 family are related from a common ancestor, although it is unknown whether Diego Martínez and Salvador Martínez, born in the second half of the 1800s, were brothers or cousins. The members of the Martínez4 family are descended from Juan Maurilio, who came from another town. There would be more in the Martínez2 group if one of Diego's children, Graciano, had not changed his surname to Aldama. In contrast, the Calixtos have a common ancestor. The origins of other surnames, such as Rufino, are unknown. Thirty-six more names, including Emiliano and Lucas, survived only as maternal surnames eventually to be forgotten. The exception is Pedro Santiago, an important person in the town's history, whose surname was no longer used when Basilia Calixto Santiago died in October 2015. Once associated with nineteen people, it lives on in the memory of half a dozen descendants with the surnames Ramírez, Bernal1, Villalba1, and Enrique. Adding the 36 surnames that did not survive, the number goes to 106, not counting those not from Ahuehuepan.

In calculating the relative size of kinship clusters, I created five categories:

1. Very large (>200 individuals): Martínez2, Marcos, Lázaro1, Mauricio, Rodriguez1;
2. large (95–200 persons): Ausencio, Villalba1, Pascual, Calixto, Bárcenas, Alejo1, Rojas, González, Ignacio, Ramírez, De La Luz, Muñiz, Natalio, Muñoz;
3. medium (25–94): Basilio1, Aliano, Isidoro, Adame, Alcaraz, Cardoso1, Martinez1, Aldama, Díaz1, Cosme, Catalán, Guzmán, Enrique, Díaz2, Esteban, Isidro, Fabián1, Felipe, Pedro, Gómez1, Isauro, Leonides, Manuel, Miguel, Morales, Nazario, Ocampo, Ramón, Rodríguez2, Román, Tomás, López, Salvador;
4. small (5–24): Alejo2, Lázaro2, Díaz2, Basilio2, Martínez4, Sebastian, Bernal1, Bernal2, Blas, Dionecio, Delgado, Fabián2, Gómez2, Hernández, Matilde, Nava, Nicanor, Ortiz, Palacios, Rios, Santiago;
5. very small (< 5): all other families, who make up 20 percent of the population.

Martínez2 is the largest category; 525 people have this as paternal or maternal surname. Given that a maternal surname drops off in the third generation, fluctuations in the size of kinship clusters is the result of an imbalance in the sex of siblings. There are 111 more individuals with Ramírez as their paternal as opposed to maternal surname, while there are 41 more maternal Basilio1 surnames. American-born children of Mexican-born women with no connection to Ahuehuepan are rarely given a maternal surname. Eight women lost their paternal surname after their marriage to someone not of Mexican descent.

Marriage is endogamous at the village level; hence family clusters are interlinked in a dense web of relationships. In fourteen cases, such links were strengthened through sibling exchange, where two brothers from one household married sisters from another, as illustrated in figure 10.1. In such cases, first cousins have the same pair of surnames. In two cases, when siblings of opposite sex from one family married opposite sex siblings, the surnames of their respective children are reversed. People have many first, second, and third cousins. One woman said: "I have so many, I do not know exactly how we are related."

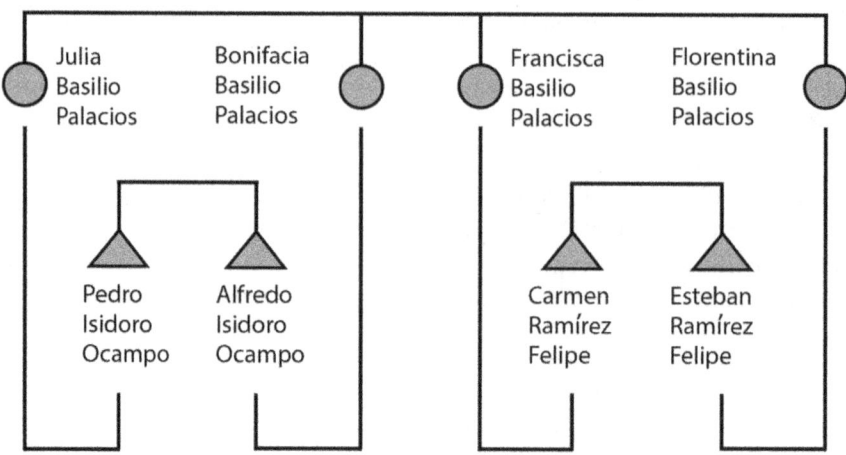

Figure 10.1. Sibling exchange.

Despite an emphasis on family unity, the rate of marriage breakups is high. My survey showed that 518 adults were separated, although fourteen have gotten together again. Given the high rate of mortality among women in childbirth, more men than women remarry with the death of a spouse. The word for a second union resulting from a separation is *kinepanowa* (placing on top of). People have affairs; the Spanish word used for lovers of all genders is *amante*. The prevalence of such unions, contrary to an emphasis on fidelity, is mentioned in orally transmitted stories (Raby 2007; 2015). In the case of one family, three brothers had affairs. Most women who have affairs continue to live with their spouses. It is a norm that a man cannot live with more than one partner in the same house. One person told me: "If a man takes on a lover who is not already married, he must arrange to get her a place where she and her children can live."

OTHER ASPECTS OF KINSHIP

The sexual division of labor has changed, with the women assuming formerly male responsibilities and vice versa. The only thing that has remained the same is that men in Ahuehuepan never cook. When I heard about a man who had lost two wives, and whose children were living elsewhere, I wondered who made his meals. None of his aunts nor his mother were alive. For two years, he had to pay a girl to prepare his meals. The Spanish expression *la alquila* (rents her) was used for this situation. This was no longer necessary when a daughter, separated in Tampico, came home with her baby daughter to live in her father's house.

Relations between family members were quite formal prior to 1990, with children never talking back to parents. While attending a party in 2006, a teacher who did not think it proper to give his father a drink asked me to offer him a glass of tequila. With schooling, the social distance and power differential between children and parents diminished. Nahuatl-speaking adults with no formal schooling were dependent on children to read documents. This dependence was replicated in the US, where those children's parents cannot read or write English.

The Absence of Parents

Juana Salvador Morales.
"Children left in the care of grandparents will not learn how to grow corn if those grandparents are too old to work in the fields."

One of the consequences of migration is the father's absence. Such separations are hard on wives, who take on extra responsibilities. Such women are not the only ones with conflicted feelings; married men returning to Mexico find it hard to leave elderly parents. A man I met on his way to collect firewood for his mother said: "I have been here since December. I have five children in the US and just spoke on the phone to my daughter who has never seen my town. I find it hard to leave; I like it here and my mother needs me. I have two grandmothers; one cries when I tell her I am going back."

The separation of couples puts a strain on marriages; sometimes a man finds another partner, forgetting about his family in Mexico. At other times, a woman gives up on a husband deported for repeated offenses. Couples who migrate may leave children in Mexico. *Isabel* left four children, from ages two to eight, with her parents when she crossed the border to join her husband. A child from an affair of an unwed mother living at home is treated as a sibling as if the unwed mother is a sister. For those cases, people use the expression *la tenían a escondidos* (they had her secretly).

My survey has data on who raises people. The category *by grandparents* constitutes 1.8 percent of the total. The breakdown includes "by both parents" (94.1%), "by mother and stepfather" (0.5%), "by a stepmother" (0.3%), "by an uncle or aunt" (0.3%), or "by a mother" (2.1%). In absolute numbers, 136 people were brought up by mothers, while 116 were brought up by grandparents. These numbers have changed; the higher percentages of those brought up by grandparents correspond to the NAFTA period. The long absence of parents is not easy for children. People do not mind looking after grandchildren when they are young, but they find it difficult to cope when they become teenagers. The proportion of those raised by a single parent was the same over time.

De Facto Adoption

Juana Salvador Morales.

"People with more resources once took in the children of poor families to help them to take care of animals, fetch water, and do chores. Nowadays this rarely happens. Parents do not like the idea of other people giving orders to their children, or they are afraid that those people would take advantage of them."

There is no formal adoption. If a couple cannot have children, they might take on the child of a close relative. The Nahua term is *tetlayookolia* (to give away). In one case, someone did not "give" but "lent" one of their children. This happened when a man in California asked another family to take care of a son when he and his wife went back to Mexico. A child may also be "given away" if he or she loses their mother. That is how one woman ended up living with her godparents. She became an orphan when her mother died. When her father could not look after her after he moved, that couple took her in.

Kinship Nomenclature

Words such as *father* and *son* can be directly translated into Nahuatl. However, there are no equivalents for *uncle*, *aunt*, or *cousin*, for which the Spanish words *tío*, *tía*, and *primo* or *prima* are used. In Ahuehuepan the word *tío* has a broader meaning, since anyone can be addressed that way as a gesture of respect. The words for brother and sister (*ikniiwtle, siwaaikniiwtle*) include half-siblings, adding adjectives (*axtopa, nepantla, xokooyootl*) to refer to the first, middle, and youngest siblings. Another set of terms, *weeweh* and *piipeh*, is used to address older siblings.[2] The word *ichpochtle* (girl, maiden) with an added possessive (*nochpoch*) is used to refer to one's daughter. The same applies to the words that are translated as young boy or son: teelpokawah or noteelpoch. A son- or daughter-in-law is *iimon* or *iisiwaamon*, and father- or mother-in-law is *iimonaan* or *iimontah*. For brother-in-law and sister-in-law, the Spanish terms *cuñado* and *cuñada* are used in Spanish, although in other towns the word for sister-in-law is *westli*. The prefix *tlakpa-*, like the English *step-* is used to name relationships resulting from remarriage (stepfather, stepmother, stepchild), although for Nahuas this prefix refers to a wider array of relationships that have no equivalent kinship term in English or Spanish: *tlakpaikniiwtle* (stepsibling), *tlakpamontle* (husband of a stepdaughter). The relationship of being the in-law of the partner of one's offspring has its own word, *wexiwtle*. If a man wants to indicate that he would like someone to marry his daughter, he might call that person *nowexiw*.

---

[2] The word *weeweh* also refers to a man who acts as mediator, while *topiipeh* is used to show respect to an old woman.

COMPADRAZGO

People create enduring bonds when someone becomes a *padrino* or *madrina* (godfather and godmother) for a baptism, confirmation, or marriage. Couples are joint sponsors. The resulting relationship can be more stable than that between a couple and their in-laws. Although an integral part of Catholicism, there is a secular version, such as when a person becomes a *padrino* for a graduation. The unique feature of compadrazgo, not associated with Catholics in North America, is that the relationship between the *padrinos* and the child's parents is as important as that between godfather and godchild.

Nahua communities have a form of fictive kinship known as *compadrazgo de medida*. I had not heard this term prior to Margarita's suggestion that I become her niece's *padrino*, and hence her brother's *compadre*. I was puzzled because I know that Basilio's youngest daughter had already been baptized and confirmed. Margarita explained that being a *compadre de medida* does not require a priest. All I had to do is buy a ribbon. I soon discovered that my new status involved a different kind of relation with Basilio, someone with whom I could no longer joke. From now on we addressed each other as "compadre," never by our first names. This form of *compadrazgo* was more prevalent in the past, usually when the parents needed to find someone who could cover the costs of a healer and medications for a sick child.

> Margarita Gómez Marcos (Ahuehuepan, 1949–2018).
> "Someone would usually ask a friend to be *padrino or madrina de medida*. That friend might go to a place where they have a powerful saint to get a priest's blessing of the *listón* [a ribbon], which must be done with holy water."

> Fulgencia Pascual Enriquez (a teacher born in Ahuehuepan).
> "Nowadays hardly anyone asks someone to be a padrino de medida, which is not recognized by the Church. I too was a madrina de medida for a boy. I bought him a present although that was not expected. One goes to the church and the *padrino* or *madrina* put the listón around the neck of the child who is going to become one's godchild [*ahijado/a*]. One prays an 'our father' in front of the of the saints."

Being compadres (co-parents) involves trust. Such "fictive" kinship ties, which shape alliances and create networks of cooperation, are part of a web of interconnections that enable people to deal with life's stresses.

Using a duplexity approach, one must examine kinship clusters, including compadres, from contrasting perspectives, giving equal weight to kinship solidarity (an ideal dimension) and to the fact that families are beset with disputes among relatives, especially when it comes to the inheritance of house plots and land. However, when examining kinship, it is easy to overlook its connection to the unequal distribution of wealth and ownership of strategic resources.

11

Kinship Clusters and *Riikos*

Extended families resemble patrilineages. Over half such families originated in San Juan Tetelcingo, while others go back to other towns. At the turn of the twenty-first century, there were eighty-five such kinship clusters in Ahuehuepan. This chapter looks at three types: those with *riikos*; those with members who made contributions to public education, politics, or entertainment; and the rest, about whom it is hard to generalize. Understanding layering between them, especially over the last few decades, gives a good picture of connection between kinship and economic class.

CLUSTERS WITH *RIIKOS/RIKIIYOS*

Pedro Martínez2 Tomás (a man in Ahuehuepan born in 1948).

"As a boy I wore a *calzón* [white cotton trousers] when some men were already using a *pantalón* [store-bought pants]. When I asked my father if I could also start wearing pants, he told me that pants were only for *riikos* like Moises [Mauricio]."

Margarita Gómez Marcos (Ahuehuepan, 1949–2018).

"In the past, women used to grind their maize by hand. Only a few had a hand-held *molino* [mill]—five of them, all *riikos*."

Juana Salvador Morales.

"Some well-off families not only took on women to help in the house and men to work in the fields but also entire families from other towns, especially Oapan and

Ahuelicán. They would stay for months, sleeping and eating in the same house as their *patrón* [boss].

"In the 1980s and 1990s, people from other towns—Maxela, Xalitla, San Agustín, and Ahuelicán—used to come to Ahuehuepan to deliver their crafts to wholesalers.

"People no longer send their children to live with rich families as *molenderas* [house maids] or *mozos* [male servants], because they found other ways of making the money that they need to take care of their own children."

Riikos, who rode horses, were the first to build bigger houses. Those who lived to an advanced age were frail by the time I got to know them. Their offspring had spent their inheritance, except for a few who obtained more wealth through strategic marriages. In 2004, eight families had *riikos*, four of whom were alive in 2021. They are associated with three clusters ranging from the biggest (the Ausencios) to the smallest (the Navas), with one medium-sized cluster (the Salvadors). Those kinship clusters show that the most likely route to ongoing economic success is through investment in the commercial side of arts and crafts. Clusters with *riikos* are not included in this chapter if they did not branch off into more lucrative enterprises.

The Salvador, Bernal1, and Nava Clusters

Manuel, the only male heir in a family of ten who inherited his father's cattle, is the original patriarch. A *riiko* prior to the Revolution, he recovered his wealth as a trader (*viajero*). An older sister, Micaela, was married to another *riiko*, Feliciano Basilio1. Their two sons, Loreto and Bernal, were also *riikos*, but in the next generation there was only one. In contrast, the wealth of Manuel Salvador ended up in the hands of his grandson Santos via his father, Joaquin, whose sister married Florentino Martínez2, a *riiko*. Santos Salvador got more wealth when he married Julia Bernal1, the daughter of Santos Bernal1, who in turn is the grandson of the wholesaler Galdino Bernal1.

The two families were once equal in wealth, but the Salvadors did better over time. Santos Salvador and Santos Bernal1 each owned cattle and had stores. The latter also owned a house in Mazatlán. Santos Bernal1's children could not replicate the success of their father, who died in a car accident. In contrast, Marcelo, Santos Salvador's son, became a merchant who now has his principal residence in Baja California. He owns the only store in Ahuehuepan that sells clothes. Marcelo married a Nava, a woman descended from Romualdo Nava. Romualdo had more money, but he was not considered to be a *riiko*. Neither Romualdo nor his son Aurelio had a lot of land, but Aurelio's son, Gerardo, obtained access to land and cattle when he married Juana Román, the daughter of Irineo, a prominent *riiko*.

Gerardo's son Norberto Nava Román, a *riiko* whose sister married Marcelo Salvador, became a vendor in Mazatlán.

The Ausencio and Martínez2 Clusters

The Ausencios, with seven *riikos*, are an example of the consolidation of wealth through intermarriage (see figure 11.1). They trace their descent back to Juan Ausencio, who lost his cattle during the Revolution, then built up his herd in the 1930s. He was not considered a *riiko* even after he got more land after his marriage to Petra Salvador. Juan Ausencio was married three times; first to Petra, second to a woman from Xalitla, and finally to Eulalia Bárcenas. Emigdio Ausencio, the oldest and only son with his first wife, inherited his father's wealth. He became a *riiko* after he started making trips to the coast as a trader. His second and third sons, Camilo and Fernando, ended up owning more land and cattle: each married a daughter of Vicario Martínez2, a man who had more land and cattle than anyone else. Vicario's only son, Roberto, was milking cows well into the twenty-first century. His sisters' share of land ended up in the hands of the next generation of *riikos*: Santos, Fortino, and Eduardo, with the surnames Ausencio Martinez2; and Francisco Ausencio Bárcenas, Camilo and Fernando's half-brother. One of Francisco's sons, Roberto Ausencio Rios, used to be considered a *riikos*, but this was no longer the case by 2005. There is a further connection between the Ausencios, Martinez2s, Bernal1s, and Navas; Camilo's daughter, Alicia Ausencio Martinez2, was Santos Bernal1 de la Luz's wife. In the third generation, Francisco's sister, Rosa Ausencio, was married to Aurelio Nava. All these people, considered to be *riikos*, are a minority within the larger family clusters to which they belong. Their spouses, siblings, and children derived benefits from their association with them.

Unless households can turn their inheritance into new sources of income, either as wholesalers or by setting up other businesses, they eventually lose their wealth. For example, only Fernando's sons, Fortino and Eduardo, did exceptionally well. Apart from running ranches, they bought a bus, a van (*combi*), a dump truck, and a truck for transporting cattle. If a person has such a business, or a wholesale operation with outlets in cities like Mazatlán, their children are not likely to leave Mexico. While some Ausencios have emigrated, no Navas and none of Fortino Ausencio's children became international migrants.

OTHER KINSHIP CLUSTERS

The Pascuals include a half dozen professionals: Toribio, a teacher and former school director; his daughter Fulgencia, who oversees the kindergarten and ran the civil

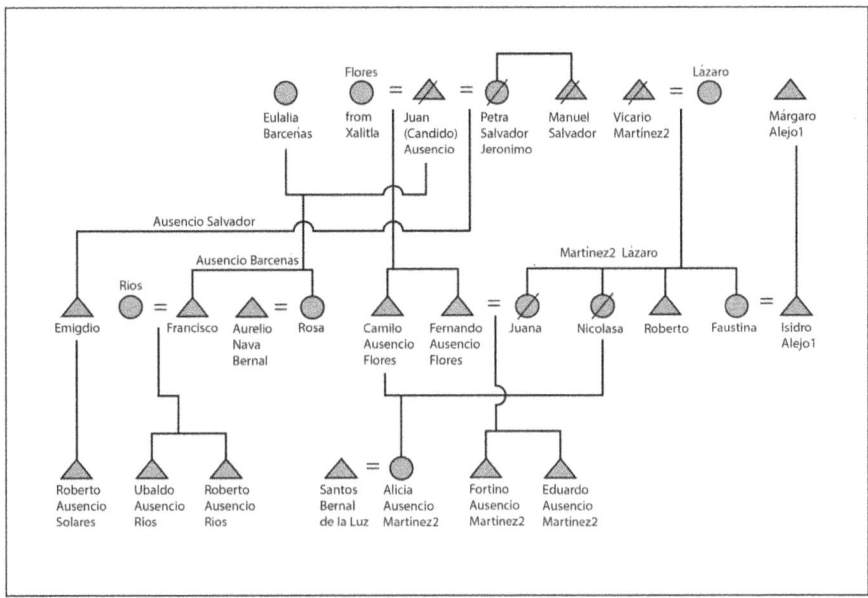

Figure 11.1. Intermarriage among *Riikos*.

registry; his son Eduardo, a priest; and Gregorio, Toribio's older brother, who once oversaw the health clinic now run by his son, Noe. Maximina, Gregorio Pascual's daughter, works as a health care worker in Xalitla and Tepecua. Other members of that family have played important roles in the Catholic church. José Domingo Pascual, Toribio's father, was the assistant of the parish priest. This man, with the nicknames *pastor* and *cantor*, was the leader in the *curista* faction in the 1960s (see chapter 5). His daughter, Salustia, is the main organizer of church activities. Her cousin Francisco and his wife lead prayer meetings called *pequeñas*, where they play the guitar.

The emphasis on formal education among members of this family bore its fruits among those who ended up as migrant workers. Agripino, another of Toribio's sons, was a manager of two pizzerias in Houston. He returned to Mexico, where he initially had a clerical job in Iguala while upgrading his schooling. He then became an English teacher in Xalitla. One of Francisco Pascual's sons, who lived in the US for twenty years, became a manager of a small textile factory before working his way up by selling food supplements for Amway. The Pascuals include vendors such as Toribio's brother, Cirilo (who died in 2020). Toribio's uncle, Alejandro, was also a vendor, with a license for selling and with a permanent stall in Tepotztlán.

The Pascual family has more well-educated individuals than the Salvadors. Juana Salvador and her husband are teachers, whose three children continued their formal schooling, but her nephews and nieces have not gone further than elementary or high school. Still other family clusters are known for their musical talents. The Miguels and the Villalba1s include musicians who combine day jobs in the US with playing in bands and composing music. It is difficult to generalize about the reputation, level of income, or occupation of other families. Most include households with members who have lived in the US, vendors, people with special talents, and those who have never left Ahuehuepan.

CHANGES IN LAYERING

Given the declining fortunes of most *riiko* families, there is no longer a sharp contrast between the haves and the have-nots. By the middle of the 1990s, ownership of cattle ceased to be the main source of economic layering; people no longer paid rents for the use of plow animals. New forms of layering relevant to fields other than agriculture or the craft industry appeared; men and women developed careers in public education and health care. Involvement in the international labor market enabled members of other families to build big houses and buy vehicles. Given the large number of intermarriages between family clusters, combined with the downward mobility of *riiko* descendants, there is now more variation within the families with *riikos* than there is between those clusters and those that have never had any.

Another way of examining social layering is to count the number of people descended from *riikos*. My ethnohistorical survey shows 4,101 (62 %) of all individuals are descended from *riikos*, of which 3,763 were alive in 2021. The last number includes 407 (21%) of the 1,923 people who were born in the US or in other parts of Mexico. A further breakdown of data pertaining to members of twenty-four, mainly large, kinship clusters, is shown in table 11.1. The first column lists the clusters in order of decreasing size, including those that never had *riikos*; it also shows the number of *riikos* in each cluster (from none to seven) in double brackets. The second column shows the total number of people associated with each cluster (those with that cluster's paternal or maternal surname) while the third column shows the total number and percentages of *riikos* to whom people are related. Columns 4 to 9 show the proportion of people who are descended from one or more *riiko* ancestors (from 0 to 5 or more). Columns 10 to 14 show the number of generations members with *riiko* ancestors are removed from the one to whom he or she is the most closely descended. Only percentages are shown in these two sets of columns, as they supply a better picture when doing comparisons.

TABLE 11.1. Family clusters with *riiko* ancestors.

Family Clusters	Total People	Total / % of Riikos	Proportion of Descendants						Generations Back				
			0	1	2	3	4	5	1	2	3	4	5
Column: 1	2	3	4	5	6	7	8	9	10	11	12	13	14
Martínez2 (5)	209	183/88%	13%	61%	8%	18%	nil	nil	18%	26%	33%	10%	nil
Villalba1 (0)	162	110/68%	32%	61%	nil	2%	5%	nil	2%	4%	11%	18%	34%
Ausencio (7)	179	166/93%	7%	17%	34%	20%	17%	5%	26%	37%	24%	4%	2%
Pascual (0)	177	125/71%	30%	52%	3%	5%	nil	nil	5%	20%	42%	3%	
Marcos1 (0)	174	84/48%	52%	32%	8%	5%	nil	2%	2%	25%	21%	nil	nil
Mauricio (2)	134	81/61%	39%	15%	39%	5%	nil	6%	20%	15%	11%	11%	4%
Rojas (0)	113	64/57%	43%	3%	33%	8%	13%	nil	nil	20%	31%	3%	3%
Rodríguez1 (2)	107	46/27%	57%	24%	16%	nil	3%	nil	13%	19%	11%	nil	nil
Bárcenas (0)	103	44/43%	57%	13%	24%	6%	nil	nil	11%	9%	5%	8%	
Ignacio (0)	102	9/9%	91%	3%	3%	3%	nil	nil	3%	6%	nil	nil	
Alejo1 (1)	99	92/93%	7%	47%	31%	7%	7%	1%	2%	19%	41%	28%	3%
Calixto (0)	93	47/51%	57%	31%	6%	6%	nil	nil	6%	22%	9%	6%	
Salvador (5)	90	78/87%	13%	10%	48%	3%	3%	23%	58%	19%	10%	nil	nil
Lázaro1 (0)	90	6/51%	48%	42%	3%	7%	nil	nil	nil	16%	19%	16%	nil
Juárez (0)	87	7/37%	63%	nil	7%	nil	nil	nil	7%	nil	3%	27%	
Muñoz (0)	87	70/80%	29%	17%	60%	3%	nil	nil	0%	33%	37%	10%	nil
Ramírez (0)	84	29/100%	nil	34%	nil	38%	nil	28%	nil	40%	41%	nil	10%
Gómez1 (0)	81	17/22%	79%	3%	14%	nil	3%	nil	4%	14%	nil	3%	nil
Natalio (0)	78	61/78%	22%	30%	41%	7%	nil	nil	22%	41%	15%	nil	
Enrique (0)	73	35/48%	52%	40%	4%	nil	4%	nil	nil	nil	16%	24%	8%
Manuel (0)	70	6/8%	92%	4%	nil	nil	4%	nil	nil	nil	8%	nil	nil
González (0)	70	35/50%	50%	21%	8%	21%	nil	nil	nil	8%	8%	33%	nil
Basilio1 (3)	67	61/91%	6%	8%	49%	23%	5%	9%	28%	8%	21%	10%	7%
Aliano (1)	54	52/96%	4%	83%	7%	6%	nil	nil	13%	19%	31%	31%	2%
Alcaraz (0)	41	13/32%	68%	nil	12%	20%	nil	nil	nil	2%	7%	12%	nil

The information included in table 11.1 should be examined in the light of information on intermarriage and social trajectories. It is not surprising that the families with more *riikos* as well as the highest proportion of members one generation removed from a *riiko*, such as the Ausencios and Salvadors, are connected through marriage to other clusters with *riikos*. Those two clusters had wholesalers alive at the time of the writing. In contrast, the two *riikos* of the Rodriguez1 cluster, a father and son, were never involved in the craft business. Like the members of other clusters (Mauricio, Alejo1, and Basilio1), they are descended from *riikos* who died prior to the advent of the craft boom. Members of the Alejo1 cluster were descended from Margaro Alejo1, a *riiko* who died in 1972. One can further compare the number of those of the first generation with the percentage of those who are three or more generations removed from *riikos*. The Ramírez cluster, with no *riikos*, has a high proportion (40.7%) of members with *riikos* ancestors, most of whom go four generations back. Although they are all descended from Pedro Santiago (the earliest *riiko*), members of the Ramírez family are poorer than other family clusters, plus they have a low proportion of members who have worked in the US (less than 2%). Yet they are proud that they are descended from that important historical figure. The prestige of being an indirect offspring of Pedro Santiago explains why many people without Santiago as one of their surnames are aware that there is a kinship connection; younger members of other clusters do not know if they are descended from *riikos*.

This chapter gives the last word to Toribio Pascual Muñoz, one of the teachers who lives in Ahuehuepan:

> "Some *riikos* own big houses with up to four stories but no bathroom. They eat tortillas with chili sauce and a bit of meat because they are stingy. They never go to a restaurant. When they go to Iguala, they pay twenty pesos for some tortillas and a bit of chili to eat in their *camioneta* [pickup]. But they spend a lot of money for an expensive band."

12

Governance and the Civil-Religious Hierarchy

Usos y costumbres refers to the recognition in Mexico's constitution that indigenous towns have autonomy, although that policy has generated contradictions. The civil-religious hierarchy or cargo system of the Nahuas, consisting of men occupying increasingly more important posts, is part of both the religious and the political fields, which is not consistent with Mexico's strict separation of church and state. To understand how this is possible, one must take the relationship between church and state plus religious syncretism into account. The first topic of this chapter is Ahuehuepan's governance system, including an examination of the town's barrios, the administrative divisions that are a part of how the cargo system is organized. The chapter then looks at the broader context of Mexico's political system, which puts limits on local autonomy. The last part examines the level of participation at the local level and beyond.

THE LOCAL SYSTEM OF GOVERNANCE

The highest authority at the local level is the *comisario municipal*. Another word for this position in Ahuehuepan is *juez* (judge). The *comisario*, who presides over meetings and settles disputes, did not receive a salary until recently when the occupants of several posts were paid an honorarium. Incumbents are divided into those who work for the town hall (the civil side) versus those who serve the *tiopan* (church). Women play a minor and indirect role. Although the duties of post holders have not changed much, different labels have been used. As the need arises, new positions are created. Some posts are more onerous; hence they are referred to as *cargos* (loads).

The Civil Side

- The *comisario municipal propietario* has authority over public affairs, including the administration of justice. He uses the town's seal to stamp documents.
- The *comisario municipal suplente* helps the comisario and may assume his duties.
- A secretary has the responsibility of writing memos and letters and keeping records.
- Two *regidores* attend meetings with the other officials; their responsibility is to advise, and when necessary criticize, the comisarío.
- Five *mayores* are assigned specific tasks, including the oversight of new projects, in consultation with the comisarío. Each mayor has two helpers.
- Ten men serve as police under the command of two officials. They are also called *policías*, *soldados* (soldiers), *caporales*, or members of the security apparatus (*cuerpo de seguridad*).
- Ten men are *auxiliares* (assistants), also known as *topiles*. They go from house to house to notify people summoned to appear in the *comisaría*.
- Two *mayordomos* sweep out the *comisaría*.
- Ahuehuepan no longer has a committee responsible for a communal granary (*tekikahle*),
- Several men who take care of the town's cattle are known as *vaqueros* (cowhands).
- Each school has a committee with a president, a secretary, and a treasurer plus *vocales* who send messages. Members of this committee take care of classroom and yard maintenance.
- The members of another committee, with a similar structure, keep the town's system of piped water (*comité de agua potable*).

Religious Posts

- The *fiscal*, who is expected to do fundraising, handles construction projects related to the church and the *curato* (a building used by the priest). He also looks after church objects, including its statues, and finds *rezanderos* (those who chant and pray).
- Two sacristanes help the priest when he comes to Ahuehuepan; they put on his robes and arrange the objects put on the altar.
- Five mayores work closely with the fiscal. The first mayor is his alternate. The others help with dusting the benches and statues inside the church.

- Ten auxiliares are helpers, two for each mayor. Their main function is to sweep the church yard and to light *cohetes* to announce church events.

All these positions are part of the duties associated with being a citizen of Ahuehuepan. The term of office for most posts is one year.

Rights of citizenship begin when a man starts living with a woman. His obligations consist of monetary contributions and assuming public posts. Men must serve their town for three years, with one year off before taking on new positions. The age they no longer must serve has been changed several times. After that point they go with the authorities during out-of-town visits and are asked for their opinion. Who hold posts shows economic and gender layering. In theory, women may attend and speak up in meetings. Although they do not to assume public posts, they play a supportive role for their husband's job in the *comisaría*, including cooking communal meals. Margarita, aware of the duties of her sister-in-law when her brother Basilio was *comisario*, commented: "a *comisario*'s wife has a lot of work, especially if the topiles don't do enough." Such women are known as *topilesiwaameh*. Men know that wives are decision-makers at home, hence they will let a woman know that a son needs to start serving his pueblo. Women also serve as *celadoras* (security guards) in the church. That position, occupied by some older men, is not part of the cargo system.

The expectations associated with the most important posts are not easy to fulfill; if their incumbents do not do much, they are subject to criticism. The fiscal, responsible for handling money, is particularly under scrutiny. The *comisario municipal* is expected to hold higher authorities accountable for the upkeep of public buildings, plus he dips into his own pocket to cover the cost of the bull slaughtered to prepare the broth served during major fiestas. He also pays for the transportation of musicians from other towns. In 2016 Leobardo Juárez spent 15,000 pesos (approximately $900 US), when he was the comisario municipal.[1] It is difficult to compare other posts in terms of time and effort. One man told me it was more difficult to be auxiliar for the church, because it involves staying for rosaries lasting all night especially after a burial.

Posts vary in level of commitment and prestige, with *auxiliar* or *topile* at the bottom. Those who hold lower posts eventually become mayor or sacristán, but few reach the highest pinnacle of *comisario*. Ideally everyone takes on both civil and religious posts, but most men assume more or fewer of each depending on preference. Nor does everyone go up in the hierarchy in the expected order. Heleodoro Martínez2's first cargo, after getting married, was as sacristán. From then on, he

---

1 He told me this in one of my phone interviews following a trip to Mexico. At that time, he was again living in Nayarit after spending a year in Ahuehuepan.

became the youngest *comisario*, in 1977, without assuming other posts in between. He had that position again in 1983; fourteen years later, he served as fiscal. Toribio Pascual was never appointed as topile, with the rationale that he helped people fill out forms. He became *comisario* municipal in 1989, at age forty-two, but assumed no other posts. His brother Gregorio, who worked in the health clinic his whole life, did not start serving until age twenty-seven, serving only the church. Men with lighter loads include members of the town band, who play on all occasions.

Election of *comisarios* takes place during a meeting in January, with a discussion of the merits of candidates, followed by a show of hands. The names of those not chosen are withdrawn and two new ones for *suplente* are presented, leading up to a new round of voting. Once the important posts are filled, the rest are selected in a closed-door meeting. Unlike national elections, there is no campaigning; it is a matter of accepting the inevitability of having to serve one's town. Men may have to be persuaded by appealing to their sense of duty, or through flattery. Marcelo Salvador served as *comisario suplente* twice before moving to Tijuana. He has since been approached to serve again.

Men living year-round in the US or in other parts of Mexico are expected to fulfill their duties as citizens. Sending money is easy but spending a year in Ahuehuepan is more difficult. The way to get around that is to find a replacement, usually a close relative. One can also pay someone, which has become a source of income. In 2015 the cost for a minor position was between fifteen and twenty thousand pesos (around a thousand dollars). Men avoid taking on the post of policeman; an old rifle is no match for an automatic rifle if you need to stop a vehicle driven by the member of a drug gang. It is not possible to use a replacement for more important post, which requires a migrant to come home for a year. Faustino Salvador came back by himself in 2010 to be fiscal. His wife did not want to leave Rincón de Huayabitos, where they were vendors. Sergio Nazario, who worked in Los Angeles, became *comisario* in 2004. He told me: "I came back to oversee the construction of a house and to take a rest, when I found out they wanted me to be the next *comisario*." He ended up staying in Mexico, where he was *comisario* again for the period 2016–2017. For the 2018–2019 cycle, Bernabe Martínez2 Ausencio brought his family from Puerto Peñasco when he served as *comisario suplente*. Before that he had not done public service apart from paying someone to be auxiliar in 2008. He accepted because he was worried that he might lose his rights as citizen.

Not everyone fulfills their duties. Some men do not send money, nor provide service, with few repercussions. On two occasions, the authorities refused to allow the relatives of one such man to have his body buried in the cemetery. They put up obstacles, but in the end relented. When those living in the US heard about the hassle involved, they started making contributions. The absence of men to assume posts makes it more difficult to find suitable candidates. Unlike the case of Zongolica, Veracruz, where women took on key religious posts (see Rodríguez 2017), only men continued to do so in Ahuehuepan. The exception is a woman who was a member of one of the school committees.

The religious and secular sides of governance are intertwined. Early in May, people converge on two mountaintops to ensure a good harvest. The topiles for the *comisaría* leave offerings in Tepeeyekapitstle, those for the church in Tepeeyewahle. Officials from the *comisaría* also take part in preparation of religious events. On March 2006, I went with the suplente to the house of Alfonso Rodríguez1, the *padrino* of the town's patron saint. We brought chickens, corn, and two cartons of beer to his house. To get further insights into how local governance works, I will let people speak for themselves:

Margarita Gómez Marcos (Ahuehuepan, 1949–2018).

"When the *comisario* wants to hold a meeting, it is crucial that people hold him in high esteem. He buys beer to hand out to those who attend, but he does not drink. That way people will respect and obey him. He must have a lot of friends who will gather in his house.

"One of our customs is that the owner of the land where another person wants to put up a hillside chapel makes no objection. They do not get angry.

"My bother Basilio is busy because one of his sons in California is supposed to make the arrangements for a *castillo* for barrio Loma. Basilio is his replacement, apart from his own responsibilities for the upcoming Quinto Viernes ceremonies."

Juana Salvador Morales.

"Most people already know whose turn it is to serve the town. They talk about it, including who will be a replacement for whom. For a few people, I am not sure if they are supposed to serve, because I have not yet heard about it.

"Sometimes, when posts are assigned, they might overlook a younger man living in the house of his parents, especially if there are many brothers in that family. Last year a decision was made that from now on young men who are not married, but old enough to be married, will be considered as citizens of Ahuehuepan."

Leonor Martínez Basilio (from Ahuehuepan; born in 1968).

"It is customary when a man enters the *comisaría* that he is offered a cigarette and then a beer. That would never happen if you were to go in to see a government official in Tepecoacuilco or in Iguala."

The way that secular and religious activities are interlinked in the complex system of local governance is also exemplified in the barrio system.

THE BARRIOS

Everyone, including migrants, has a connection with one or more of four barrios (Tlatsintlan–San Juan, Tlakaltech–San Agustin, Tlalpitsahko–San Miguel, Loomah–Guadalupe), each of which is associated with a specific neighborhood. Figure 12.1 shows their location. Their main function is to organize the annual Quinto Viernes celebration. In contrast, the *comisaría* does the fundraising and organizing of other fiestas. Sometimes this system is used to coordinate secular tasks, such as when a main street was paved in 2002. Although they cooperate, there is also rivalry. There is no endogamy, although a woman is more likely to marry a man from another barrio. Moreover, membership does not always coincide with an expected geographical location. In most cases men belong to the barrio where they grew up, even if they moved to another one with their parents. Migrants' children, including those born elsewhere, have a symbolic connection with their parents' barrios unless they start living in Mexico, at which time they must support a barrio after marriage.

It is possible to generalize about which kinship clusters are associated with each barrio. Most of the Juarez live in Tlalpitsahko, the Gómez1 in Loma, and the Marcos1 in Tlakaltech, while the Alianos and Salvadors are associated with Tlatsintlan. Tlatsintlan was the original barrio of the Enriques, who later moved to Loma. The small Rios cluster has been associated with Tlalpitsahko since the time when the system was created. Barrio clusters include migrants who live in various locations in the US as well as in Mexico, where few are overrepresented in any city. The exception is the Villalba1s from Loma; many of them now live in Puerto Vallarta.

Each barrio has a committee with a secretary who records who has paid their yearly contribution. An examination of the notebook for Tlakaltech, with minutes and budgets going back to 2006, gave me an idea of its operation. The amount recommended for each household head stayed the same (350 pesos) from 2006 to 2014, then jumped to 1,000 pesos in 2014, and went up even higher, to 3,000, in 2016. This inflation reflects the prosperity of its members, as shown by the monetary contributions for major expenditures: the bull slaughtered; paying the owner of a ranch that supplies the bulls and riders in the rodeo; the purchase of tortillas, beer, the *castillo* (an elaborate fireworks display), flower arrangements, cigarettes, and candles; payments to dancers; and a cash contribution to the *comisaría*. In theory each man is supposed to pay the same amount, but not everyone does so. In 2009 the contributions varied from 100 to 1,250 pesos. The men who gave the biggest donations are documented migrants with stable incomes. The money collected in Tlalpitsahko, whose members have fewer resources, is lower; it went from 300 to 400 pesos in 2016.

GOVERNANCE AND THE CIVIL-RELIGIOUS HIERARCHY 115

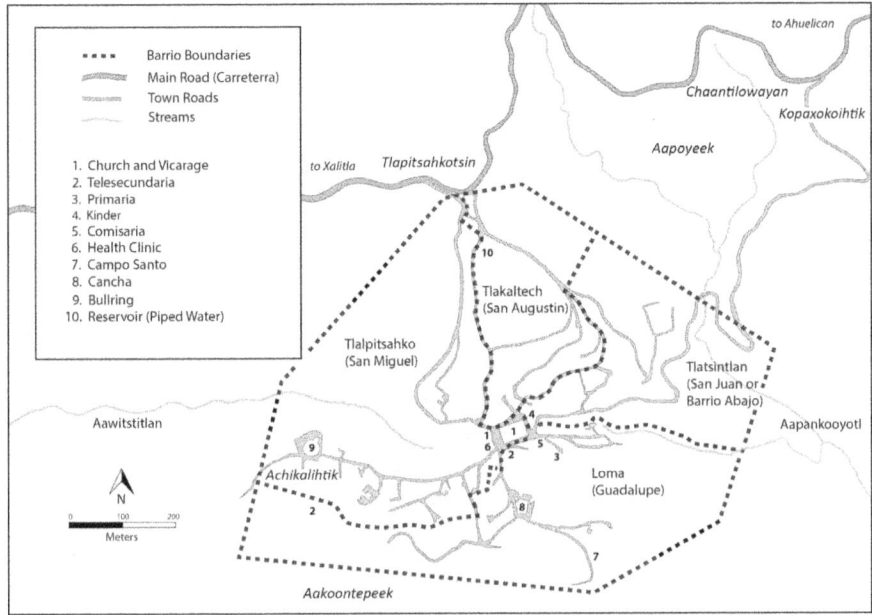

Figure 12.1. The town of Ahuehuepan—barrios and town features.

Outsiders, including teachers who live in Ahuehuepan, are not aware of the existence of the barrio system. Even the town's professionals either do not know or tend to mix up their Spanish and Nahua names. The confusing answers I received from people who are not full participants, plus the fuzzy criteria of membership, show its ad hoc nature. Most children born in the US would not know to which barrio they belong. However, it is the place they will stay for short-term visits.

THE NATIONAL POLITICAL SYSTEM

The barrio system and other parts of the civil-religious hierarchy work under the umbrella of a broader system of governance. Mexico is a republic with a presidential system. After years of authoritarian rule, with a de facto one-party system, Mexico is today a multiparty democracy, although the Institutionalized Revolutionary Party (PRI) still prevails in parts of Mexico. In theory, states and municipalities are "free and sovereign," but in practice, Mexico's administration is centralized. Ahuehuepan's *comisario municipal* reports to the *presidente municipal* in Tepecoacuilco. Only one person from Ahuehuepan, Toribio Pascual, has occupied a position at that level. The participation of people at the municipal level could not happen until the introduction of formal schooling, greater contact with the outside world, and facility in Spanish. Mexico's administrative system can be daunting; few people understand the way administrative and electoral boundaries overlap. Ahuehuepan is part of the judicial district of Hidalgo and of the electoral district of Iguala, while the neighboring town of Ahuelicán belongs to the respective districts of Bravo and Chilpancingo.

The first state institution whose presence became noticeable is the one overseeing access to land, with the redistribution of landed estates in the 1920s, culminating in a form of land tenure called the *ejido*. It provided people with secure access to land previously rented from landowners. Such land recipients, known as *ejidatarios*, elect a committee, the *comisariado ejidal*, with its parallel supervisory counterpart. Another part of land reform was the legalization of village lands going back to the colonial era. That is how Ahuehuepan gained legal recognition of its *terrenos comunales*. The people who farm in that land elect representatives of a committee with a similar structure. It is also headed by a president (*comisario*), a secretary, and a treasurer. The term of office of those committees is three years. The men who controlled these committees sign off for funds for development projects. There are thus three *comisarios*: the one described and two in charge of land issues.

The expansion of the Mexican state resulted in more programs and institutions. The town's health clinic, with a paramedic, is run by a national program, IMSS (Mexican Social Security Institution). That man, who dispenses medication and treats minor injuries, is seen as a doctor. His salaried position is not part of the cargo system, nor is the job of running the local branch of the civil registry. Other national programs include Procampo, created in 1994 to supply support for poor farmers, followed by Progresa, a social welfare program of payments in exchange for regular school attendance and health clinic visits. Initiated in 1997, its name was changed to Oportunidades, then Prospera, which was eventually replaced by Becas para el Bienestar Benito Juárez, a scholarship program. The most recent government initiative is designed to help people visit their migrant children in the US.

> Juana Salvador Morales.
> "Some people recently made trips to the United States to visit their children under a new program designed to further such visits. Many are waiting to see if they will be approved."

Another institution, public education, started with state schools, which reached Ahuehuepan in the 1940s. Several decades later, a sub-branch of a national system geared to Indigenous regions was created. The two exist side by side, although federal schools are sometimes closed, to be replaced with an *escuela bilingue*. Designed for indigenous children, it is based on the philosophy of *indigenismo* of the central government, although the two types of schools are almost identical. Bilingual teachers can communicate with their students in their native language, but they are not trained to teach students how to read and write in Nahuatl. The only unique, but purely symbolic, feature is that students sing the national anthem in Nahuatl.

Not everyone has a birth certificate, voter's identification (*credencial*), or an identification card called CURP (which translates to "unique population registry code"), with periodic campaigns to get people to obtain such documentation. For example, in 2012, the National Electoral Institute (INE) tried to standardize addresses of all voters. Street names, which do not appear on signs in Ahuehuepan, are superimposed on a satellite image in Google Earth. I also found documents in the civil registry in which people have reported their street and a number; however, most people list *domicilio conocido* (known residence) as they did in the past. Few people know about those streets, nor can they agree where one ends and another begins. For most, such names are irrelevant; yet people cannot ignore that they are national citizens, especially in the case of migrants, given that the federal government covers the cost of their repatriation if they die in the US (García and Celestino 2015, 44).

OVERALL LEVELS OF PARTICIPATION

When designing my census, I created a variable, PSTS (public posts), to measure level of participation, whether through involvement in the civil-religious hierarchy or by holding local posts not part of the cargo system: 0 = "never or not yet," 1 = "minimum," 2 = "average," 3 = "above average," and 4 = "high." In assigning these values, I took into account the fact that not every post has the same weight. The value assigned to a woman is the same as that of their husband's, on the assumption that they do much of the work associated with public posts assigned to their husbands. The wives of the holders of more important posts were assigned a value of one less than that of their husband. Women married to men in the US were assigned half the value of that of their husbands; part of their monetary income goes to support their husband's expenses for paying substitutes. Duties such as being *celador* in the church are counted separately for men and women. The values of the variable PSTS were derived from data that includes people for whom there was complete or partial information. The value of 2 (average) was assigned to people from earlier cohorts for whom much this information was not available. The value of 66 ("not applicable") was given for children, those born in the US, and outsiders.

The final breakdown for PSTS, in percentages, is as follows: never, 31.7 percent; minimal, 11.7 percent; average, 46.3 percent; above average, 8.8 percent; and high, 2.1 percent. The percentage of people not holding public posts increased over time, with minor fluctuation. Minimal participation stayed the same, while average participation fluctuated, then went down significantly in the last cohort. This pattern is replicated for above-average participation, which went down to 1 percent in the last cohort. Likewise, high participation consistently declined until it reached zero. The most dramatic decline is for those whose participation is average, from a high of 294 (36.8%) in the postrevolutionary period, to a low of 29 (3.65%) in the last cohort. This last number shows how mass migration, indicative of the latest form of globalization, has resulted in an overall decline in involvement in the town's governance.

My census data also includes information on the participation in the national politics of people from different social layers in different time periods (cohorts). An overwhelming majority (96%) of those in the last cohort do not have any political affiliation, nor do they take part in national politics, which is not surprising given that most of them live in the US as undocumented workers. They cannot vote, while their counterparts in Mexico have little interest. It was only possible to measure to what extent members of the two cohorts support different political parties given that competition among rival parties is a recent development. Although I have data on membership in five parties, plus no party affiliation, I recoded the data as one with two variables (the PRI and the PRD). The proportion of adherents of these two parties is similar for different layers, although slightly higher for individuals from the lowest layer, who are more likely to support the PRD than those of the middle social layer, who in turn are more likely to adhere to the PRI. Those results are consistent with the leftist orientation of the PRD. Once all parties are included, a higher proportion of those in the upper layer support the PRI, while a few are PANistas. What is more striking is the low level of participation of people overall, consistent with the decline in political involvement beyond the required minimum.

Apart from considering how people in Ahuehuepan view their local system of governance, this chapter has paid attention to various complementary facets of governance. It also shows that the declining involvement of people in politics has been shaped by forces beyond their control, particularly the new forms of globalization resulting in the increase of border crossings. Migration has likewise had an impact on people's connection to the land.

13

Land Use and the Changing Landscape

Migrants once worked in the fields. This chapter starts with an overview of maize production, followed by an outline of the town's terrain, including its transformation. Data from interviews, archival research, and GIS (Geographic Information System), reveals that practices are not consistent with legal categories. The last section addresses the issue of whether it makes sense to talk about peasants, or *campesinos*, in today's world.

THE MILPA

Miihlan ("milpa" in Spanish), an extension of *miihle*, refers to Mesoamerica's system of swidden (slash-and-burn or shifting) cultivation revolving around the cultivation of maize in combination with squash and chili. People consider working in the fields as the town's main occupation, although they recognize that some migrants did not live in Mexico long enough to learn how to do so, and that some migrants who became vendors stopped growing maize:

Jose Domingo Pascual (a man in Ahuehuepan born in 1925).
"The milpa is our life."

Margarita Gómez Marcos (Ahuehuepan, 1949–2018).
"People who grow corn want to have *elotes* [fresh corn], with some of it left over for *maíz* [ripe corn] for making tortillas."

Pedro Martínez2 Tomás (a man in Ahuehuepan born in 1948).

"When I started growing my own crops, I sowed maize and squash (*tlayoohle waan ayohtle*), the *ayotle* in between. I also sowed *ajolín* (sesame). It was a way to make some money, until its price plummeted."

Juana Salvador Morales.

"A person must go to the fields for four consecutive years to learn how to grow maize. Children whose parents took them to the fields two or three times but then left cannot be said to know how to do so. A woman who left at a young age visited a milpa for the first time during a return visit, as part of an outing, but she would not have been able to help much."

Toribio Pascual Muñoz (a teacher whose wife grows maize).

"Many people no longer want to grow maize, because it is expensive to buy fertilizer and insecticides. There are more costs—all for getting just three or four bushels of corn. They prefer to go away to sell crafts."

Many people use the expression *titookah xoopantlah* ("we sow [corn] during the rainy season"); yet they report to outsiders that "no one grows maize nowadays," which really means that they no longer do so as a way of earning money. When I asked if someone grows maize, he or she would often say, "that family does not grow corn," even if it turns out its members once learned how to do so. Others give the answer "only for *elotes*," which downplays the importance of corn production. A duplexity approach expects such inconsistent answers. I have heard people say that Ahuehuepan is the exception, yet I know that maize is grown in other towns.

The amount cultivated fluctuates depending on the level of remittances, rainfall, and government subsidies. I estimate that almost half (145 out of 287 individuals) grew maize in 2014. That proportion remained significantly lower in the 2018–2019 cycle. More precise information is included in my census: never (112; 19.8%); learning to work in the fields when growing up (994; 13.4%); cultivating maize at some time (727; 11%); substantial, "most of their life, until now" (1562; 23.6%); uncertain, or possibly (6; 1%); not applicable (children, strangers without a connection) (2,202; 30.3%); and unknown (117; 1.8%). Those numbers will change when older people no longer go to the fields and if return migrants start growing maize again.

Although people sow genetically modified corn, they prefer the local varieties named after their color: *kostik* (yellow); *chiichiilik* (red), also known as *xokoyolin*; *tliltik* (black) or *yaawtsiin*; and white (*isták*). For modified corn bought in Iguala, with smaller kernels but better yields, the use of fertilizer is essential. Beans (*yetl* or *frijol*) are grown in separate parcels. Given the dry climate, only one crop can be grown. People do the first plowing early in May and start sowing on May 20, later if it does not rain. Weeding and plowing continue until August 20. Chilis, planted close to home, are then transplanted. On September 13, people perform rituals to assure a good harvest. They bring home fresh corn (*yeelotl*), but most maize plants are left to dry for another two months.

There are two ways of working the soil. *Tlakooloohle* refers to cultivation with the use of a digging stick. It is the only way one can grow crops on steep hillsides, as opposed to plow cultivation, which can be done on both flat and hilly land. Plowing with a team of oxen and a yoke (*yunta*) was prevalent up to forty years ago. Doing so with mules, using a different kind of plow, has since become more common; in 2016 only two men were still plowing with a yunta. Another form of agriculture, practiced on riverbanks, is the cultivation of herbs and vegetables in *huertas* (gardens) (see also Good Eshelman 2005).

TOPOGRAPHY, BOUNDARIES, AND ACCESS TO LAND

Juana Salvador Morales.

"In Aapankoyootl people own land that once belonged to Oapan. They originally asked for permission to use it and even offered to buy, but the people in Oapan were insulted and did not want to talk to them, so the men from Ahuehuepan just appropriated the land and divided it up among themselves.

"When Isidro Alejo died, the seal that shows he is the representative of the small property owners passed into the hands of Reynulfo Morales. When he died, his son, Hipolito, handed it over to the authorities in the *comisaría*. I do not think anyone has done anything else. I believe that committee does not function anymore."

Every piece of land has a name, few of which appear on maps. There are places with more than one name: Chaachiwtepeek is also known as Xoochitepeek; Tepeeyekapitstle is the same as Cerro Picudo. In nine cases, one name refers to two, or even three, places. Figure 13.1, a simplified version of a larger map I left in the town hall, shows terrain features not shown in the town map in chapter 12, including boundaries with other towns, types of land ownership, roads, mule trails, plus rivers with their corresponding ravines. Pipes carrying water pumped up from a river run parallel to the hydro line installed on one side of an old dirt road.

Figure 13.1 shows six sections of land: larger *propiedad* parcels (*propiedad*/propiedad de Pedro Santiago); an area registered as a single property jointly owned by people who call themselves *pequeños propietarios*; two sections of former estates expropriated and redistributed in two stages as *ejidos*; communal land, including a slice under dispute between two towns; and a section I call "ambiguous," which does not have a clear legal status, although it appears in some documents as *pequeña*

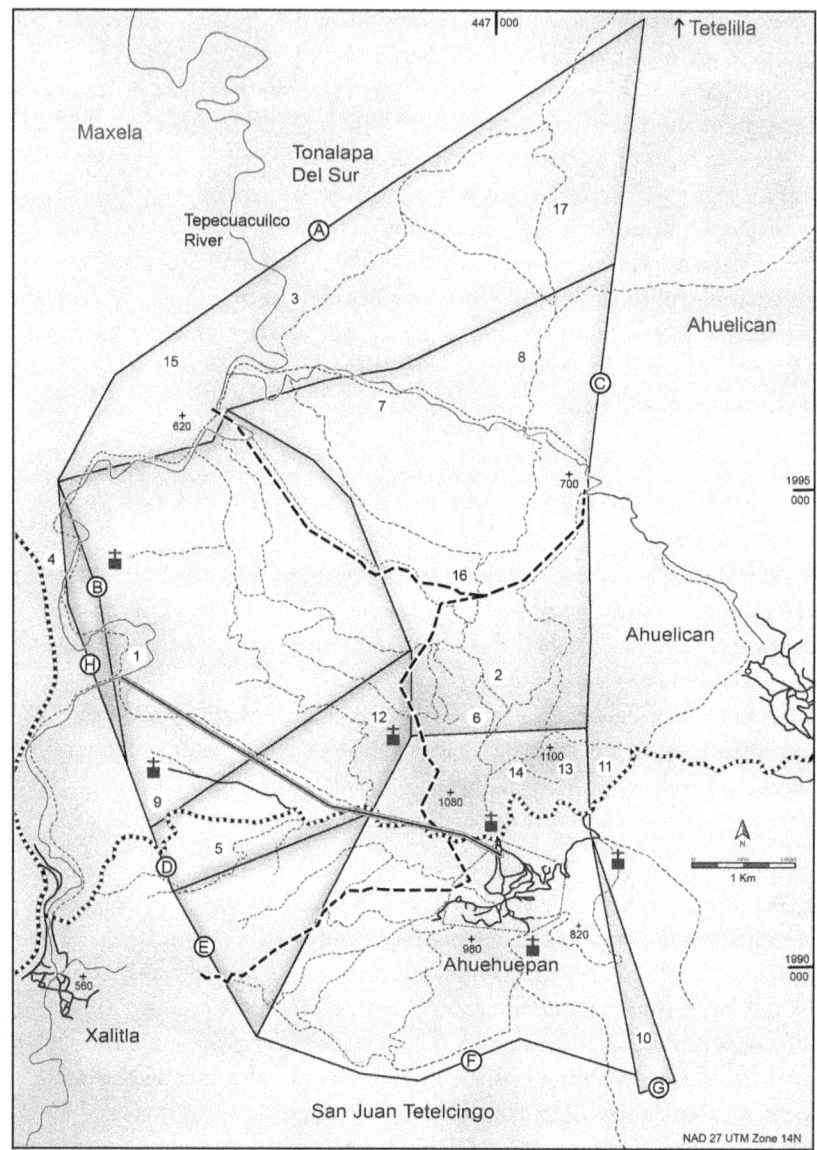

Figure 13.1. Land boundaries and Corral Común.

propiedad. That legal term refers to both bigger properties (*propiedad*), up to two thousand hectares (which could be labeled as *ranchos*), and small plots of land. The first type would resemble the land bought in the name of Pedro Santiago, while the second type consists of land that got smaller over time (*minifundismo*). An example of the second type is Ahuelicán's land, shown as *pequeñas propiedades* in several maps, but which appears in other sources as its share of communal lands held jointly with Oapan (Amith 2005, 1068). It has been de facto private property since at least the middle of the nineteenth century. A section of Ahuehuepan's land contiguous with that of Ahuelicán has a similar history. It is shown as "pequeñas propiedades de Ahuehuepan" in the archives of the Registro Agrario, even though my guides considered that land to be communal. That section of land is shown as being ambiguous (communal or *pequeñas propiedades*).

Legal forms of ownership do not correspond to what happens on the ground. Ejido parcels could not be sold until a recent change in the law, unlike communal land that can be sold, but only to other *comuneros*. Ejido parcels are supposed to be the same size, as opposed to communal plots, which vary in size and can be subdivided. Yet there are government documents that use only one term, *tierras de uso común*, for both types. Lists of those with rights of possession are rarely complete. Meetings are periodically held to revise them, striking off names, but it can take up to fifteen years for the lists to be updated. Few are familiar with the legal distinctions—even my guides could not agree on the status of the land in the ambiguous zone that includes Kuwiaantlan and Xaalmeeya—yet anyone who grew up in Ahuehuepan knows who "owns" different pieces of land. At least a third of the people with land have documents: certificates issued to *ejidatarios* and comuneros, land titles in the name of dead people, and bills of sale regardless of legal status. In practice, people buy and sell every type of land, including to members of neighboring towns. Moreover, not everyone has legal rights. Most people must wait until a parent dies to inherit, while some, like Eliseo González, may never own their own land; his father, an outsider who moved to Ahuehuepan, rented a team of oxen from Vicario Martínez2, and Eliseo uses his wife's land in Iaapan Parra. *Manuel Victoriano* did not inherit land because it had already gone to his half-brother. Yet people without legal rights to land can always find some to rent, given the number of people who are too old to use it or because they are absent.

My survey has information on land ownership going back to the nineteenth century. Of the 4,226 persons born in Ahuehuepan, land was of no significance for almost a half. Of the remaining 2,137, the number of people who had titles to land was 885. The other 1,252 had access to land through kinship or rental. The 444 farmers who at one time rented the land of absentee landowners within what is now Ahuehuepan's ejido, or in the valley of Iguala, make up less than a third of those farmers. Other numbers show the relative importance of various forms of land ownership: ejido (540; 24.2%), communal (674; 30.3%), ambiguous (i.e., communal or pequeñas propiedades; 245; 11.1%), pequeña propiedad (73; 4.1%), and larger parcels of land (*propiedad*) (102; 4.6%). People have more than one type of land, hence a single number, taking size and quality into account, is a better indicator of how much land people "own." The breakdown (for all periods combined) is "none" (29; 2.6%), "little" (210; 19.4%), "some" (526; 47.8%), "average" (3 or 4 pieces; 235; 21.3%), "above average" (67; 6.1%), and "a lot" (2; 7%). Land ownership has become more polarized over time. Between 1975 and 1995, the proportion of those with an average amount of land declined from 16 percent to 9 percent. Once people started emigrating, land was abandoned, while larger properties were divided up among their owners' descendants. By the turn of the century, the only category left was *some land*.

THE CHANGING LANDSCAPE AND LAND USE

Over the past fifty years, agricultural practices and the environment have been transformed. The most dramatic change is the disappearance of a communal fence (*corral común*) that existed for more than fifty years. Used by all the towns, it consisted of a rotation between pasture and cultivation, putting cattle into one area to eat the stalks left over after the harvest. The plowing for the next cycle started on the other side. The way the fence was managed, and levels of cooperation between farmers and those who own cattle, varied. The communal fence was already under strain when it was ended in 1994; an increase in out-migration made it more difficult to find enough people to keep supporting it. Those who did not own land refused to cooperate in a system from which they did not benefit. When that fence disappeared, cattle roamed freely. Many people started putting up fences, which made it difficult for people to gain access to their fields, resulting in conflict as well as negotiation. Some owners put up gates that anyone can open by untying a string, while others use padlocks so that only they can enter.

The landscape was transformed in other ways. Once covered with a canopy of trees, the Alto Balsas experienced deforestation. Up until thirty years ago, every hillside was cultivated. Overuse and insufficient fallowing resulted in erosion whose effects are visible today.[1] Further soil erosion and deforestation were averted with increasing migration. People stopped using land far from the town, such as Tsopilotepeetl or Weei Aatlahko (see top of map). By 2010, it was shrub. Those with four-wheel vehicles drive along the old road from Kontlahko to Ahuelicán during the dry season for picnics or to bathe in the river. The only places cultivated are the foothills of the two mountains close to town. When they go to their fields, people

---

1 Fallow land is arable land either included in a crop rotation system or kept in good agricultural condition, whether worked or not, but which will not be harvested for the duration of a crop year.

bring back dry branches. They no longer cut down trees. There has been a comeback of deer, but there are no more mountain cats and wild boars. How raw materials are extracted also changed. Today one can see the remnants of lime-making operations. Lime was made by digging a hole to serve as a lower chamber. The extraction of wax, tallow, or clay is also no longer practiced. The last thirty years have seen the erection of a half dozen wooden crosses and chapels. My larger map shows thirty man-made places that are sources of water, each of which has its own history, from ancient wells to water tanks. Some are more recent, while others have fallen into disuse. Other fabricated structures include houses that were provisional shelters, storage sheds (*galeras*), and cattle pens (*corrales*), none of which are used today.

Once, everyone knew how to get around and how to grow maize. They were familiar with the names of landmarks. Given the high rate of recent migration, people are today acquainted with at best a few ravines and mountains. Those born in the US or who left when they were small children know none. They are not likely to become peasants by any definition. Ahuehuepan's territory does not have relevance for them unless they want to go to see a cave or a place with a pleasant view. People with land farther away have not visited their properties for a long time. Older people liked the map I left in the *comisaría*; however, one man who spent his life as a vendor told me, "What use is that map, showing all those trails? No one uses them anymore."

THE DUPLEX NATURE OF THE PEASANTRY

The fate of the peasantry, as well as how that term should be defined, has long been a topic of debate. Political economists predict their disappearance, leaving capitalist farmers and a rural proletariat. In contrast, other scholars argue that the peasantry will not disappear. Starting in the 1960s, this argument took the form of a debate between two schools of thought: *campesinistas* versus *decampesinistas*. The former, including Angel Palerm (1972), Luisa Paré Ouellet et al. (1979), and Armando Bartra (1979), changed the definition of peasantry to include vendors and artisans. Later scholars, including Lynn Stephen, were ambivalent about the term and related expressions such as *peasant community* (1991, 276 fn.). The category *peasant* or *campesino* does not fit well when looking at men in Oaxaca who use their American earnings to pay women to do piecework weaving. By the 1980s, only 11 percent of the households in her study had full-time farmers (Stephen 1991, 72). Twenty-five years later, Michael Kearney, who declared *peasant* to be an outmoded category (1996, 58–59), proposes the word *polybians* to refer to people with a plurality of occupations. I opt to not discard the term *peasant*.

Peasantry, which is an analytical category as well as referring to a social identity, must be examined from both emic and etic perspectives, even more so if doing so engenders incompatible conclusion. From an etic perspective, the term *peasant* refers to people involved in subsistence agriculture, including those who combine farming with other ways of making a living. A researcher using only that approach might reject the term by pointing out that growing corn is now more of a hobby than a means of making a living, at best the last possibility left for surviving. Investigators using an emic perspective will argue the opposite; they draw attention to the importance of maize in Nahua cosmology and the preference for local varieties, to explain why people continue to grow it. For them, the word *campesino* is still relevant, because those who once grew maize and are now vendors nevertheless report it as their occupation, a declaration that cannot be dismissed. In "Farewell to the Peasantry?" Gerardo Otero (1999) mentions that even third-generation wage workers consider themselves as *campesinos*. In a survey of beach vendors, Tamar Diana Wilson (2017, 220) reported that twenty-five of thirty-two sons of peasants, including vendors, said they would like to replicate their father's career. The same can be said for migrants who grew maize when growing up and continued to do so before they emigrated. Such diverse and contradictory replies are expected from a duplexity perspective.

14

The Religious Field, Cosmology, and Folklore

I started off my research by recording folktales as a way of tapping into beliefs and feelings. To get a better sense of what matters to people, I visited home altars and talked to those who work in the US. People from other Nahua towns provided me with more information. This chapter begins with several quotes of people from Ahuehuepan and other Nahua towns to illustrate the diverse perspectives on religion, followed by a short summary of stories from Ahuehuepan. To put those in a broader perspective, I present an overview of what scholars have labeled as the syncretic nature of the beliefs of indigenous people, followed by a discussion of the cult of the saints. The chapter next talks about the conversion of people in the region to other religious denominations. Only then do I present an overview of the Nahua worldview and how that has been altered. That section is largely based on the research of several outsiders who did fieldwork in Mexico on that topic. I end this last chapter of part 3 of my book with the words of a migrant from Ahuehuepan now living in California on levels of religious devotion.

DIVERSE PERSPECTIVES

People from the Alto Balsas comment on, reflect on, and also explain to strangers what people believe.

An artist living in Cuernavaca (born and raised in a Nahua town).

"The devil is like God. My painting portrays the role the devil plays in helping the moon go around the earth and supplying life. The large woman is mother earth."

A middle-aged man from Oapan.

"The (Protestant) charismatics say that the *santos* in the church are only pieces of wood, that they are not gods. I know that there is a god who lives in heaven, but the *santos* are also gods who look after us. Why else do we have masses and leave offerings in the church (*templo*), and not out in the open or in the fields? It is what our ancestors did."

Basilio Gómez Marcos (a man who lived in Ahuehuepan most of his life).

"I believe that San Lucas will help you get more animals, but you must have faith. Some people, who are not believers (*creyentes*), think that they can get what they want only by going through the motions."

Margarita Gómez Marcos (Ahuehuepan, 1949–2018).

"Everyone used to help when we grew corn for Juan Evangelista. It was used to feed people during his feast day, but we have not done so for eight years. A committee in charge of a communal milpa now collects money to pay for his lights in the church. That saint, who is rich, has millions of pesos in a bank account. When people come here for his fiesta, including those from the States, they pin money on his vestment—$50 and $150 in bills. Money is also collected for Tonaantsin (our lady of) Guadalupe in December.

"When people eat in the house of the person who has a santo on its feast day, the *padrino* and family members eat at the table. They are served on a full plate. The rest, including visitors, eat on the ground.

"On their trip back to the world of the living on the Day of the Dead, ancestors are guided by candles on the way to the houses where their descendants live. The dead cannot eat, but they do smell, which is why the food prepared should be spicy and savory.

"All Saints (Todos Santos) begins with eight days of vigil, when we leave offerings: first for the children—coffee, buns; the following two days, rice, chocolate, watermelon, on small plates. We light candles for those who died at an old age. I address my father, Silvano, his wife, my siblings, my uncles and aunts, and cousins. For the Day of the Dead, there is a lot of *sempoalxoochitl* [a kind of flower]."

Juana Salvador Morales (teacher from and in Ahuehuepan)

"Many of the cantors [*rezanderos* and *rezanderas*; literally those who pray] learned how to read enough to follow what they have copied in their notebooks, even though they never went to school."

STORIES (*CUENTITOS*) AND RIDDLES (*SAASAANIHLE*)

Oral tradition is a source of further insights into how people see the world. The titles and content of several well-known stories include Pedro de Malas (Bad Peter), a mischievous man who cheats people until God turns him into a stone; the poor boy who marries a king's daughter after many trials, including killing a serpent with seven heads; the man who is almost eaten by a snake, until he is saved; and Flor Blanca (White Flower), a girl who helps her father after he loses his money on a bet. Such stories express moral values, such as one by Esteban Gómez:

> A traveler used to leave his wife behind. When he discovers after a trip that she has died, he smashes the statue of a saint and wanders off. He meets an old man, who helps him find his wife in the realm of the dead, on the condition that he restores the saint he smashed. The old man transports him instantly, telling him to blink after asking him to climb on his back. When the traveler sees his wife, she tells him not to touch her, but he ignores what she says. As soon as he embraces her, she crumbles into pieces because she is made of bones. The man picks up the pieces and puts them together.

The moral of the story is that a married couple should not be separated for long, that their duty is to stay with and support one another.

Every town once had renowned storytellers. With schools and television, storytelling is disappearing. In contrast, riddles, part of a ritualistic dialogue, were until recently included in the school curriculum. Several women in Mexico and two men in California gave me examples. One person starts by saying "saasaanil, saasanil," to which someone replies "teentetl" (big mouth). The riddle, often with sexual connotations, consists of guessing the name of an object, a body part, or an animal. If someone does not know the answer, they are subject to ridicule (see also Flores Farfán 2009, 438 fn. 4). Such riddles are not just a diversion; they serve to preserve the Nahuatl culture (Flores 2009, 439.). Yet many young people growing up in other parts of Mexico or in the US have never heard about them.

THE REPORTS AND VIEWS OF SCHOLARS

Scholars, both outsiders and indigenous professionals use the term *syncretism* to characterize the blending of Catholic and pre-Hispanic features, combining elements drawn from a broad repertoire of symbols. According to Johanna Broda (2001, 17), this can be detected in the way rites associated with the agricultural cycle in the Aztec calendar continue under a new guise under Christianity. The feasts dedicated to the Holy Cross coincide with the changing of the seasons. On the third day of May (the feast of Santa Cruz), people climb to the tops of mountains to invoke the coming rain. The feast of John the Baptist, a saint assimilated into pre-Hispanic deities with dominion over the realm of water, involves prayers to the wind spirits that carry the water necessary for the growth of plants (20). In Ahuehuepan its statue is brought out during droughts (Hémond 2003, 396).

The worldview of people who did not attend school, and who do not draw a distinction between what is worldly versus what is sacred, is different from those immersed in an urban society. Henry Kammler (2010, chapter 3) and Alan Sandstrom (1991, chapter 6) present accounts of a Nahua cosmovision that is bound to be tentative, as explained by Sandstrom (236):

> The Nahuas ... are not very articulate about the philosophical underpinnings of their religion. They communicate through the medium of myths and ritual, through concrete examples in which basic principles are repeatedly worked out and expressed in religious performance.[1]

According to scholars, a common element of Nahua cosmology is that everything that affects people's lives belongs to interconnected realms. One can communicate with supernatural beings who live in *ilwikatl* (the sky) on the tops of mountains. The heavens are the source of maize, a plant that links humans with the sun because its heat is transformed into the energy associated with the vital force (*chikaawalistle*) that people lose if they do not eat corn that is carried in their blood (Sandstrom 2011, 246–47). All realms are associated with benevolent and malevolent forces that are associated with caves, the dwelling places of snakes. Vultures go back and forth between them. Spirits in the shape of air (*yeyeekameh or yeyeekamaires*) cause illness.

Folk tales from many sources mention the devil: *xkwaahle tlaakatl* (bad man), *tiaachkaaw* (evil lord from up high), *xyektle* (bad), or *diaabloh* (devil—a Spanish loanword). To explain how someone suddenly gets rich, people are said to sell their soul to the devil. Another aspect of Nahua cosmology is the way personhood is conceptualized. Kammler (2010, 127) refers to four concepts about a person's immaterial components: *aalmah, toonal, yoohloh,* and *tlamachilistle*. *Aalmah*, a Spanish loanword, is an overarching category that refers to an animating principle separate from the body. *Itoonal*, the possessive form of *toonahle* (day, sun, heat), is a mobile soul that can be separated from the body, resulting in the weakening of the aalmah, manifested in insomnia and listlessness. That can happen because of fright (*susto*), as when someone wakes up from a dream or falls.

---

[1] In later publications that focus on the ritual use of paper cuttings, Alan and Pamela Sandstrom (2022a, 2022b) put more emphasis on the function of pilgrimages as reinforcing traditional values in the face of onslaught of external forces.

People who die maintain *yoohloh* (heart or life), a life force that enables someone to exert their will, and *tlamachilistle* (wisdom), which includes intuition, foresight, and the ability to make the right judgments. *Yoohloh* allows ancestors to interact with the living.

Like all beliefs transmitted orally, words related to the soul have different meanings. Margarita used *aalmah* and *toonal* indiscriminately, although she used the latter more in a ritual context. She told me that my soul will become tired after I die, since it would retrace the steps of all my journeys. According to traditional beliefs, the dead, who end up in a faraway place, are not reunited with their bodies in heaven as a reward for good behavior. Only acculturated individuals with a worldview closer to Christianity believe they will go there to live with Jesus.

THE CULT OF THE SAINTS

The religion of Nahuas resembles Catholicism to some extent. In Catholicism, saints mediate between the laity and God. In contrast, Nahuas treat different versions of Mary, Mother of God, and of Christ (the Redeemer, the King) as distinct supernatural entities whose powers are associated with specific locations. People adore the *santos* through prayer and with incense to assure good health and prosperity. Those saints are capricious; one can plea and negotiate with them, and as a last resort, make threats (Gamio [1916] 1982, 85–86). Their sphere of influence is different than that of their counterparts in Catholicism; Saint Luke the Evangelist (San Lucas), one of the twelve apostles, is officially the saint of physicians and butchers. For Nahuas, he ensures fertility. His worshippers visit a chapel to ensure that many calves will be born. The highlight is when older women start dancing, waving small wooden bulls over their heads. They chase and pretend to stab any man who gets in the way with the bull's horns. They wrestle a man personifying a bull to the ground. That ritual has nothing to do with Roman Catholicism.

Each saint has a designated day when household altars are adorned with wreaths, *rosquetes* (sweet buns), and colored paper. People likewise worship the saints in the church. The most important one is John the Evangelist, Ahuehuepan's patron saint. Other include La Virgen de Guadalupe (December 11, 12) and San Juan Bautista (June 24). In 2016 a new feast day, also for Juan Evangelista (December 27), was added. Less prominent ones include that of Kolotlipan (the Scorpion), on the third Friday of Lent. Each saint has its sponsors. Guillermo Manuel and Gregorio Delgado, who live in Los Angeles, go to Mexico once a year as the *padrinos* of Niño Jesus (the Christ child), celebrated on December 24. These festivals dedicated to saints have their practical side, including feeding spectators and the collection of money. Outsiders who are compensated for their services include the cowboys in the *jaripeos*, and the men who make the firework displays. The corresponding beliefs and norms are diverse. Religious specialists, including a priest from Xalitla, do not always share the same beliefs as those who train dancers or play instruments. Nor are any of them subject to the same expectations. People's level of devotion also varies; yet all citizens, including those in the US, contribute money.

CONVERSION TO OTHER DENOMINATIONS

Cleotilde Alcaraz Martínez (a vendor from Ahuehuepan born in 1969).

"I am a *Testigo* (Witness of Jehovah). I no longer believe in paying for religious fiestas, but I want to help with public projects. The authorities locked me up even though I was the secretary of the *ejido*. I pointed out how I served the town for many years, so why punish me just for not following their traditions?

"In Ahuelicán, which has many religious denominations, it is acceptable for people to belong to different religions. They are united in cooperating for the good of their town."

Unlike in other towns, few people in Ahuehuepan have joined other denominations, thereby renouncing the customs described in this chapter. Even when that is not so, as for a man who joined a breakaway Catholic Church, they are seen as *Protestants*, a term with negative associations. Until recently converts were given a hard time. Catholics with a more charitable view use the term *separated brethren*.

NAHUA WORLDVIEW

According to Henry Kammler (2010, 188–90), who examined a broad set of practices, a Nahua worldview emphasizes the need for an intense ritual life to achieve the right balance among competing forces that consists of several elements: fatalism; the anthropomorphism of sacred entities, including merciful but moody saints; the localization of all sacred beings; and a sense of mutual obligation between the generations. His synopsis resembles five key principles outlined by Alan Sandstrom (2011, 319), who did fieldwork in the Huasteca. Alan and Pamela Sandstrom (2022, 329) add pantheism and the centrality of the notion of equilibrium, as does Hémond (1999, 36). Hémond (1994, 391) also argues that reciprocity, as a form of moral symbolism, assumes that an increase in a person's wealth is linked to the impoverishment of the community. A related notion is that the maintenance of social equilibrium requires making offerings to superior beings.

The Transformation of Nahua Cosmology

The village studied by Sandstrom did not have craft production, hence he analyzed the rituals and beliefs of its inhabitants in terms of how people dependent on growing corn make sense of life and cope with its challenges. Kammler (2010), who examined the rupturing of such a worldview in three towns (Ahuelicán, Oapan, and San Miguel Tecuiciapan), points out that a traditional worldview meets the needs and expectations of subsistence farmers, then argues that a drastic decline in the ability to make a living from the land leads to increasing anxiety; when people can no longer rely on traditional ways of making a living, they adopt a new worldview once it becomes available.

In looking at the emergence of an alternative worldview, one cannot leave out formal schooling, which, alongside exposure to large urban centers and mass media, is bound to alter people's mindset; yet migrants above the age of forty hold many elements of an older worldview. One explanation is the persistence of dispositions formed during early socialization that continue to shape how people act and think long after they move from an agrarian to an industrial urban setting, as shown by Bourdieu's study (1982) of migrants from Algeria who moved to France. However, strongly held beliefs associated with a traditional worldview will not carry over to the next generation, much less those raised in the US, as told to me by a man born in Ahuehuepan. That man, who made a career as a gardener, speaks Nahuatl and Spanish. He keeps abreast of what is happening in Mexico; yet much of his outlook on life is not that different from that of other people brought up in an urban environment. He recognizes that he can never have the same depth of devotion, nor the inner feeling, of his grandparents:

> Nowadays, when the authorities go to the top of Tepeeyewahle in May to give offerings, they no longer hand out a handful of maize kernels of four colors. That ceremony does not have the same meaning as it did for our forefathers. Recently people living in Lincoln started celebrating San Lucas the way they do in Ahuehuepan, where people believe that the dance with the bulls promotes fertility. Here it is an amusing pastime. People like my grandfather had real faith. They were convinced that the dead would come back to visit them on the Day of the Dead. We are not sure whether that is the case. We have lost that faith.

While a traditional worldview is bound to change as people become exposed to an urban, industrial way of life, it is not inherently incompatible with a drive to get ahead, as mentioned in my discussion in the introduction. To show that is the case requires following people from Ahuehuepan who have migrated to other parts of Mexico and to the United States.

Part Five
Going beyond Ahuehuepan

15

Zooming Out to the Rest of Mexico

People from Ahuehuepan are found all over Mexico, particularly on the Pacific coast. The artisans initially did not stay long in any place. Esteban Gómez, who started as a vendor in Mexico City, later went to the Yucatan. On his first trip with a friend, they ran out of money and slept on the beach. Others stayed away longer. The late Rodolfo Martínez4, whom I interviewed in San Marcos, California, went to Mazatlán at age sixteen with his father. He continued to do so after he was married, traveling to other places: Mérida (three times), San Blas (in passing), Cancún, and Puerto Escondido. Amado Fabián1, who uses gourds to make animal figures, goes to Puerto Vallarta. Many people eventually remained in the same place. Other vendors first emigrated, later returning to Mexico.

This chapter, starting with the words of two people from Ahuehuepan, describes the presence of people from their hometown in each of several Mexican regions.

> Juana Salvador Morales (a teacher who spent part of her life in other parts of Guerrero).
>
> "Before 1950 no one left, because they did not know Spanish and because they were afraid, including of the risk of getting infected with malaria.
>
> "Most move around to find customers. One man who went to Puerto Vallarta had earlier been in La Peñita, Nayarit. Many members of the Lázaro family still live in Vallarta. One of them told me that they had bad experiences and plan to go to Tampico.

"The older children of people living in Mexico do not join their parents after emigrating, for several reasons: they are continuing their education and would not be able to get the access to internet services, or they are already married or cannot get away for their jobs."

Pedro Martínez2 Tomás (a vendor who lives in Ahuehuepan; born in 1948).

"I never went to the United States; instead, I used to go back and forth to Ensenada, Baja California, to sell masks and wooden fish figures. I bought them in San Francisco and in other towns. I also sold in Mazatlán, San Felipe, Puerto Peñasco, and Guadalajara. In some places, gringos bought on the beach where I had my wares spread out on the ground. That was when the dollar was worth two and a half pesos. Groups of four or five customers would gather around to look at my wares. They liked what I had to sell."

NAYARIT

More *Ahuehuepeños* have gone to the Riviera Nayarit than to any other destination. People take alternate routes to get to several towns via Tepic. Those who arrive after a six-hour bus ride from Guadalajara are picked up by relatives, who take them to La Peñita de Jaltemba and to Rincón de Huayabitos. A nearby town, San Blas, gets Mexican visitors and low-budget American travelers who like its Miramar beach. My ethnohistorical census shows a total of 439 people with a connection to La Peñita, including 96 who were born there; 158 people have a connection to San Blas. It is hard to say how many migrants lived there at any time, since many come and go. Most families rent rooms, while eight own houses. Their children work as vendors or find jobs in stores that cater to tourists, as described by a man who went there:

Arón Alejo Leonides (a vendor from Ahuehuepan, born in 1962).

"About seven hundred vendors, including thirty from Ahuehuepan, sell on this beach in Huayabitos. It is very competitive, but the sun shines on all of us. I like where I am living, because it is quiet and no one bothers me. I built my own house here; I have not yet finished it, but I no longer need to pay rent. For twenty years, I rented a house and walked back and forth to the beach every day. Recently I bought my small truck [*carrito*], which I use to go back and forth between here and Ahuehuepan."

The histories of migrants in Nayarit are intertwined. Victor Tomás, who went to Huayabitos, was followed by Alfredo Isidoro. When he arrived, Alfredo saw that other vendors were already there, so he went to San Blas. His brother Pedro and his wife followed suit. The two families became closely connected when Alfredo married Pedro's wife's sister. One of Pedro's sons, Florencio, married a woman from

Oapan. He went to Sacramento for seven years, which enabled him to build a house in San Blas. His wife has never been to Ahuehuepan, but Florencio makes regular visits home with his Nayarit-born children. Members of thirteen families, including the Lázaro1s, Alejo1s, Díaz1s, and Ramóns, are well set up in La Peñita. When Leobardo Juárez arrived in 1995, he found more people from Ahuehuepan than those living there today. That year many people decided to move to the US. When I asked him why he never did the same, Leobardo told me, "In Mexico, life is easygoing, and one can get by if you give it a try." Antonio Ignacio spent eighteen years in Nayarit, returning to Ahuehuepan with his family. Others, who first stayed in La Peñita and Huayabitos, went to Bucerías, close to Puerto Vallarta. Many of the 132 people who were there have since gone to Houston, Texas. The four remaining families go back and forth to nearby towns and their beaches, including to Las Varas.

NORTHERN MEXICO'S PACIFIC COAST

In the 1980s, fifty men found jobs in construction in the city of Culiacán, Sinaloa. Seven of them went from there to the US. *Adolfo Gregorio*, then eighteen years old, did not join them. Instead, he went to Tepic, where he sold wooden fish. *Adolfo* spent the rest of his life in Ahuehuepan, growing maize and working as a *reemplazo* for migrants. His career stands in stark contrast to those who ended up in the port city of Mazatlán. Unlike towns in Nayarit, with few people from the Alto Balsas, Mazatlán has vendors from Copalillo, Ameyaltepec, and Oapan. One hundred and sixty-five people have a connection to Ahuehuepan. The first vendors left their merchandise at stores or sold it directly to tourists. Initially they traveled by bus, bringing their wares in carton boxes. By the 1990s, they were spending most of their time there.

Commercial success depends on kinship connections. Santos Bernal1 was already settled in Mazatlán. His wife, Alicia Ausencio, is the sister of Fortino, a wealthy man who was once a vendor. His children, Alicia and Fortino, also lived there. Santos Bernal1, Santos Salvador's nephew, was a vendor in Mazatlán and Tijuana before retiring in Ahuehuepan. Other people, including Aurelio Nava, the son of Gerardo, a wholesaler in Tijuana, are likewise related. Aurelio's maternal grandmother, Rosa Ausencio, is Francisco Ausencio's sister. Some of those vendors in Sinaloa augmented their savings by working in the US. Francisco Ausencio's son Ubaldo was in Houston before he followed his father's footsteps. He built a house on the edge of town, but he never sowed corn; instead, he became a wholesaler supplying crafts to vendors in Mazatlán, where he built a second house. The families who did not do so well are not related to them. *Francisco Martínez* rented land in Zacacoyuca before becoming a vendor. His oldest son tried to do likewise, but that did not work out; the five thousand pesos he spent on buying merchandise, in addition to what he paid for food and accommodation, was more than what he earned. Pedro went back to Ahuehuepan, and his son emigrated to the US.

The second destination in this part of Mexico is Puerto Peñasco, Sonora, where 208 people including transients have a connection to Ahuehuepan. Cleotilde Alcaraz made his first trip in 1986. On his second trip, he traveled by bus to Guadalajara and from there to Peñasco by train. That year three women were already there. More people arrived in the 1990s, staying during the height of the tourist season. Eventually they only returned for major fiestas. In contrast, Cleotilde often goes to Ahuehuepan, where all his children were born. Another case, somewhere in between, is Esteban Calixto. He has not been back since he and his wife moved there as a newly married couple. Nevertheless, he continues to support his hometown. In 2016 Esteban sent his oldest son, Jobani, to Ahuehuepan to serve in the *comisaría* on his behalf.

Many other people told me stories about how they ended up in that part of Mexico, with more information about those places:

Tourism and Conservation in Puerto Peñasco

The development of tourism goes back to the early 1950s, when the shrimping and fishing economy of Peñasco was transformed into one based on real estate, sport fishing, and ecotourism. Highway 8, a scenic route between Sonoyta and Peñasco, is the quickest way for people from Arizona to reach the Gulf of California to go whale-watching. That highway skirts a biosphere reserve (El Pinacate y Gran Desierto de Altar) recognized by UNESCO (United Nations Educational, Scientific, and Cultural Organization), which draws visitors from all over the world. People from Ahuehuepan discovered its potential in 1990. In 1998 they were joined by families from San Juan Tetelcingo, followed by vendors from Copalillo. Business boomed, but by the second decade of the twenty-first century, a downturn in the economy and a drop of tourism triggered tensions between the government of Sonora, local Indigenous clusters, newcomers, and conservationists.

Prior to the arrival of "people from the south," a term referring to migrants from Guerrero, Sonora set up programs to help its Indigenous people, including the Tohono O'odham (Pápagos), a binational Indigenous cluster. Its territory includes the biosphere reserve. Like the Mayos and Yaquis, they received support from a commission to mitigate the impact of the recession. People from Guerrero live in Colonia Obrera, a neighborhood of three hundred migrant families, who formed an organization to fight for the right to be recognized as Indigenous residents, with their own traditions legally enshrined as *usos y costumbres* (Castellanos and Johnson

2017, 9–10). Esteban Calixto played a different leadership role, in the creation of a sense of territoriality, including spaces for the performance of rituals. He once visited the top of a volcanic peak, where he saw a blue wooden cross next to a statue of San Judas Tadeo. That night San Judas appeared to him in a dream with an invitation to make offerings. From then on, Esteban and others started to use that place for worshipping the Holy Cross.

The Tohono had no objection when the Nahuas made pilgrimages to three mountaintops. The story of how that started and how Nahuas ran into problems with the reserve's guards illustrates the contradictions between the actions of state agents, whose job is to conserve ecologically sensitive territory, and the ritual practices of newcomers (Castellanos Domínguez and Johnson 2017). They negotiated with the land's owner about the logistics of putting up a small base ("to hold the candles"). People from Ahuehuepan and San Juan Tetelcingo made pilgrimages, putting up a patio that could accommodate several hundred people. They gave up on converting it into a permanent shrine after the reserve guards demolished the patio and removed their offering. A few years later, they were again making pilgrimages to the site of the blue cross, but no longer built permanent structures (see Castellanos Domínguez and Johnson 2017).

I learned more about Puerto Peñasco from other people:

A son of a former vendor in Ahuehuepan.

"I left my parents' home and now sell crafts in Puerto Peñasco. It is a forty-eight-hour bus trip to Tijuana. I get off in Sonoyta; from there to Peñasco. There are beaches with tourists, especially from Arizona, as well as Canadians, Japanese, and people from Europe. We are thirteen vendors from Ahuehuepan, more from San Juan."

A young man (a former migrant, born in 1990).

"I was in Rancho Cordova for seven years. I went there at age fifteen in 2005. Unfortunately, I fell into a gang and was deported. Back in Mexico, I ended up in Baja California, were some cousins helped me. I was there for two and a half years before I returned to Ahuehuepan, where I met and married my wife in 2013. Together we came here to Puerto Peñasco, where our two children were born. My life has changed completely—no gangs, no drugs, zero vices—now it is only hard work to make sure that my family can make progress."

Juana Salvador Morales.

"Many people living in Puerto Peñasco and other places are no longer interested in coming to Ahuehuepan for visits, even during major feasts. They prefer to stay where they are vendors. Some have their own houses there."

BAJA CALIFORNIA

Puerto Peñasco is close to the border towns of Mexicali and Tijuana. Sixty-nine people, from seven households, lived in Mexicali in 2021. Fourteen were associated with Tijuana. Those with stands in nearby Rosarito include Gerardo Nava, who lives in Tijuana with Nicolasa Mauricio. Of their four children, his son Norberto makes frequent trips to his hometown to visit his mother.

Traveling south into the peninsula of Baja California, one does not find as many Ahuehuepeños. Five people have passed through Ensenada, but no one stayed there for longer than a day. At the southern tip of the peninsula, Los Cabos consists of Cabo San Lucas and San José de Cabo. In 2018, when I made a short visit to the area, sixteen migrants lived there. Five families, including that of Santos Ausencio, own houses. The son of a *riiko*, Santos was a wholesaler before settling down in Cabo San Lucas, where he was joined by his wife and children. Another family, Rosalba Ramírez and her husband from Ameyaltepec, also own a house. *Salustia Atilano* had been in Melaque before going to Puerto Vallarta and finally Cabo San Lucas. She has a booth in a craft market, where I met her son *Saul Eleodoro*, who has been in the US. His younger half-sister sells from another booth. Another half-sister and her husband from Oaxaca rent a stall in San José de Cabos. It is where I met a man who works as a security guard. He and his wife, with three children born in San José, all speak Nahuatl and Spanish. Adding in anyone who has stayed there for a short time, the number goes up to fifty.

A man from Oaxaca married to a woman from Ahuehuepan told me: "We live in Cabo San Lucas and take the bus to San José, arriving at nine and leaving in the evening. To cover our costs, we need to sell at least $100 a day. Wholesalers come here to supply items on credit. If a product sells well, they bring us more."

Juana Salvador Morales.

"Baja California is getting dangerous, with many kidnappings. Last December one of Alfonso de la Luz's daughters came back after staying in Cabo San Lucas."

The other place in the peninsula with people from Ahuehuepan is San Felipe. Of the twenty-eight people who once lived there, most moved elsewhere, leaving only the family of Cristino Martínez1. When he made his first trip, he and a cousin rented a room. After several years, Cristino and his wife took their children to Baja California. That family goes back to Guerrero for several weeks around Christmas. In 2020 Cristino spent a year in Ahuehuepan to serve as *comisario municipal*.

PUERTO VALLARTA AND THE REST OF THE PACIFIC COAST

Back in the mainland, vendors are scattered along the rest of that coast. According to my census, 245 people have been in Jalisco, 200 in Puerto Vallarta. Luciano Lázaro used to stay for two months at a time, then for much longer. Some members of that family got jobs serving people in restaurants. Vallarta has more vendors from Tetelcingo, with their own neighborhood. As in other cities with vendors from many towns there is fierce competition. A good proportion of Ahuehuepeños (I calculate, a quarter) opted to emigrate to the US.

Melaque and Barra de Navidad (Jalisco)

Melaque, also known as San Patricio, with hotels catering to tourists, does not have many vendors from Ahuehuepan. Twenty-nine people live in rental accommodation. At first the late Alfonso Díaz and his wife, Teresa Aliano, sold the crafts she made together with her daughter. Alfonso later started selling in Manzanillo in the neighboring state of Colima. That couple first went to Atlanta, Georgia, saving up enough money to return to Mexico to become vendors. Alfonso went to Tampico, then started selling in Huayabitos, and afterwards found more customers in Melaque. By that time, he was going back and forth to Manzanillo and Melaque, where hotels organize tours for tourists to Barra de Navidad, a fishing village on the northern tip of Colima. In 2016 a young unmarried man and two couples were living and selling in Navidad, including a man who was in California. None of their children have been to Ahuehuepan.

Colima and Michoacán

Thirteen people from Ahuehuepan have been to Colima. Two men did not stay long; they went to Tampico and Puerto Vallarta. In 2018 several migrants connected to Ahuehuepan lived there longer, including a woman born in Oaxaca. She attended school in Manzanillo, then worked as a salesclerk in a beach resort. Her parents and twenty others have sold crafts to tourists, including a man who did so in 1982 at age sixteen. Three years later, he was in Riverside, California, cutting almonds. Back in Mexico, he did not go back to Manzanillo, but he did sell bracelets in Bucerías for a while.

Juana Salvador Morales.
"There are no longer vendors from Ahuehuepan in Manzanillo, Colima, because there was too much competition, with many vendors from other places, who were well established."

The state of Michoacán used to have some people from Ahuehuepan, including two men in Lázaro Cárdenas. They were both in the US, where they ran into trouble with the law. Five others also went there as vendors; it is not far from Zihuatanejo, with six from Ahuehuepan as well as people from Tetelcingo. Further south one is back in Guerrero, whose principal coastal city is Acapulco, a place with too much competition with many vendors from other places.

Acapulco and the Costa Chica

Acapulco de Juárez has been a port city since the colonial era. After the completion of the highway from Mexico City to the Pacific coast in 1928, it became a destination for tourists. The forty-four people who made regular day trips there include Juventino Juárez, who spent many years in Mazatlán and then Acapulco before returning to Guerrero, where he started baking bread. In 2010 Roberto Pascual was the only vendor making trips there. No one from Ahuehuepan has Acapulco as their main destination today. The Pacific coast between Acapulco and Oaxaca, the Costa Chica, was the place where *viajeros* once obtained salt. One will not find any vendors there, because it does not have good beaches, unlike the coast of Oaxaca, farther south, which is the destination for thirty-five vendors from Ahuehuepan,

THE YUCATAN PENINSULA AND THE ATLANTIC COAST

People from Ahuehuepan are also found on the other side of Mexico, in Quintana Roo. Alfredo Isidoro used to go there, supplying crafts to stores in Cancún and Isla de las Mujeres. Five other vendors, including Cirilo Pascual, made stopovers in Merida and in Cozumel, while seven high school graduates work in a variety store (OXO) in Cancún. Adding in vendors who went there brings the total to fourteen. I am not aware of people from Ahuehuepan in nearby Tabasco. In contrast, there are 194 vendors in Tampico, farther up along the Atlantic coast.

Tampico, Tamaulipas, was the main port for export in the early part of the twentieth century. There are more Mexican than non-Mexican visitors, including Canadians at a language institute. The first person who went there did not stay long before moving to Las Varas, Nayarit. The second, Juan Martínez1 Muñoz went there after working in Atlanta, Georgia.[1] The third person, Esteban Gómez, was followed by others, including several women with children. They rented houses after first living in tar paper shacks. Esteban and his wife, who arrived in 1987, made

---

1 I did an interview with him in March 2016. He provided me with information on Tampico.

trips home up until the last years of his life. In 2008, during one of his return visits, Esteban told me what life is like for a typical vendor:

> "I sell in the market, where we have stands, each day on a different street, except Mondays. Permits used to be 200 pesos, but they kept going up. On the beach, where I sold every second day, I used to pay 500 pesos. There you see ordinary Mexicans (*mexicanitos*) from Monterrey, Reynoso, and San Luís Potosí. There are not a lot of gringos."

I got more information by talking to his sister Margarita, who made clay necklaces sold by her brother. By 2005 Esteban was barely able to cover the costs of rent, hence he was unable to give his share of what he owed as a *padrino* for Juan Bautista. The authorities let him wait one more year. He and his wife used to come home in the fall, a slack period with harsh weather and few sales, but he never stayed away long because most of their belongings were in Tampico, where they continued to pay rent.

THE INTERIOR OF MEXICO AND THE NORTHERN BORDER

There are not a lot of people from Ahuehuepan in Mexico's interior or in the northern border region.

Hipolito Morales Ausencio (a vendor in Ahuehuepan, born in 1977).
"I am the only one who went to Reynoso, Tamaulipas, where I sell what I paint. I have also been to Laredo and towns in between, like Miguel Aleman. At first, I went by bus, but later I started going there with my pickup truck (*camioneta*). It was difficult at first, figuring out where to go. Now I send everything I make to wholesalers. I get phone calls telling me how many pieces and what type to send."

The only craft vendor who was in San Miguel de Allende, Guanajuato, Cristino Martínez1 Marcos,[2] once delivered merchandise for resale to vendors from other towns. People did not stay long in Cuernavaca, where migrants board flights to the border. In the 1960s and 1970s, several wholesalers made short trips. Only one family lives in nearby Tepotztlán. In my census, I included them in the thirty-one people with a connection to central Mexico. Further south we are back in Taxco, Guerrero, close to Iguala. A colonial mining city with cobblestone streets, it is a popular destination for tourists. At least twenty Ahuehuepeños have been there at one time, including wholesalers who buy silver. Juan Catalán, who later moved to Tonalapa, learned to make *castillos* in Taxco.

---

2 He used to supply the wooden boxes used to transport the bodies of people who died in the US. I spoke to him several times, including when he served as *comisario municipal* in 1990. He died of COVID-19 on July 5, 2021.

None of the other cities in central Mexico, not counting Mexico City, have seen more than a smattering of vendors as well as a few manual laborers, clerical workers, and students from Ahuehuepan: Chilpancingo, Monterrey (Nuevo Leon), and Guadalajara (Jalisco), each with three people; Pilcaya (Guerrero), Tepic (Nayarit), and San Francisco del Rincón (Guanajuato), each with two; and the rest, including Hermosillo and Nogales (Sonora), Matamoros (Coahuila), Reynosa (Tamaulipas), and Morelia (Michoacán), with one person each. They are included in the eighty-one people who spent some time in other parts of central Mexico.

Mexico City (DF)

It is worth taking a closer look at Mexico City, also known as DF (Distrito Federal). Once known as Tenochtitlan, it has long been the seat of power. Many streets have Nahua names. At one time the largest city in the world, Mexico City is the headquarters of national institutions. People from many parts of the world land at its international airport. It is where children born in the US are picked up by their relatives in Ahuehuepan. There has never been a significant presence of Ahuehuepeños. The number of people who have lived there since 1990 is 42: 14 craft vendors, 12 manual laborers, 3 clerical workers, and 13 students.

Prior to 1950, Mexico City did not have much relevance for Ahuehuepan. Apart from the four men who traveled there in 1935, people viewed the DF as a distant and dangerous place. There were rumors that people might be beaten up. That mentality disappeared with schooling and an awareness of opportunities. Esteban Gómez, Miguel Alejo1, and José Domingo Pascual were the first to go there as craft vendors. Esteban sold amates made by women in Maxela, while Miguel sold masks. They had already picked up some Spanish, but these men still had to learn how to navigate the city's subway system. Some people went there for reasons other than selling crafts. In 1967 Pedro Martínez2 first went there to work on a construction project. On his third trip, he met up with several men selling animal figures carved out of wood. He followed their example, realizing he could earn money as a vendor. Pedro soon found out that his customers preferred antique, handmade masks. Ponciano Fabián2 Mauricio[3] showed Pedro how to make the masks look old. Once he learned to paint amates, Pedro sold them in subway stations, then found customers in an office complex, where he was given an identification card.

After Mexico City was hit by a devastating earthquake (in 1985), most vendors started going elsewhere. By 2006 only a handful were selling there, including

---

3 Ponciano, who used to go to San Francisco to buy masks, died in 2020, the year he served as a member of Ahuehuepan's water committee.

Alberto Canuto and his wife, Tomása Felipe, who brought along their children. When Alberto died in 2009, Tomása and her children stayed. That year two men were selling there: Eliseo González and his brother Pablo González. Eliseo, who sold masks, first went to Francisco to buy them, then traveled to the DF, where he sold them in the Plaza San Domingo. Between 2010 and today, few other people went there, excluding those who only passed through on their way to other places.

SUMMARY

Internal migration is the spatial dimension of the field of arts and crafts, which gradually became more closely linked to commerce. The involvement of people in those intertwined fields has become the main form of social layering, culminating in a polarization of wholesalers versus beach vendors. In contrast, people working in construction and the service sector constitute a tiny part of internal migrants. Many vendors, facing stiff competition, emigrated to the US, contributing to an increase in external migration.

16

Crossing the Border to Earn Dollars

People go to the US thinking they will return—until they realize that will not happen.

They want to keep their jobs but don't want to risk going back and not being able to reenter. That is why few no longer go back and forth. Men used to go to Mexico to visit their families. After NAFTA, with stricter border controls, more women joined their husbands and young couples started migrating, resulting in more children being born in the US. This chapter, whose focus is on people's experiences crossing the border and the kind of jobs they find, will also touch on several related topics: learning English, the loss of an ethnic identity, and a comparison of migrants and people who stay at home. As in earlier chapters, most of the information was provided by people in or from Ahuehuepan:

Pedro Martínez2 Tomás (a man who never left Mexico, born in 1948).

"Most of the better houses were made by people who started working north of the border. That is how many people with few resources, like the sons of Ruben Ignacio, were able to pull themselves up with their bootstraps [*levantarse*]. Before that, they lived in a straw hut."

Margarita Gómez Marcos (Ahuehuepan, 1949–2018).

"My niece *Ana* and several friends were escorted to the border by a *woman coyote*. They left Iguala at noon and arrived at Reynosa at midnight. Only one, Ronny, was imprisoned and sent back. The others arrived in Hidalgo, Texas, the next day and stayed in a hotel, arriving in Houston, where my niece's sister picked her up in her car. *Ana* stayed with her for three days while waiting for more people before the coyote could take them to Los Angeles, where she handed *Ana* over to her partner, who took her to Rancho Cordoba, where *Ana's* sister helped her find a job.

"A man I know once worked in Los Angeles without a work permit or a visa. He is trying to get them. He is now in Ahuehuepan to serve as sacristan in the church. He plans to take it easy for two months but wants to leave again.

"Four years ago, one of my nephews was in prison for several months, first in one near the border, then in Sacramento. They supplied meals and a change of clothes, but it was a prison uniform. They then took him back to Mexico, leaving him in Tijuana. He wanted his wife and children who were in the US to join him, but she did not want to come, so he went back to the border by himself. There, members of a criminal gang found him. My nephew only had $50 to pay them off, but they wanted more and took his clothes, practically leaving him naked. Someone he knew gave him used clothes, and he went back to Ahuehuepan. He stayed for a year, then went north again, this time with a coyote. He stayed in California for six years before returning for another visit with the whole family."

Juana Salvador Morales (retired teacher; interviewed in 2020).

"Vendors who no longer have customers are getting more desperate. They need to find other ways of making a living. Some are moving to the States, others find work in restaurants.

"I know one man who lost many head of cattle in Ahuehuepan when he was working in the States, because his wife did not do a good job taking care of his animals."

A vendor in Nayarit (born in Ahuehuepan in 1962).

"I was in the US for one year. I went back to Mexico because my wife did not want to join me. She said she is 100 percent Mexican and does not want to live anywhere else. I love my wife, nor did I want my children to be without their father any longer."

A teacher from Ahuehuepan.

"I told my oldest daughter I wanted her to start helping us a bit more because my salary is not enough to support the family. She wants to buy expensive clothes in Iguala and a new cell phone. She could not get a decent job, so she went to the US."

A woman from Ahuehuepan (born in 1963).

"Some coyotes deceive people. When some of us wanted to cross the border, they kept us indoors while waiting to cross, which was supposed to be the following day. The coyote said he was waiting for more people, so another day went by. By the fourth day, we were desperate, so we looked for another coyote."

A young man in Ahuehuepan (born around 1998).

"The only person in my family who went to the States is my brother. He left when he was young and was there for four or five years. He died and they shipped home his body."

It used to be easy to cross the border. One man told me: "It was not difficult, because there was only one barrier, and you could jump across. I crossed on the first try." Migrants sometimes succeeded in entering the US by pretending that they lived in San Diego or El Paso. After the 1986 amnesty, it became easier for the relatives of those legalized to enter the US without a coyote. Another man told me: "My uncle had his papers, so he would drive to Mexico and pick me up in Tijuana. When he drove back across the border, I would pretend to be his son." Throughout the 1990s, costs crept up and more people were returned. *Feliciano Nuñez*, born in Ahuehuepan, recounted: "When I went to Los Angeles in 1994, I paid $350. When I went back for my wedding in 1997, it cost me $450. In 2003, I went to surprise my father on his birthday. That cost $1,700. Afterwards it became more expensive, with greater risks."

Migrants are creative in finding ways to enter the US. *Baltazar Miguel*, who crossed the border several times, arranged for someone to pick him up at an inspection station. The driver knew that for the three minutes when a new shift started, no one minded the checkpoint. It was not that easy for everyone. Some traversed by walking over the hills near Tijuana. *Angelina* found her first trip in 2006 difficult: "We were walking at night, everyone holding on to a rope. We carried sticks so that we would know where we were stepping. Sometimes the person walking behind would hit the person in front by mistake." Her sister-in-law faced other challenges. She and three other women took a bus to Tijuana but did not find a suitable coyote. Food and hotels were expensive. *Jessica* ran out of money and couldn't even make a phone call. She finally made it across and has so far not returned. Her nephew *Cruz* fainted when he was walking up a steep hill. His friends had to carry him. Another young man was not so lucky; he died of dehydration crossing the desert in Arizona. Some do not want to take the risk anymore; yet despite new measures to deter illegal entry, young people have not given up hope. They keep trying. Twenty high school graduates traveled to the border in the summer of 2011, but only three reached their destination. This was a dramatic development, since before that time, those who entered the US far outnumbered those who did not make it across.

WORKING IN THE UNITED STATES

Each person has their own story of finding their first job, what kind of work they did, and getting along with coworkers and employees. Everyone mentions that their life in the US revolves around work. Some talk about how stressful the jobs are; at the same time, they recognize that it allows them to get ahead. The time between arrival and finding a job varies. *Isidro* found jobs quickly. He got a job in Texas, then found a better one in California. Others had different experiences:

> A man born in 1961 (interviewed in Ahuehuepan, 2013).
> "I left Ahuehuepan after finishing three years of grade school [*primaria*]. In California I was a helper in landscaping. Next, I learned to be a bricklayer, using a trowel to put up bricks that are very different than the ones used in Mexico. I got other jobs, putting in insulation, plastering ceilings, and roofing. I do not like working with drywall, because it is heavy and you must hold a screwdriver while you are balancing a sheet of gyprock on your head. I came back to take a two-month rest, but I plan to go back to California."

Most employers do not do job training. Those who went to Los Angeles had no prior experience in sewing, so they had to learn on their own. *Feliciano Nuñez* took lessons in a private school founded by a former employee. Several months later, he found a textile factory where the sewing was not as difficult. However, that job did not pay well, so he got a job in another factory, where *Feliciano* became more proficient. His wages went up. His wife, *Ofelia*, who also works in the fashion district, had a different story about how she learned to sew: "Like other workers, I started off trimming. One day my boss asked me if I wanted to work with a sewing machine. She showed me what to do and left me to practice on my own time. I did not have to go to a sewing school like my husband." *Magdalena Lázaro*, who came to the US at age fifteen, had a different kind of job, working in a donut shop. She was not paid for working overtime, nor did she receive holiday pay, but she did get some on-the-job training.

Although many women are employed in the service sector, some have physically demanding jobs, as in the case of *Jessica*. When I first met her in Ahuehuepan, I overheard her telling her mother-in-law about her job, showing the scars on her knees from kneeling while grafting plants. The legal status of other members in the same workplace varies considerably. Sometimes it consists entirely of Spanish-speakers, including supervisors and in some cases owners.

While migrants from Ahuehuepan work in six states, they mostly go to three metropolitan centers in Texas and California. In downtown Los Angeles, they work in textile factories. The Sacramento area offers a wider selection of jobs in construction, restaurants, and yard maintenance. Few migrants live in the city of Sacramento, although sixteen have been in the city's suburbs; the vast majority are in Lincoln (901), Rancho Cordova (388), Roseville (251) and Citrus Heights (41). The total for the whole area is bigger (>1,580) once we include nearby locations with one or two families, such as Carson City, Folsom, Newcastle, Riverside, and Winters. There were once almost as many *Ahuehuepeños* in Los Angeles as in the Sacramento area (over a thousand each). Starting around 2014, over twenty families who were in Los Angeles moved to the Sacramento area. A much smaller number (16 households) live in the San Diego area, mainly in San Marcos (102) and nearby Oceanside (22). The third destination, with 294 migrants, is Houston, Texas, and nearby Katy (9), followed by Atlanta, Georgia. Some of those in Atlanta had earlier been to Houston. Most of the 27 people there belong to three families whose members work in the suburbs and in nearby Lawrenceville, Duluth, and Doraville. Migrants have also gone to Florida (10) or further north, to Chicago, Illinois (20 people), and Seattle, Washington (15).

The first migrants rented apartments. As many as eight men shared one- or two-bedroom units. When whole families started arriving, they moved farther away, resulting in a dispersed settlement pattern. Over time, families rented townhouses, with other relatives moving in. Once settled down, migrants rarely move to another state. People make comparisons: one man thought it was better in Sacramento because one can earn more money than by working in Los Angeles. Someone else pointed out that it costs less to live in Los Angeles, where rents are lower. Textile workers living downtown are not dependent on cars to get to work. The advantage of Sacramento is greater exposure to English.

Conditions of employment and relationships of migrants with employers, some of whom are themselves immigrants, vary. In downtown Los Angeles, textile factories are owned by Koreans, some of whom speak the Spanish they learned in Argentina. One of these owners, *Jon-wo*, who knows how to gain the trust of his workers, adopted the Spanish name *Nicanor*. *Feliciano*, a man who likes and got along with his former boss, is aware that *Nicanor* is running his business outside the law. *Feliciano* did not hesitate to leave to work in another factory when he saw a better opportunity, but he keeps on good terms with former boss. He is aware that *Nicanor* is vulnerable: "He does not have insurance and gets nervous when inspectors come around. By law we are only supposed to work for eight hours, but sometimes we work much longer." The fate of people working for big companies is determined as much by decisions made in the head office as by the whim of a manager. One person who lost his job did not understand how he could later get hired by another company, using the same documents.

The way undocumented workers get paid takes many forms: checks, with or without deductions; cash under the table; or a combination of checks for regular hours, with cash for overtime. Employers tap into the migrants' network of friends and relatives to recruit more workers, preferring to take on people from the same town. When *Paula* drove me around Houston, she explained that they work for the same chain of donut shops, the men as bakers, the women as cashiers. *Angelina* had insights into why employers prefer workers belonging to a close-knit circle of people of the same background: "The bosses know that we are good workers. The company used to employ native-born Americans, but most of them stayed for only a while. The owners know that we are going to stay for a long time." I asked her whether she and her coworkers can take unpaid holidays or miss work when they get sick: "Yes, we can get permission to take time off work. In my case, I explained I would be away for two months for my wedding." If an employee must take time off work, he or she tells the manager whom to hire as a replacement. That is what happened when *Paula* was hired. She got her job through a cousin, to the chagrin of the head office, who did not like losing control over hiring. Jacqueline Hagan (1994), who conducted a study of a Mayan community in Houston, saw similar control over the allocation of workers.

Further Comparisons and Group Identity

People make comparisons between those working and living in Ahuehuepan versus those in the US:

A man who has lived in both places (born in Ahuehuepan in 1972).
"I liked working in the States, because I paid only $250 a month in rent and earned that much in a day. However, when you cannot work for a couple of days, you must still pay for gas, rent, food. It is very different in Ahuehuepan; you do not need to work all the time and you have fewer expenses. That is why I am thinking about staying in Mexico."

Eugenio Ausencio Alejo (has never been in the US; born in 1974).
"Most people in Ahuehuepan speak a mishmash of Nahuatl and Spanish, just like the people from Mexico use a defective form of English mixed with Spanish in the US."

Working in the US is bound to shape people's identities as well as how they communicate. Older migrants feel more comfortable speaking Nahuatl; however, mastery of Spanish through interactions with other Mexicans is changing their social identity. Those who have spent a good part of their lives in the US see themselves as Mexicans. In places with few people from Ahuehuepan, migrants only keep in touch with close relatives. Once elderly relatives die, there is no reason to visit Mexico or places in the US. In contrast, in places in the US with a concentration of migrants, a hometown identity is kept over several generations. People send videos to relatives in Mexico, who become acquainted with people they have never met. During a phone call with Margarita in November 2012, I found out that couples were having their weddings in the US instead of in Mexico. Margarita's sister-in-law, who had recently seen a video, recognized members of the wedding party and who was dancing with whom.

Migrants cannot afford to cut off ties if they want a place they can return to. Consequently, they try to fulfill their duties as citizens of their hometown, including making contributions for its festivals, but only if they are gainfully employed. A decline in remittances affects the entire town; in 2010 only three instead of four *castillos* were lit for Quinto Viernes. People in Ahuehuepan continue to see all migrants as its members even if those migrants no longer perform their duties as citizens and stay away for a long time. However, once it becomes clear that they will never come back, they will be treated as strangers.

It is difficult to answer the questions of whether undocumented workers are exploited and taking away the work of Americans who can do the same job, and if the advantages of living and working in the US, even if people cut off all ties with their hometown, outweigh those associated with staying in Mexico. Economists and sociologists have different answers, with the former putting more emphasis on the benefits of earning more money, while the latter would dwell more on the loss of contact with loved ones in Mexico. Mexican migrants, their employers, and investigative journalists each have their own viewpoint. Migrants would argue that most people born and raised in the US would never take on the jobs they do, the employers deny that they exploit migrant workers. Journalists tend to have diverse views depending on their own political orientation. Only a study placing equal importance on diverse methods of investigation that generate different answers can give a complete picture.

17

Children of Indigenous Migrants

Children of migrants are mentioned in earlier chapters. The ones with whom I interacted, including school-age students born in the US, undocumented teenagers born in Mexico, and American-born children living in Mexico, have little in common. Many are now adults. One migrant from Ahuehuepan who came to California at age twelve is proud of his ability to speak Nahuatl. In contrast, the American-born offspring of other migrants understand, but do not speak, their parents' mother tongue. For example, the children of *Alejandro* speak both English and Spanish but not Nahuatl. His ten-year old son told me:

> "I was taught English in school but do not speak Nahuatl, although I understand a bit. My parents spoke it with each other but not with us. When I visited Mexico, my cousin used Nahuatl with her parents at home. While showing me around, we spoke Spanish."

The stories of many other young people, of different ages, are too many to include, so I randomly selected few:

> A young man originally from Ahuehuepan (born in 1986).
> "My parents took me to Roseville, California, when I was twelve years old. As children, we helped our parents while going to school. I worked part-time in a restaurant and gradually got used to working. I am now working in landscaping."

> Pedro Martínez2 Tomás (a man in Ahuehuepan, born in 1948).

"I told my son that he should arrange to have his house built here, since I am getting older. He went to the States to earn money and then return, just like all those who plan to do. However, most do not come back, because they have children who were born there. They won't want to live in Ahuehuepan, because they are used to eating American food and speaking English. Here we only eat tortillas with chili."

A young woman born in the US (in 1986).

"My parents and all my uncles used to speak to me in Nahuatl when I was growing up in the US. That was before I started my schooling in Ahuehuepan. That is why I never learned to speak English very well."

A woman from Ahuehuepan (born in 1973; emigrated in 1988).

"In Lincoln where we live, we used to speak Spanish with our children, but they prefer to speak English among themselves. Recently I started to speak to them in Nahuatl. I want them to learn, because if they do not understand it, children in Ahuehuepan will poke fun of them."

Juana Salvador Morales.

"Some children born in the US whose parents sent them back to Ahuehuepan did not learn how to work in the fields or how to paint. Why would their grandparents teach them if those children's parents are sending money for them to take care of their children and if those parents do not think that was important?"

Some children are ashamed of the language their parents speak. In one of the households where I stayed, a boy poked fun at his mother when she scolded him in Nahuatl. Regardless of their exposure to or feelings towards Nahuatl, the English-speaking children of migrants born in the US identify as Americans although they are aware that they are not the same as others of Mexican descent. They take part in ceremonies that are not the same as those of other migrants.

Family relations and courtship are different between the two countries. It is easier for young people to date without the scrutiny of parents, especially if one or both parents are living in Mexico. However, once they start living together, they must follow rules that apply to their hometown, as in the case of a migrant's son who started living with another migrant's daughter. In the eyes of their parents, they had eloped. One *weewe* living in the US and one in Mexico did the negotiations. Mexican-born children who did not join their parents in the US until later faced other challenges, especially when it comes to language. One boy who barely finished grade three in Mexico told me: "I could not understand my teacher, who spoke only English. The other Mexican kids would poke fun at me because I did not speak much Spanish or English, which I did not learn until middle school." Older children who master Spanish before arriving in the US learn English within a few years, which makes them trilingual. However, as more children were born in the US, a generation of young people grew up speaking no Nahuatl. Their grandparents complain they cannot communicate with them. Such children have no trouble speaking Spanish, but do not know how to write it.

It is not easy to bring up children in the US. It costs more to buy clothes and food. The network of relatives available for babysitting is smaller. In Mexico parents are more demanding and expect their children to do more chores, but they do not restrict their movements. Their counterparts in the US do not allow their children to leave the house when they come home from school. When I asked *Ana*, then fourteen years old, if she and her brother ever left their apartment, she said, "No—our parents don't allow that, nor can our friends come and visit us. We are stuck at home." Given the existence of gangs of juveniles, parents are very protective. Those same parents do not worry when their children visit Mexico. *Pedro*, the fifteen-year-old American-born son of *Jessica* and *Gabriel*, flew there to attend Ahuehuepan's annual festival in 2011. He had been there only once before when the family went back for a visit. *Pedro* had a wonderful time when he hung out with several cousins. Two teenagers from another family stayed at their grandmother's house for several weeks in 2012 while visiting an aunt, who later told me about the conversation:

> "When my niece and nephew came to visit me, I asked them what they thought of our town. My niece, who is older and more capable for expressing herself, told me that life here is not as hectic as in the United States. She liked the freedom she had here, that she could leave her grandmother's house whenever she wanted."

Those who go to the US as teenagers will have finished six years of school, which means that they are literate in Spanish. However, the English they learned in Mexico is minimal. *Raul*, who was fourteen when he became an undocumented worker, told me:

> "I started working for a Taco Bell right away but had a tough time because I did not know much English, so I went to high school for one year, which helped me a lot. I now work as a cashier for Burger King. I stopped working in the kitchen like so many of the kids who only went to grade school in Mexico."

Once they start working, such children may be living at home, where they must obey their parents. In 2012 I met *Leonardo*, *Jessica* and *Gabriel*'s eighteen-year-old, Mexican-born son. He had a part-time job but spent a lot of time playing computer games. His mother gets angry when he drinks. He was once involved in a car collision but has never been deported. But she thinks that her son has turned out alright, even though he went through a difficult period as a teenager. Other young men were not as lucky. I heard about *Cristino*, *Leonardo*'s cousin, during one of my trips to Houston. I met him for the first time after he was deported for drinking while driving. *Cristino* had worked in a supermarket and paid off what he owed to his *coyote*. In Mexico, I saw him using a shovel to mix sand and cement. He did not like the fact that he earned less per week than what he did in a couple of hours in the US. A year later, *Cristino* was back in Houston.

Migrants in California have large gatherings where they celebrate baptisms and other rites of passage. People eat together, followed by dancing, including the dance of the bottle I saw in Mexico. The children of recently arrived migrants meet American-born cousins; however, they do not share many interests. *Leonardo*, who came to the US when he was a toddler, told me:

> "I do not have much contact with my *paisanos*. My friends are Americans, including Americans of Mexican descent. I am very different from my cousin *Daniel*, who came here four years ago. We are about the same age, but we have little in common."

Over time, *Leonardo* and *Daniel* will likely get to know each other, yet they will continue to live in different worlds. Their tastes in music and the people with whom they associate will be different. I predict that *Leonardo*, who is single, will marry someone with no connection to Ahuehuepan. *Daniel* is already married to someone from his hometown.

I got a good sense of cross-cultural differences by looking at Facebook. Young people who went to school in Mexico use Spanish, unlike their American-born cousins, whose postings are in English. Only the former use phrases in Nahuatl or refer to their hometown. Religious images are found in postings by young people in both the US and Mexico, but the profiles and postings of those who were born and raised in Mexico are easier to recognize; they show landscapes, including panoramic views of Ahuehuepan, and refer to Mexican bands. In contrast, those who were born in the US make comments on, and post pictures of, American sport teams.

VISITS TO AHUEHUEPAN

The offspring of migrants go to Ahuehuepan for various reasons, including for weddings, getting deported, or family visits:

> Saul Ignacio Manuel (born in the US in 1986).
> "This is my first visit to Ahuehuepan. Although I was born in the States, my parents spoke to me in their language, which I can understand but not speak. I came here to get married and will go back to the States to work. I plan to eventually come back to live here. This is my village. My fiancée, whom I met in Lincoln, was born and raised here."

A single man now living in Ahuehuepan (born in 1989).

"This is the first time I am back. I left Ahuehuepan after finishing school. I am not going to return to the US, because I was put in jail for two years. If I return, they will put me back in jail for a long time, since I committed a felony. It is like, two strikes and you're out."

A married woman living in Houston (born in 1976).

"Two years ago, my son made a visit to Ahuehuepan. He did not like staying with my mother-in-law. He was bored because he spent most of his time in her house. My mother-in-law often makes trips to other towns, but she never took him along, nor did she ever go with him on a mule to climb to the top of one of the mountains. He spoke to us often by phone, begging us to arrange his return, but we bought a return ticket, and it would have been expensive to make a change. His grandmother in Ahuehuepan complained that she could not understand him half the time. Two of his cousins, who were also there for a visit, used to come over to see my son, and they would speak to each other in English. My mother-in-law spoke to them in Spanish, but she used words in Nahuatl that my son did not understand. In contrast, my uncle's children liked their visit to Mexico, especially his daughter Fanny. She stayed with her grandmother, who took her to meet other people."

Some young people go back to Mexico to avoid trouble with the law but might later go back the US. In contrast, other children born in the US may not see Ahuehuepan until they are teenagers. *Germán* and *Santa* live in downtown Los Angeles. *Apolinar*, one of their American-born sons, had a record when they sent him to Ahuehuepan to live with *Germán*'s parents. They hoped that he would be reformed if he were to spend some time in a supportive environment. They thought that their son would enjoy the fresh air and learn how to work. However, he was bored, missed his friends, and was not allowed to smoke. He gave his grandparents a hard time.

Some migrants die in the US, only coming back once their corpse is shipped to Mexico. In some cases, a baby who does not survive is buried in Ahuehuepan, as I found out from Margarita Gómez during a conversation in 2014:

Last year, a baby who died in the States was shipped back in a small casket. Parents prefer such a burial in Ahuehuepan, but they must both agree. Another dead baby, one of the grandchildren of the late Leonardo de la Luz, came back around the same time. The baby's father was married to someone he met in Lincoln. She is not from Ahuehuepan, yet she came here for the burial. She came again a year later, as is customary for what we call the *cabo del año* [the tail end of a year].

When talking about specific individuals and families, it is easy to overlook the larger picture of kinship clusters over several cohorts, which is done in the next chapter.

18

Transborder Families

This chapter follows six life trajectories to illustrate how migration enables women to avoid poverty and how some people lose contact with their hometown. It also shows to what extent people descended from *riikos* have a competitive advantage when covering the cost of relocation. The final paragraph provides information on a kinship cluster with a mix of international migrants, professionals who have spent their lives in Ahuehuepan, and internal migrants who are vendors. I first allow people connected to Ahuehuepan to speak for themselves. One of the aims of this chapter is to portray as much diversity as possible and to capture the complementary nature of social life.

Pablo Gómez Marcos (has traveled only within Mexico; died in 2014).
"I have two children in Los Angeles and four in Mazatlán [Mexico]. The ones in Mazatlán, who visit me every year, are coming to see me in October. The ones in the States, who don't come as often, are planning to be in Ahuehuepan for Quinto Viernes."

Guadencio Marcos Manuel (lived his whole life in Ahuehuepan, 1943–2007).
"I have sons in the United States who send me darn [*pinche*] bills [*billetes*]— hundred, a hundred and fifty at a time. It is not much, but enough for me since I live by myself. My children, who no longer visit me, have invited me to join them, but I don't want to leave my house. I remain alone, just knocking back [*chupando*] alcohol."

Dili Calixto Pascual (English teacher, born in 1994).

"I was born in Ahuehuepan. My parents took me to California when I was six. When I started school in Lincoln in 2001, I already spoke Spanish, which my father spoke to me. It took me less than a year to learn English. Back in Mexico, I did my *bachillerato* in Xalitla, where I also attended their technical school [Escsectec Carlos Darwin III]. After that I studied English in the Windsor Institute in Iguala. My father is planning to go back to the United States."

Juana Salvador Morales.

"A month ago [2019], a member of the Rojas family returned with his family and their belongings. They realized that the life of an undocumented person is too complicated. Luckily, they have a house here."

For other people, I only know their stories secondhand. *Lucia Segundino Julian*, born in 1961, was orphaned at age six. Her mother, *Febronia*, did not get any support from her second husband, and none of her children went to school. *Lucia*, married early to *Gregorio Fidencio*, was also an orphan with little schooling. At first this couple lived with *Lucia*'s mother in a thatch-roofed house, then moved into an adobe house that had belonged to one of *Gregorio*'s grandparents, a *riiko*. *Gregorio* and *Lucia* had nine children (three boys, six girls), who likewise became orphans when *Gregorio* died the year their oldest son turned thirteen. The following year, *Lucia* left to work in a textile factory in Los Angeles, leaving her children in the care of her mother. Some of them finished their schooling before joining their mother. *Lucia* sent money to Mexico for the construction of a better house; her older children helped when they started working. Her mother, *Febronia*, who supervised the construction, continued to raise her daughter's younger children.

The story of *Lucia* and her children, which is my first case of a transborder family, is typical of examples where almost the entire third generation ended up in the US. One of *Lucia*'s daughters, a teenager when she arrived in the US, married a man from Ahuehuepan. They have not been back. Another daughter, who went to Houston after marrying a man from her hometown, has also not been back. Only one of *Lucia*'s daughters now lives in Ahuehuepan. She returned after her separation from a man from Guatemala whom she met in Los Angeles, bringing back two boys born in the US. They started attending the school where their mother was once a pupil. They were still in Ahuehuepan in 2021. They speak Nahuatl and Spanish but not English.

My second case illustrates how the lives of people scattered throughout a continent are intertwined. *Esteban* is one of nine children of the late Carmelo Ramírez Felipe and Francisca Basilio1. Carmelo, three generations removed from Pedro Santiago, did not inherit any of his great-grandfather's wealth, but he did gain access to the land and cattle that his wife inherited from her father, Bernal Basilio1 Salvador, who was a *riiko*; hence their ten children are descended from two *riikos*. The fact that *Esteban*'s wife was the granddaughter of a *riiko* gave that couple a head start, making it easier for them to first migrate, move to another location in the US, and then become vendors in Mexico. Most of their children ended up spending the rest of their lives north of the border.

Esteban and his wife initially grew corn and made crafts. Five children attended school until 1996, when their parents took them to Los Angeles, where they had two more children before the family moved to Lincoln, where more children were born. A few years later, *Esteban* and his wife went back to Mexico to become vendors in La Peñita, taking three of their sons and their youngest daughter with them. Two of those sons did not stay long before going back to the US. The American-born daughter, *Jessica*, and one of her brothers continued their schooling in Ahuehuepan, where they lived with their mother while their father went back and forth between Ahuehuepan and La Peñita. *Jessica* later returned to the US to live with an older brother. She worked at Taco Bell and McDonald's while finishing high school. After meeting her husband, she went to Houston, where she got a job as a cleaner. Half of *Jessica*'s siblings, who stayed in Sacramento, got married to people with no connections to Ahuehuepan. They have not returned. Only one of her brothers, a bachelor, is back in Mexico.

The third story illustrates the close-knit nature of cross-border families. Born in 1940, Bonifacio Marcos made charcoal and painted the amates he sold in Mexico City. His mother, who died when he was growing up, was the oldest daughter of Fructoso Morales, a *riiko*. Bonifacio inherited his parents' large urban lot house and a house, where six daughters and a son were born. A combination of being the only male heir and the fact that he is the oldest grandson of a *riiko* meant that his children grew up in a secure environment that enabled them to cope with setbacks. Magdalena, the first of Bonifacio's ten children, went to Los Angeles, returning to Mexico after a separation. She spent the rest of her life in Ahuehuepan, working in the fields as well as painting carved wooden fish used to make mobiles. After her mother died, Magdalena cared for her father, including when he was recuperating from an operation after a collision. She supervised the final construction of three more rooms, which remained closed for a long time. They were financed through the remittances sent by her brothers. When living in one of those rooms in 2005, I saw that they conducted weekly phone calls in Nahuatl with other family members. In 2018, Bonifacio and Magdalena moved to Rosarito to be close to another daughter, who earlier lived in California. One of Magdalena's brothers and his family live close by, in Puerto Peñasco. A sister, who was in the US for a long time, is also back in Sonora, where she looks after her husband's sick mother.

That extended family is an example of the role played by grandparents and collateral kin in the raising of children and the care of sick relatives. When Magdalena's brother, the second oldest, moved to Los Angeles, he left his wife and their first son in Bonifacio's house. His wife stayed there for five years, then left that son with his grandparents. *Pedro*, another of Bonifacio's sons, had four children who were also born in Mexico. He went back and forth a lot, but his wife did not join him in Los Angeles until a decade later. That couple's last, American-born, daughter, was sent to live with her relatives in Mexico eight months after she was born. She started kindergarten, then went back to California. Bonifacio has a total of twenty grandchildren, born in Ahuehuepan, Los Angeles, Lincoln, and Puerto Peñasco; all speak Spanish, and a handful also speak English or Nahuatl.

The fourth story traces the lives of three siblings with no connection to a *riiko*. I got to know their father, Gaudencio Marcos, in 2003. He was living alone, eating with a couple from Tepecoacuilco who had set up a vegetable stand in the patio of his house. Gaudencio's three sons in California sent him money, but he did not want to join them. By 2020 one of those sons, whom I met in 2016, had returned after his father died in 2008. He then married a woman who had never left Ahuehuepan until that couple started going back and forth to Nayarit. They had three boys, one of whom entered primary school. Gaudencio's other two sons, who are in California, are both married. Their children have never been to Mexico.

My last two cases provide further examples of kinship clusters with no *riiko* ancestors. The first is a blended family with ten children. *Eugenio Martinez* and *Jocelyn Villalba* had both been married before they got together. It took them longer to get ahead in life. *Jocelyn* and her first husband lived for several years in Zacacoyuca, where people from Ahuehuepan rented land to grow corn and other crops. One of their three children was born there in 1987, while the other two were born in Ahuehuepan while their father went back and forth to the US. They lost their father in an industrial accident in Lincoln. His corpse was sent back around the same time that his youngest daughter was born. *Jocelyn*'s siblings and half-siblings live, or have lived, in California. In contrast, all six of her children spent most of the rest of their lives in Puerto Peñasco, including a son from her first marriage, who was in California for several years.

Jocelyn, who learned to make crafts from her mother, took her children to Puerto Peñasco, where she went with her second husband, *Eugenio*. They sold crafts to tourists with the help of *Jocelyn*'s children. That part of the family illustrates a couple who carved out a niche for themselves in other parts of Mexico. All the children under her care finished their schooling at the primary and secondary levels, and four went further. *Jocelyn*'s oldest daughter, who did her first two years in the *primaria*, got as far finishing her BA (*licenciatura*) in Sonora, specializing in business administration. She got a job working for Telcel, Mexico's wireless communication company. In the fall of 2000, two sisters and one brother were studying at the level of *preparatoria* or *licenciatura*, also in business administration. That brother is now running his mother's business. Their life trajectories illustrate how the offspring of migrants with no connections to *riikos* can get ahead through schooling. *Jocelyn* has eight grandchildren, including her oldest daughter's three sons, who speak Spanish but understand the Nahuatl spoken by their maternal grandmother.

The last case typifies a family in my middle category of social layering. I was able to trace their descent to Miguel Sebastian, born in 1921. Having access to land in four places plus owning forty head of cattle was not enough to be considered as a *riiko*, nor did he ever milk his cows. He and his wife had five children, three boys and two girls, none of whom married anyone related to a *riiko*. That family had their share of tragedies. Their oldest son died from malaria in 1949. Their second son, who played the trumpet in the town's band, died in a collision when the truck in which he was a passenger tumbled into a ravine. Of the remaining three children, I selected Pascual Sebastian Antonio, who died in 2020 at the age of eighty-one, for closer scrutiny. The story of that man and his children provides insights into the division of labor among people with diverse talents, the interdependence of people on both sides of the border, and the ongoing relevance of cattle ownership.

Pascual, a man who is a storyteller and a healer, assumed various public posts, including looking after the town's communal granary. He and his wife made candles and ran a small store in their house. She also made clay necklaces and mobiles. That second-generation couple had three daughters but no sons. The two oldest, living in Pascual's house, never had life partners, while the youngest one went off to Los Angeles with her husband, leaving their five young children in the care of her two sisters. She and her husband worked in textile factories, sending home money, part of which was used to build their own house in another barrio. Its construction was supervised by her mother, Macedonia. The sale of the cattle they inherited enabled the family to buy a sewing machine, which Macedonia used to make clothing for people. That youngest daughter returned to Ahuehuepan after she contracted what they thought was a fatal illness, staying after she recovered. She lives in the same house as her sisters, while her husband continues to work in California and to send money. The house they built in another barrio is not abandoned; she and her sisters use it as a pen for their hogs and poultry. They often go there during the day but sleep and eat in their original family home.

The sale of more cattle plus remittances allowed the family to buy a pickup truck, registered in the name of one of Pascual's unmarried daughters. The driver, one of two nephews, uses it to go to Iguala for errands but not for selling crafts. His two aunts sell what they make to wholesalers. That nephew became a bricklayer. Together with a younger brother, they managed their grandfather's remaining cattle and continued to do so after Pascual died in 2020. Married since 2016, the driver and his wife live in the same house where he was raised by his grandparents. He is a part-time musician who plays the flute in the town's musical ensemble. One of his older sisters also lives in Ahuehuepan. Another sister went to another part of Mexico, where she is a vendor. The third sister and her husband continue to paint and grow corn in Ahuehuepan. The driver's younger brother went to Los Angeles, where he joined the father to whom he had so far only spoken by phone.

The Pascual kinship cluster, whose members trace their descent back to Pedro, born around 1905, is unique in terms of the mix of occupations and destination. In many other respects, it is typical of most transborder families spanning several generations. Although not a *riiko*, Pedro owned enough cattle and land to leave more than enough to his three sons who survived to adulthood: Jose Domingo (also known as Ponciano), Alejandro, and Roberto. Each of them became vendors who sold crafts in other parts of Mexico while they continued to work the land. Ponciano, born in 1925, had eleven children, two of whom died as children. Of the remaining nine (four men and five women), three live in the States, as do their spouses, although one is now back in Ahuehuepan. A daughter who never left Ahuehuepan is married to an international migrant. Two sons and one more daughter have never gone to the States, although one of those sons, Cirilo, travels to other parts of Mexico as a vendor. We have already met the other son, Toribio Pascual Muñoz, a teacher born in 1947, who spent most of his life commuting back and forth between Ahuehuepan and Tetelcingo as a teacher. Although never a migrant, he made trips later in life to visit his daughter in Texas. Of his eight children, one of whom died early, three never migrated: one son became a priest, a daughter became a teacher, plus another daughter has a husband who works in the US. Of the two sons who emigrated, one later returned. He was living in Ahuehuepan in 2022 with a woman from another town after they got married. He found a job teaching English in Xalitla with the qualifications he got in Iguala. Toribio's other daughter lives in Texas, where she works as a cashier. Ponciano's brother, Alejando, born in 1932, had four children, including a son who also became a vendor like his father. Roberto (1936), the third son of Pedro Pascual, had eleven children, including three sons who spent most of their lives in the US. Looking at all the men mentioned so far, they include about the same number of professionals as successful merchants (3 and 4 respectively), plus a slightly larger number of international migrants who spent most of their lives in the US (6), not counting the four men who suffered from health issues or who had disabilities.

While the cases so far presented provide snapshots of transborder families, the next chapter provides a different perspective by presenting a statistical analysis of various sides of social and geographical mobility of everyone with a connection to Ahuehuepan.

19

Patterns of Geographical and Social Mobility

A statistical analysis of my ethnohistorical census shows how broader forces shape people's geographical mobility, and how various forms of layering, plus other variables such as leadership, are related.[1] That census, with information on geographic mobility for 3,651 people, excluding outsiders who have never lived in Ahuehuepan, plus the children of outside teachers, has the following four categories (percentages only):

1. people who traveled within the region where they were born (local; 59.1%);
2. people who went farther, to other parts of Guerrero, nearby Morelos, or Mexico City or within the same state in the US (3.9%);
3. people who migrated to more distant places within Mexico or from one American location to another American state (13.8%); and
4. people who traveled even farther within North America (including the US) (23.2%).

I did a breakdown for each of five periods or cohorts (1830–1910, 1911–1940, 1941–1975, 1976–1995, and 1996–2021; see introduction). Looking at the last three periods (after 1940), all the numbers go up, except for the *local only* category, which makes sense given that few people went anywhere before that date. Focusing on

---

[1] A more technical account of the kind of statistical methods used to come up with those results can be found in the appendix.

those who traveled farther, during the last two periods, the proportions are even higher (15–28 percent), which is consistent with the fact that there was noticeable increase in international migration after 1994.

Information on economic layering, combining data on living standards, income, and ownership of the means of production, was broken down into five categories. The numbers and percentages are as follows: poor or destitute: 323, 4.9 percent; low middle: 5,895, 88.2 percent; middle: 236, 3.6 percent; upper middle: 59, 9 percent; and upper (*riikos*): 44, 7 percent. Babies and very young children who died were not included, while students were placed in the category of *low middle* on the assumption that they would later enter an economic layer the same as or lower than their parents.

Numbers for overall economic layering gloss over long-term changes; hence I did a comparison of the five cohorts. The percentages of the very poor or destitute have been consistently low (ranging from 3.6% to 2.4%), with the highest (9.2%) in the third cohort. The numbers for low middle, starting at 83.4%, decrease, then increase, in the last two cohorts (to 90.1%, then 96%); the corresponding absolute numbers, starting with 427, keep increasing, especially in the third cohort, until they reach 3,957. The high percentage of 96 for the most recent time (the fifth cohort), together with a dramatic decrease in the percentages of high middle over the last two periods, from 2.8 percent in the second cohort to 0.5 percent, then nothing, combined with a decline in *riikos* (from sixteen in the second cohort to zero), reveal a pattern of increasing class polarization. Given the small numbers for poor and upper middle, it makes sense to use just three categories: low (including low middle), middle, and high (including high middle).

It is important to take intergenerational mobility into account: downwards (compared to one's parents), comparable (or too early to tell), and upwards (higher than both parents). The total number of cases, including all five periods, is 6,438 (excluding 179 unknown), with percentages of 86.3 percent (comparable), 3.4 percent (up), 9.7 percent (down), and 0.5 percent (not applicable). Those numbers also vary by cohort.

Table 19.1 displays the percentages for each of the five categories of economic layering for each cohort, including three for intergenerational social mobility. An examination of that table complements the town's history. Comparison of the first two columns reveals the differential impact of the revolutionary period. Not all prerevolutionary *riikos* and their offspring recuperated their wealth, yet newcomers did well, hence the proportion of the population that belongs to this layer stayed almost the same (3 percent). The percentages for the middle layer increased (from 1.9 to 2.8), showing that people belonging to that layer fared well in the transition to the postrevolutionary period, when people got access to more land. This increase

TABLE 19.1. Layers and social mobility over time

	Cohorts (%)				
Layers and Social Mobility	1	2	3	4	5
High	10.6	8.3	1.8	2.0	0.3
High-Middle	2.7	3.6	3.5	2.0	0.3
Middle	13.3	17.6	11.4	4.4	5.0
Low-Middle	70.0	67.0	77.3	91.3	96.0
Low	3.5	3.6	6.0	3.8	3.5
Up	21.0	21.5	9.6	3.8	1.4
Same	73.0	63.5	67.7	79.5	9.1
Down	6.0	15.0	22.7	16.6	7.4

includes people whose families were low middle before the land reform. The negative impact of the chaos and destruction of the Revolution and its aftermath explains the increase in the proportion of the people who were poor or destitute (low; from 3.6% to 8.1%.), as well as a dramatic increase in the percentage of downwardly mobile (from 7.2% to 17.3%).

A comparison of numbers on social mobility for cohorts 2, 3, and 4 provides insights from the period starting with a craft boom and ending in economic decline and a crisis at the national level. People were not aware of the impact of that decline until toward the end of the fourth period. While the proportion of people who did not experience either upward or downward mobility went up, that of people in the middle layer declines by almost 10 percent, while the size of the low middle layer shows a significant increase. This shows overall polarization. Upward mobility declined because of the downward mobility of most *riikos*' families; the proportion of people in that upper layer (high) fell to just half a percent. The further decrease in the percentage of *riikos* to zero during the last period is misleading, because the members of the uppermost layer who grew up prior to 1995 do not appear in that table. By the turn of the century, there were few older *riikos* left. By 2020 the three remaining middle-aged ones are less than a half a percent (their presence appears in square brackets). The same can be said for the *high middle* category.

Going back to the third cohort, the high middle layer experienced a small decline in size alongside a 10 percent decline in overall upward mobility. The most dramatic change occurred during the NAFTA era (the fifth cohort), which saw a decline in social mobility from almost 12 to 3 percent. The size of the middle layer shrank to an insignificant proportion while the low middle now constitutes 97 percent of the population. Most work in dead-end jobs in the US, while the rest eke out an existence making crafts for wholesalers or as beach vendors, day laborers, and subsistence farmers in Mexico. The poor or destitute stayed at 2.4 percent, which is indicative of the social benefits provided by the federal government. Were it not for that aid, that percentage would have gone down even more.

EDUCATIONAL AND OTHER FORMS OF CULTURAL CAPITAL

Level of educational capital (mainly formal schooling), a form of layering, consists of seven values, from 0 (none) to 6 (for college or beyond), with a breakdown of none (698; 12.5%), part primary (1,345; 24.1%), full primary (1,303; 23.3%), part *secundaria* (514; 9.2%), full *secundaria* (1,580; 28.3%), *bacchillerato* or *preparatoria* (120; 2.1%), and college or university (26; 0.5%). A related factor is talent, which includes basic literacy, because some people who have spent several years in school do not know how to read and write, while others have learned to read even though they did not go to school.[2] My census has information on thirty-two talents for 5,993 people, including basic literacy (4,436; 68.1%), singing (in public), playing a musical instrument (43; 0.7%), folk dancing, chanting, healing (e.g., bone-setting), using a sewing machine, driving (226; 3.8%), painting, drawing, or carving (1,712; 28.6%), taming horses or plow animals, lassoing (33; 0.6%), castrating a chicken, and being an electrician, master bricklayer (34; 0.6%), baker (25; 0.4%), storyteller, hunter, or *weewe* (mediator) (19; 0.3%). Well over half (3,464; 57.8%) had no special talents.

Since some people have more than one talent, I took number of extra talents into account: none (1,486; 24.9%), one extra (4,000; 66.6%), two extra (7.4%) and three or more (1.0%).

OTHER FACTORS

More variables include leadership (LDRS), and public posts (PSTS). A discussion of PSTS came up in the chapter dealing with governance. Both are dependent on age and sex, since women do not take on public posts, with few exceptions. People under the age of fourteen and outsiders with few connections to Ahuehuepan are excluded. LDRS has to do with reputation (a subjective part), which reflects the ability to have influence. Coded as three values ("none," "some," and "a lot"), that variable consists of leadership and organizational ability in various fields, including religion, the arts, and making improvements in physical infrastructure. Leaders

---

2 Students in grade school who start off knowing only Nahuatl would not be able to read and write Spanish until after grade four.

may or may not hold important political posts. The final breakdown of LDRS, in percentages, excluding those coded as missing or not applicable (n/a), are as follows: none, 96.3 percent; some, 2.9 percent; and a lot, 0.7 percent. Those numbers show that while most citizens of Ahuehuepan make financial contributions, as well as serving the town through participation in the running of its affairs, those considered to be leaders are small. In looking for trends over time, their proportion has gone down, especially if we look at the last three cohorts, when the percentages for the last two categories went down from 9.5 to 2.3 and finally to less than 1 percent. The low percentage for the last cohort reveals the consequences of the new form of mass migration; there are hardly any people available for leadership.

CORRELATIONS

In doing an analysis of the way spatial mobility is associated with economic and other forms of layering, I found no significant correlations. People who go farther away and who set up a second household in another part of Mexico have more resources. The same is true for international migrants, on the assumption that people with more economic capital can afford to travel to, and live for part of the year in, more distant locations. However, the relation between spatial and social mobility is not straightforward. People in the highest income bracket, the *riikos* and their family members, are more likely to have gone to distant locations in Mexico, but they do not need to cross the border. People with moderate resources are more likely to become international migrants, although a lower proportion have gone to other parts of Mexico as vendors. If one looks at another form of spatial mobility, that is, how often a person moved to live somewhere else (never to seven times or more), there is even less association between that and social layering. The correlations, while not significant, are reversed; those with fewer resources travel more often because they need to do so to find work. Wholesalers and successful craft vendors are more likely to visit and do business in many locations, but they also have a more permanent home base, which means less travel overall.

Looking at both types of migration, the interplay among geographical mobility and social layering gets more complicated. Level of schooling is associated with income and property to only some extent. Most *riikos* do not emphasize such education even if they can afford to pay for it. The association became more significant after the introduction of secondary schooling. Having high school has become essential for making a living. Literacy in Spanish and numeracy is vital for young people even if they enter the lower end of the job market. Going beyond that allows migrants to get somewhat better jobs as cashiers. Continuing one's schooling opens opportunities in the fields of education and health care, allowing students from poor families to move into the *high middle* category. The relationship between schooling and economic layering reveals further complexities. A minority of young adults have a lot of formal schooling but without a correspondingly higher income or ownership of property, while a tiny proportion of middle-aged people have both economic and cultural capital. Having special talents plus formal schooling makes it more likely that a person ends up going farther away. In doing comparisons between men and women, I discovered that a somewhat higher proportion of men have migrated, while three times more women stayed in Ahuehuepan compared to men. That is consistent with married men emigrating when it was easier to go back and forth across the border.

CLOSING REMARKS

In my statistical analysis of a survey of those with whom I interacted, I supply information on spatial and social mobility and other sides of social life. Correlations reveal tendencies consistent with what I learned from fieldwork, interviews, and archival research. Statistical analysis also gave some surprises, such as the fact that level of formal schooling plus special talents explains most of the variation in the level and type of geographical mobility, and for socioeconomic layering to a smaller extent. However, the time people stay away and how often they come back, which are bound to shape their attachment and commitment to Ahuehuepan, are difficult to quantify. Overall, census data provides evidence of the negative consequences of the mass migration that coincided with the implementation of NAFTA.

20

Different Perspectives on Transnationalism

This final chapter of part 4 summarizes the published work of scholars who examine international migrants from Mexico who have kept contact with the people they left behind. The expression *transnational community* refers to the involvement of migrants in the politics and social life of both country of origin and destination. Robert Courtney Smith (2006), who talks about transnational life, argues that migration does not lead to a loss of past loyalties. In his study of migrants from Ticuani, Puebla, in New York City, he explores people's involvement in hometown organizations. Smith gives examples of youth who returned to their parents' hometown to attend festivals, which changed how they saw themselves. Transnationalism also takes the form of the transport of nostalgia food that enables people to combine the best of two worlds. Judith Hellman (2008, 225) uses the example of return migrants in Zacatecas who grow prickly pears for export. They work abroad to accumulate the capital to set up businesses in Mexico.

The connections between transnationalism and assimilation are not simple. Smith (2006, 7–8) distinguishes between a negative form resulting in migrant youth quitting school and entering dead-end jobs, and positive assimilation involving more schooling and better jobs. I argue that the transnational life of documented migrants is more likely to lead to positive assimilation, while undocumented migrants are more prone to negative assimilation. With strict border controls, members of transborder communities cannot be involved in a meaningful way in the politics of the community of origin. Ongoing contact by telephone and sending money without showing up in person are weak forms of transnationalism.

The level of interaction between people in an American city and those in Mexico is higher in the case of the migrants studied by Smith than it is for *Ahuehuepeños*. Thirty to forty percent of people connected to Ticuani travel to Mexico every three years (Smith 2006, 283). In contrast, the percentage is less than 5 percent for Ahuehuepan. One migrant with a ranch does not have enough time to manage his enterprise. The business of a man who transported goods between Mexico and California did not work out. Two men who have documents took part in, and oversaw, the construction of a new statue in 2016. They can take off time to visit dying parents in Mexico; however, their actions are not comparable to those of members of a committee in Ticuani who contributed to public projects and influenced the outcome of elections. The explanation for this difference is that a larger proportion of the latter have work permits and residency status.

Michael Kearney and Caroline Nagengast offer a distinct perspective by drawing a parallel between transnational communities, such as the diaspora of Mixtecs, and transnational corporations (1989, 8). Mixtecs, who first migrated to Baja California to work in farms run by transnational agribusinesses, developed a broader identity. They set up pan-Mixtec associations (Nagengast and Kearney 1990, 84) to promote development projects in Oaxaca. Transnational communities and multinational corporations are both involved in productive activities in two or more national spaces. Both "escape the impress of the national state to inform their sense of collective identity" (Kearney 1991, 59). From that perspective, transnationalism is not so much a trait of migrants as it is part of a global economy with an ethnic and racially divided international labor force. The resulting transnational identity coalesces as ethnic consciousness (62–63).

For Scott Cook, anthropologists are in a good position to examine "the ever-increasing complexities of daily life within the Mexican branch of the North American (and global) capitalist division of labor" (Cook and Joo 1995, 55). Roger Rouse, who did fieldwork in Aguililla, Michoacán, shows how that town functions as "nursery and nursing home for wage-laborers in the United States" (1991, 12). Aguililla is part of a network of settlements including an outpost in Redwood City, California. Their inhabitants aspire to run family-based businesses in Mexico but can only do so with an influx of dollars. I would add that they also need work permits and residence status that allow them to easily cross the border. Rouse sees such communities as "sites in which the transnationally organized circuits of capital, labor and communications intersect with one another and with local ways of life" (16). He calls this the "social space of postmodernism" with its "crisscrossed economies, intersecting systems of meaning and fragmented identities" (8). I talk about a topology of a multidimensional social space with its interconnected clusters, fields, and layers. The creation of national borders gives rise to new forms of layering and clustering, and it alters existing social fields that exist on the local, national, and international levels.

Each transnational social field has its own dynamics. Evangelical denominations and the Catholic Church can be found on both sides of the border, although that religious field is segregated along linguistic lines: in the US, Catholic churches may hold separate masses in Spanish and English, while Pentecostal congregations have either Spanish-speaking or English-speaking worshippers. In the case of music, the migrants' musical talents are recognized in the US, where they can play in bands within a subfield of music similar in both countries, although legal restrictions impede their movement across the border. In the world of visual arts, their artistic talents are not of much use in the US, because they do not have the legal status or the linguistic skills to engage in that type of exchange. At the same time, American dealers are in a position where they can profit from the art gotten from amate painters in Mexico. Likewise, social layering along ethnic lines takes a different form on opposite sides of the border.

TRANSNATIONALISM AND INDIGENEITY

Stereotypes differ between Mexico and the US. Migrants from the Alto Balsas went down several notches, from being "rich Indians" to being despised "wetbacks." The exception is the way some social activists may admire Nahuatl-speaking migrants. The same holds for higher education. Indigenous people with university degrees are valued in international studies. There are other connections between transnationalism and indigeneity. The term *Aztlán*, used at a conference in Santa Barbara where students presented "The Spiritual Plan of Aztlán," gave rise to an organization, Movimiento Estudiantil Chicano de Aztlán (MEChA). That notion, highlighting the arbitrary nature of borders, threatens the categorical integrity of the nation-state (Kearney 1991, 69). One of the slogans used by many who identify with Aztlán is "we didn't cross the border, the border crossed us" (Hansen and Tlapoyawa 2020).

Indigeneity and transnationalism are connected although they have different dynamics. Neither are opposite sides of binary oppositions although Indigenous versus nonindigenous has often been treated as such. In the case of transnationalism, it does not make sense to talk about a continuum, with transnational versus national as opposites of a spectrum. People from Ahuehuepan, including its migrants, are both transnational and not transnational, depending on the perspectives used.

Conclusions and Final Remarks

Ahuehuepan is an indigenous community according to any definition, yet most of its inhabitants do not identify as such but rather see themselves as citizens of Ahuehuepan and as *masewaahle*, a word that suggests something different than *indígena*. Everyone is aware of, and has experienced, some level of prejudice. Only a handful remember the movement against the building of a dam in the early 1990s. Two-thirds of its population live and work elsewhere, in other parts of Mexico or in the US, with few or no return visits.

My study shows how the forces of global capitalism are played out on the local level, and how exposure to diverse lifestyles and new gender roles is altering social identities. To get a good picture of how Ahuehuepan has changed, I relied on a diverse set of tools: ethnography, oral histories, documents, and an ethnohistorical census. A statistical analysis of geographical and social mobility revealed complex patterns. Ongoing polarization between rich and poor, with a shrinking of the middle layer, alongside an overall rise in standards of living and expectations, went together with spatial dispersal. Such trends, not unlike those on the national and international levels, give globalization a fractal quality.

People with a connection to Ahuehuepan think of themselves as unified, but they are not homogenous in terms of language or other traits. They belong to distinct social layers. Men known as *riikos* used to dominate an economy based on the cultivation of maize. Today a handful of wholesale merchants descended from them buy crafts on commission from neighbors who are too poor to buy their own art supplies, much less afford travel to places with tourists. The rest of the population, including descendants of the *riikos*, live and work as undocumented workers in the US or sell crafts in Mexico. Some people are well educated, and a minority is illiterate, yet the latter are more knowledgeable about Ahuehuepan's traditions than the former. Those in Guerrero are divided by rival political factions. Some no longer consider themselves as Catholics. Most can read and write Spanish, and many understand Nahuatl. Some speak English.

When I first visited the town in 2003, I knew that many people had become craft vendors who put down roots in other parts of Mexico. They kept ties with their town of origin while developing connections with other ethnic clusters and economic subfields. Many joined those who went to the US, where they became part of an international labor force. It is not possible to properly examine my primary cluster, people associated with Ahuehuepan, without taking globalization and migration into account. Migration goes hand in hand with the emergence of broader fields and new forms of layering and clustering.

In this book, I use a duplexity approach that requires the use of diverse techniques and perspectives as a way of tapping into the complementary nature of social life. One of those perspectives consists of the views of people in remote parts of rural Mexico, including the ones not consistent with those of academic researchers who are not native to the Alto Balsas. As a theoretical and methodological orientation, duplexity offers insights into phenomena in a global context, including indigeneity. Globalization transforms livelihoods and worldviews in a way that has as much to do with what social scientists see and analyze as with the perspectives of the people under study.

FINAL REMARKS

In the future of Ahuehuepan there are bound to be further changes in physical infrastructure, including more washroom facilities and better internet access, changes perceived as improvements, but mainly among younger people and long-term migrants. An increasing number of US-born children will not know much about their parents' hometown. After three more generations, they will identify as Latinos, but they are not likely to be thought of as Indígenas by either anthropologists or more recent migrants, although some offspring of migrants may identify as both Latin@ and indigenous.

The number of students continuing their education after high school will remain small; yet as it becomes more difficult to cross the border, more will stay in Mexico to become professionals, most of whom will not end up living and working in the region, much less in Ahuehuepan. For many years, they will continue to try to cross the border, but most will not succeed and instead become vendors. They will come home for visits, but few of their children will follow their parents' careers. Over time fewer internal migrants will serve their hometown or build houses there. People will continue to marry someone from their hometown for several generations, but not after that. People whose worldview resembles that of their ancestors will decline. Most will still hold a romantic picture of Ahuehuepan. Of the people born in Mexico, I doubt whether any of their great-grandchildren will speak Nahuatl. But who knows? Life is full of surprises.

I give the last word to several people in Ahuehuepan, whose thoughts about the future and perspectives on change differ, as would be the case for most towns.

> A craft merchant who has never been to the US.
> "In the future, a small number of people born here will not know Nahuatl, just like now; but our language will survive in Ahuehuepan, even if more people end up going to the US, just as in the case of Ahuelican, where people still speak in Nahuatl among themselves even though many more than here started going to the other side of the border. I think that will be the case even if we might no longer have the *escuela bilingue*."

> A middle-aged woman who once spent a lot of time in the US.
> "I don't know if anyone in Ahuehuepan will speak Nahuatl a hundred years from now—probably not, but who knows?—maybe that will happen if more poor people from the *Montaña* come here to stay or if fewer people succeed in crossing the border. Some people might become even richer, like some of the craft vendors in Ameyaltepec, but most will end up as poor people who work as *peones*."

> A retired teacher who spent most of his life in Ahuehuepan.
> "After a couple of generations, no one in Ahuehuepan will speak or understand Nahuatl, nor will they see themselves as Indígenas. But they will always consider themselves as citizens of Ahuehuepan and be proud of our town. We will become richer overall."

Appendix

A researcher's personal contacts are bound to influence the nature and quality of the information gathered. I have mentioned key people, particularly Juana Salvador and Margarita Gòmez, who were the source of much of the information I collected. Other information was supplied by the many other people I met and with whom I interacted, including those alive during the time I was in Mexico, California, and Texas. Those interactions ranged from long interviews to short conversations.

TYPE OF CONTACT AND SOURCE OF DATA

CNT1 refers to type of contact, showing numbers and percentages. For the vast majority (76.7%), I only heard about them, while I met and spoke to 639 people. Of those 639, 195 people had contact with me solely by phone or email; for yet other indviduals, the only source of information was Facebook (7) or archival documents (78). Furthermore, 88 individuals, whom I have only seen, were identifed by someone else. An additional 600 cases are inferred, where I made an educated guess that such individuals exist. I use the conservative estimate of 2 children for migrant couples in the US and 3 children for couples in other parts of Mexico. In many cases, people had already told me "their parents must have had children." When I obtained more accurate information, it was almost identical to what I guessed. A half dozen of those inferred cases are people who lived in the nineteenth century. In those cases, I deduced the values from what I already knew about a person's parents and from where they came.

CNT2 measures the level of contact with the 768 people with whom I interacted in some way: minimal (439); low (229); medium for some guides (less than three trips) and people interviewed only once (78); high for most of the guides and people whom I did several interviews, plus lots of conversation (19); and very high for three people whom anthropologists call main informants. I consider about 16, or 3 percent, of those 768 people as collaborators, who gave me their views, insights, and opinions. I had no contact at all with 5,848 people, yet the time spent with the rest does not necessarily correspond to the amount of information I obtained. For that reason, I created CNT3 to indicate the quantity of data: bare minimum (less than 10 lines of text) for most people; low (10 to 50 lines) for over a hundred people; medium (close to a full page, to a page and a half of text, plus a short life history) for twenty-nine people; high (over a page and a half and a lot of extra short notes) for nine; and very high (including an extensive life history) for five individuals.

TECHNICAL SIDE OF THE STATISTICAL ANALYSIS

The data included in my census came from a variety of sources: written documents, official census data, observations, and what people told me. Some numbers are best guesses (e.g., age of birth). Accuracy is included as one of the columns in a SPSS (Statistical Package for the Social Sciences) spreadsheet. The percentages for those whose birthdate are precise versus a best guess were 48 and 52 percent. The percentages for level of accuracy of year of death are 40 and 60 respectively.

Individuals' attributes were treated as nominal, ordinal, or interval variables. Layering (CLASS) is an ordinal variable with 5 values that were converted into 3 values. Given that standards of living increased over time, I took quality and size of house into account for each of five cohorts, to enable more meaningful comparisons. Ownership of cattle is an indicator of economic layering for all but the last thirty years. Access to and ownership of land was coded as a separate ordinal variable, as were the levels of public education (only relevant when there was access to a school). With further filtering, I homed in on people associated with different periods, labeled as COH1. I did not calculate the number of friends and *compadres*, which is almost identical for most people of the same age. Political affiliation (POL1) is a nominal variable (5 categories) that was converted into a dichotomous one (POL2). I included several computed interval variables, such as family capital (FMCAP), with a range of values from 0 to over 20. FMCAP is a good variable for lineal regressions. For statistical analysis that needed nominal variables, FMCAP was recoded to KINCAP2, with four values (from 0 to 4). Other variables were also recoded in various ways. Treating spatial dimensions (different forms of GMOB) as independent variables is a useful way of generating added insights. In running a series of regression, in conjunction with cross-tabulations, I discovered that, while gender (SEX), literacy (LITC), FMCAP, and social class CLASSA play a role in shaping geographical mobility, none allowed me to create a model showing who migrated to various locations at a level of statistical significance. The best nonsignificant but still insightful predictors were TALT$_2$ (special talents) and EDU$_1$, suggesting that people with more schooling and skills are more likely to go elsewhere.

The relationships between layering and cultural capital, and between layering and social mobility, are nonlinear. Given that some data does not fit a normal distribution, I used Kendall's tau-b test for significance of nonparametric correlations. Binary logistic regressions were used for dichotomous dependent variables. Correspondence analysis (CA), a noninferential technique, made it possible to do an exploratory analysis when the data was not normally distributed. It is a way of generating biplot diagrams for showing people sharing similar attributes. For example, such a diagram was used to visualize the relationship between CLASSA, a variable that consists of 3 values (high, mid, and low) and BARRIO$_2$, a 4-category variable (one for each barrio). The row point for "mid" (layer) was close to the column point for Tlakaltech, in the bottom left quadrant, which is consistent with what I know from an inspection of the barrio notebooks. Filtering made it possible to exclude people born in other places, those under the age of fourteen, and those inferred. The results thus obtained were similar to those from my examination of the total population.

References

Aguirre Beltrán, Gonzalo. (1967) 1991. *Regiones de refugio: El desarrollo de la comunidad y el proceso dominical en mestizoamérica*. Obras de Antropología, vol. 9. Universidad Veracruzana, Gobierno del Estado de Veracruz.

Alonso, Ana M. (2007) 2020. "El 'mestizaje' en el espacio público: Estatismo estético en el México posrevolucionario." In *Formación de indianidad: Articulaciones raciales, mestizaje y nación en América Latina*, edited by Marisol de la Cadena, 173–96. Colombia: EnVíon.

Amith, Jonathan D. 1995. "La Historia de las Comunidades Nahuas en la Cuenca del Río Balsas / The History of the Balsas River Basin Nahua Communities." In *The Amate Tradition: Innovation and Dissent in Mexican Art*, edited by Jonathan Amith, 129–44. Chicago: Mexican Fine Arts Center Museum.

Amith, Jonathan D. 2005. *The Möbius Strip: A Spatial History of Colonial Society in Guerrero, Mexico*. Stanford: Stanford University Press.

Archer, Margaret Scotford. 1995. *Realist Social Theory: The Morphogenetic Approach*. Cambridge: Cambridge University Press; London: Verso.

Barad, Karen. 2007. *Meeting the Universe Halfway: Quantum Physics and the Entanglement of Matter and Meaning*. Durham: Duke University Press.

Barad, Karen. 2011. "Erasers and Erasures: Pinch's Unfortunate 'Uncertainty Principle.'" *Social Studies of Science* 41 (3): 443–54.

Barnard, Alan. 2006. "Kalahari Revisionism, Vienna and the 'Indigenous Peoples' Debate." *Social Anthropology* 14 (1): 1–16.

Bartra, Armando. 1979. "La explotación del trabajo campesino por el Capital." Mexico: Editorial Macehual: Comité de Publicaciones de los Alumnos de la Escuela Nacional de Antropología e Historia.

Bartra, Roger. 1974. "El problema indígena y la ideología indigenista." *Revista Mexicana de Sociología* 36 (3): 459–82.

Béteille, André. 1998. "The Idea of Indigenous People." *Current Anthropology* 39 (2): 187–92.

Blackwell, Maylei. 2012. "The Practice of Autonomy in the Age of Neoliberalism: Strategies from Indigenous Women's Organizing in Mexico." *Journal of Latin American Studies*, no. 44, 703–32.

Blackwell, Maylei. 2017. "Critical Latinx Indigeneities" (introduction). Special issue, *Latino Studies*, no. 15, 126–37.

Bonfil Batalla, Guillermo. (1987) 1996. *México Profundo: Reclaiming a Civilization*. Translated by Philip A. Dennis. Austin: University of Texas Press.

Bohr, Neils. 1937. "Causality and Complementarity." *Philosophy of Science* 4, no. 3 (July): 289–98.

Bourdieu, Pierre. 1982. *The Algerians*. Translated by Alan G.M. Ross. Boston: Beacon Press.

Bourdieu, Pierre. 1984. *Distinction*. Translated by Richard Nice. Cambridge: Harvard University Press.

Bourdieu, Pierre. 1985. "Social Space and the Genesis of Groups." *Theory and Society* 14 (6): 723–44.

Bourdieu, Pierre. 1991. *Language and Symbolic Power*. Cambridge: Harvard University Press.

Bourdieu, Pierre, and Loïc J. D. Wacquant. 1992. *An Invitation to Reflexive Sociology*. Chicago: University of Chicago Press.

Brading, David Anthony. 1988. "Manuel Gamio and *Oficial Indigenismo* in Mexico." *Bulletin of Latin American Research* 7 (1): 75–89.

Broda Prucha, Johanna. 2001. "La ritualidad mesoamericana y los procesos de sincretismo y reelaboración simbólica después de la conquista." In *Cosmovisión, ritual e identidad de los pueblos Indígenas de México*, edited by Johanna Broda and Félix Báez-Jorge, 14–28. México: Fondo de Cultura Económica / Consejo Nacional para la Cultura y las Artes.

Brysk, Alison. 2000. *From Tribal Village to Global Village: Indian Rights and International Relations in Latin America*. Stanford: Stanford University Press.

Castellanos, Bianet, Lourdes Gutiérrez Nájera, and Arturo J. Aldama. 2012. *Comparative Indigeneities of the Americas: Towards a Hemispheric Approach*. Tucson: University of Arizona Press.

Castellanos Domínguez, Alex R., and Anne W. Johnson. 2017. "From Nahua Migrants to Residents in Sonora, Mexico." *Third World Thematics: A TWQ Journal* 2, nos. 2–3: 141–56.

Cook, Scott. 1993. "Toward a New Paradigm for Anthropology in Mexican Studies." *Mexican Studies / Estudios Mexicanos* 9 (2): 303–36.

Cook, Scott, and Jong-Taick Joo. 1995. "Ethnicity and Economy in Rural Mexico: A Critique of the *Indigenista* Approach." *Latin American Research Review* 30 (2): 33–59.

Cotera, Maria Eugenia, and Maria Josefina Saldaña-Portillo. 2015. "Indigenous but Not Indian? Chicanas/os and the Politics on Indigeneity." In *The World of Indigenous North America*, edited by Robert Warrior, 549–67. New York: Routledge.

Cowan, Tyler. 2005. *Markets and Cultural Voices: Liberty vs. Power in the Lives of Mexican Amate Painters*. Ann Arbor: University of Michigan Press.

Cruz Manjarrez, Adriana. 2013. *Zapotecs on the Move*. New Brunswick: Rutgers University Press.

de la Cadena, Marisol. 2008. "Alternative Indigeneities: Conceptual Proposals." *Latin American and Caribbean Ethnic Studies* 3 (3): 341–49.

de la Cadena, Marisol, ed. (2007) 2020. Introduction to *Formación de indianidad: Articulaciones raciales, mestizaje y nación en América Latina*, 7–34. Colombia: EnVión.

Delgado-P., Guillermo, and John Brown Childs, eds. 2012. *Indigeneity: Collected Essays*. Santa Cruz: New Pacific Press.

Dietz, Gunther. 2009. *Multiculturalism, Interculturality, and Diversity in Education (an Anthropological Approach)*. Münster, New York, Berlin: Waxmann.

Duran Matute, Inés. 2018. *Indigenous Peoples and the Geographies of Power: Mezcala's Narratives of Neoliberal Government*. New York: Routledge.

Emerson, Robert M., Rachel I. Fretz, and Linda L. Shaw. 2011. *Writing Ethnographic Fieldnotes*. 2nd ed. Chicago: University of Chicago Press.

Escalona Victoria, José Luis. 2019. Review of *Los indígenas de la nación*, by Paula López. *Estúdios Sociológicos*, no. 37, 822–28.

Fallaw, Ben. 2013. *Religion and State Formation in Postrevolutionary Mexico*. Durham: Duke University Press.

Flores Farfán, José Antonio. 2009. "Za Zan Tleino." In *Destiempos: Revista de curiosidad cultural*, no. 18, 437–55.

Fox, Jonathan, and Gaspar Rivera-Salgado. 2004. "Building Civil Society among Indigenous Migrants." In *Indigenous Mexican Migrants in the United States*, edited by Jonathan Fox and Gaspar Rivera-Salgado, 1–65. La Jolla: Center for US-Mexican Studies, UCSD.

Friedlander, Judith. (1975) 2006. *Being Indian in Hueyapan: A Study of Forced Identity in Contemporary Mexico*. New York: St. Martin's Press.

Gamio, Manuel. (1916) 1982. *Forjando Patria*. Mexico: Porrúa.

García Ortega, Martha, and Eustaquio Celestino. 2015. "El otro viaje: Muerte y retorno de los migrantes nahuas de México." *Liminar* 13 (1): 41–55.

García Valencia, Enrique Hugo. 1995. "Spanish Social Anthropologists in Mexico." In *Fieldwork and Footnotes: Studies in the History of European Anthropology*, edited by Han F. Vermeulen and Arturo Alvarez Roldán. New York: Routledge.

Glazer, Nathan, and Daniel Patrick Moynihan, eds. 1975. *Ethnicity and Experience*. Cambridge: Harvard University Press.

Gomberg-Muñoz, Ruth. 2011. *Labor and Legality: An Ethnography of a Mexican Immigration Network*. New York: Oxford University Press.

Good Eshelman, Catharine. 1988. *Haciendo la lucha: Arte y comercio nahuas en Guerrero*. Mexico: Fondo de Cultura Económica.

Gutiérrez Chong, Natividad. Gamio, Manuel (1883–1960). First published: 30 December 2015 https://doi.org/10.1002/9781118663202.wberen184.

Hagan, Jacqueline María. 1994. *Deciding to be Legal: A Mayan Community in Houston*. Philadelphia: Temple University Press.

Hale, Charles. 2006. *Mas que un Indio (More than an Indian): Racial Ambivalence and Neoliberal Multiculturalism in Guatemala*. Santa Fe: School for Advanced Research Press.

Hansen Pharao, Magnus, and Kurly Tlapoyawa. 2020. "Aztlán and Mexican Transnationalism: Language, Nation and History." In *Handbook of the World Language Map*, edited by Stanley D. Brunn and Roland Kehrein, 667–84. Switzerland: Springer.

Hellman, Judith Adler. 2008. *The World of Mexican Migrants: The Rock and the Hard Place*. New York: New Press.

Hémond, Aline. 1994. "'Indiens' ou 'civilisés': L'Affaire de barrage San Juan Tetelcingo (Mexique)." *Cahiers des sciences humaines* 30 (3): 391.

Hémond, Aline. 1999. "Héros ou Victimes? L'Innovation technique como transgression sociale aux Mexique." *Technique & culture* 33: 29.

Hémond, Aline. 2003. *Peindre la révolte: Esthétique et résistance culturelle au Mexique*. Paris: CNRS Editions.

Hémond, Aline. 2004. "Factions et parties politiques: La mécanique des groupes dans un village indien de Mexique." *Ateliers*, no. 27: 111–46.

Jacobs, Ian. (1982) 2004. *Ranchero Revolt: The Mexican Revolution in Guerrero*. Austin: University of Texas Press.

Jenkins, Richard. 1992. *Pierre Bourdieu*. London: Routledge.

Juelskjaer, Malou, and Nete Swennesen. 2012 "Intra-active Entanglements: An Interview with Karen Barad." *Kvinder, Køn and Forskning*, nos. 1–2: 10–23.

Kammler, Henry. 2010. *Kulturwandel und die Konkurrenz del Religionen in Mexiko.* Stuttguard: Verslag W. Kohlhammer.

Kearney, Michael. 1991. "Borders and Boundaries of State and Self at the End of Empire." *Journal of Historical Sociology* 4 (1): 52–74.

Kearney, Michael. 1996. *Reconceptualizing the Peasantry: Anthropology in Global Perspective.* New York: Westview Press.

Kearney, Michael, and Caroline Nagengast. 1989. "Anthropological Perspectives on Transnational Communities in Rural California." Working Group on Farm Labor and Rural Poverty, Working Paper 3, California Institute for Rural Studies, University of California at Davis.

Kirby, Vickie. 2011. *Quantum Anthropologies: Life at Large.* Durham, Duke University Press.

Knauft, B. M. 1996. *Genealogies for the Present in Cultural Anthropology.* New York: Routledge.

Knight, Alan. 1990. "Racism, Revolution, and Indigenismo: Mexico, 1910–1940." In *The Idea of Race in Latin America, 1870–1944*, edited by Richard Graham, 71–138. Austin: University of Texas Press.

Kuper, Adam. 2003. "The Return of the Native." *Current Anthropology* 44 (3): 389–95.

Levaggi, Abelandro. 2001. "República de Indios y República de Españoles en los Reinos de Indias." *Revista de Estudios Histórico-Jurídicos* (Valpariso), no. 23: 419–28.

Leza, Christina. 2019. *Divided Peoples: Policy, Activism and Indigenous Identities on the US–Mexico Border.* Tucson: University of Arizona Press.

LiPuma, Edward. 1993. "Culture and the Concept of Culture in a Theory of Practice." In *Bourdieu: Critical Perspectives*, edited by Craig Calhoun, Edward LiPuma, and Moishe Postone, 14–34. Chicago: Chicago University Press.

López, Felipe H., and David Runsten. 2004. "Mixtecs and Zapotecs Working in California: Rural and Urban Experiences." In *Indigenous Mexican Migrants in the United States*, edited by Jonathan Fox and Gasper Rivera-Salgado, 249–78. La Jolla: Center for US-Mexican Studies, UCSD.

López Caballero, Paula. 2010. "The National Utopia of Diversity: Official Multicultural Discourses and Their Appropriation by the *Originarios* of Milpa Alta (Mexico City)." *International Social Science Journal* 6 (22): 365–76.

López Caballero, Paula. 2017. *Indígenas de la nación: Etnografía histórica de la alteridad en México Milpa Alta, Siglos XVII–XXI.* Mexico: Fondo de la Cultura Económico.

Marak, Andrea M. 2009. *From Many, One: Indians, Peasants, Borders, and Education in Callista Mexico, 1924–1935.* Calgary: University of Calgary Press.

Martínez Cobo, José. 1986. *Study of the Problem of Discrimination against Indigenous Populations.* https://www.un.org/development/desa/Indigenouspeoples/publications/martinez-cobo-study.html.

Martínez Novo, Carmen. 2006. *Who Defines Indigenous? Identities, Development, Intellectuals, and the State in Northern Mexico*. New Brunswick: Rutgers University Press.

Martínez Novo, Carmen, and Paval Shlossberg. 2018. "Lasting and Resurgent Racism after Recognition in Latin America." *Cultural Studies* 32 (3): 349–63.

Merlan, Francesca. 2009. "Indigeneity: Global and Local." *Current Anthropology* 50 (3): 303–33.

Molina Enríquez, Andrés. 2016. *Los grandes problemas nacionales*. Ciudad de México: Secretaría de Cultura, Instituto Nacional de Estudios Históricos de las Revoluciones de México. (Originally published in 1909 by A. Carranza e hijos, México.)

Muñoz, Maria L. O. 2010. "Forging Destiny: Populism, Indigenismo, and Indigenous Mobilization in Echeverría's Mexico." In *Populism in Twentieth Century Mexico: The Presidencies of Lázaro and Luis Echeverría*, edited by Amelia M. Kiddle and Maria L. O. Muñoz, 122–34. Tucson: University of Arizona Press.

Murphy, Robert F. 1971. *The Dialectics of Social Life: Alarms and Excursions in Anthropological Theory*. New York: Columbia University Press.

Nadeau, Robert, and Menas Kafatos. 2003. *The Non-local Universe: The New Physics and Matters of the Mind*. Oxford: Oxford University Press.

Nagengast, Caroline, and Michael Kearney. 1990. "Mixtec Ethnicity: Social Identity, Political Consciousness, and Political Activism." *Latin American Research Review* 25 (2): 61–91.

Negrín Da Silva, Diana. 2012. "Wixárika Youth Activists: Unfixing the Geographic Imagination of the Indigenous." In *Comparative Indigeneities of the Americas: Towards a Hemispheric Approach*, edited by Bianet Castellanos, Lourdes Gutiérrez Nájera, and Arturo J. Aldama, 139–54. Tucson: University of Arizona Press.

Otero, Gerardo. 1999. *Farewell to the Peasantry? Political Class Formation in Rural Mexico*. Boulder: Westview Press.

Overmeyer-Velásquez, Rebecca. 2010. *Folkloric Poverty: Neoliberal Multiculturalism in Mexico*. University Park: Pennsylvania State University Press.

Palacios, Guillermo. 1988. "Postrevolutionary Intellectuals, Rural Readings, and the Shaping of the 'Peasant Problem' in Mexico: El Maestro Rural, 1932–34." *Journal of Latin American Studies* 30 (2): 309–39.

Palerm, Angel. 1972. *Agricultura y sociedad en mesoamérica*, no. 55. México: Sep-Setentas.

Paradis, Louise Iseult. 1995. "La Historia Precolombina de la Región de Mezcala / The Pre-Columbian History of the Mezcala Region." In *The Amate Tradition: Innovation and Dissent in Mexican Art*, edited by Jonathan Amith, 113–28. Chicago: Mexican Fine Arts Center Museum.

Paré Ouellet, Luisa, Armando Barta, Sergio de la Peña, Héctor Díaz Polanco, Javier Guerrero, Jorge Montalvo, Sergio Perelló, and Warman Arturo.1979. *Polémica sobre las clases sociales en el campo Mexicano*, edited by A. Bartra et al., 85–96. Mexico: Ediciones Macehual.

Pelican, Micaela. 2009. "Complexities of Indigeneity and Autochthony: An African Example." *American Ethnologist* 36 (1): 52–65.

Poole, Deborah. 2020. "Mestizaje, distinción y presencia cultural: La visión desde Oaxaca." In *Formación de indianidad: Articulaciones raciales, mestizaje y nación en América Latina*, edited by Marisol de la Cadena, 197–232. Colombia: Envion.

Raby, Dominique. 2007. "The Cave-Dwellers' Treasure Tales: Folktales, Morality and Gender in a Nahua Community, Mexico." *Journal of American Folklore* 120 (478): 401–44.

Raby, Dominique. 2012. "Sur les ailes du vautour: Genre, violence et 'résistance' dans un récit Nahua de voyage á Chiknáujtipan, le monde des morts (Mexique)." *Journal de la Société des Américanistes* 98 (2): 167–97.

Raby, Dominique. 2014. "Herencia de los ejemplas Jesuitas: Homenaje a la obra de Danièle Dehouve." *Desacatos, revista de antropología social*, no. 44, 181–87.

Raby, Dominique. 2015. "Es que aqui hay mucho *machismo*: Representación de las masculinidades como modelo explicativo nahua de la violencia intrafamiliar en el Alto Balsas, Guerrero." In *Múltiples Formas de ser Nahuas*, by Catherine Good and Dominique Raby, 195–219. Zamora: El Colegio de Michoacan.

Ramírez Celestino, Cleofas, and José Antonio Flores Farfán. 2008. *Huehuetlatolli náhuatl de Ahuehuepan: La palabra de los sabios Indígenas hoy*. Mexico, DF: CIESAS.

Redfield, Robert. (1930) 1973. *A Mexican Village: A Study of Folk Life*. Chicago: University of Chicago Press.

Reynoso Jaime, Irving. 2013. "Manuel Gamio y las bases de la política indigenista en México." *Andamios* 10 (22): 333–55.

Riding, Alan. 1984. *Distant Neighbors*. New York: Vintage Books.

Rodríguez, María Teresa. 2017. "Mujeres indígenas y sistema de cargo en el siglo XXI: Un acercamiento desde la Sierra de Zongolica, Veracruz, México." *Diálogo andino: Revista de historia, geografía y cultura andina* 52 (March): 45–55.

Rouse, Roger. 1991. "Mexican Migration and the Space of Postmodernism." *Diaspora: A Journal of Transnational Studies* 1 (1): 8–23.

Rus, Jan. 1994. "The Comunidad Revolucionario Institucional: The Subversion of Native Government in Highland Chiapas, 1936–1968." In *Everyday Forms of State Formation: Revolution and the Negotiation on Rule in Modern Mexico*, edited by Gilbert Joseph and Daniel Nugent, 265–300. Durham: Duke University Press.

Saldana Portillo, Maria Josefina. 2016. *The Indian Given: Racial Geographies across Mexico and the United States*. Durham: Duke University Press.

Saldívar, Emiko. 2018. "Uses and Abuses of Culture: Mestizaje in the Era of Multiculturalism." *Cultural Studies* 32 (3): 438–59.

Sandstrom, Alan R. 1991. *Corn in Our Blood: Culture and Ethnic Identity in a Contemporary Aztec Indian Village*. Norman: University of Oklahoma Press.

Sandstrom Alan R., and Pamela Effrein Sandstrom. 2022a. "Paper Figures and Nahua Conceptions of the Divine: Art and Revelation in Pantheistic Religion / Figuras de papel recortado y concepciones nahuas de lo divino: Arte y revelación en la religión panteísta." *Estudios de Cultura Náhuatl* 64 (July–December): 15–62.

Sandstrom Alan R., and Pamela Effrein Sandstrom. 2022b. *Pilgrimage to Broken Mountain: Nahua Sacred Journeys in Mexico's Huasteca Veracruzana*. Denver: University Press of Colorado.

Sanjek, Roger, ed. 1990. *Fieldnotes: The Making of Anthropology*. Ithaca: Cornell University Press.

Saugestad, Sidsel. 2004. *The Inconvenient Indigenous*. The Nordic Africa Institute.

Schryer, Frans J. 1980. *The Rancheros of Pisaflores*. Toronto: University of Toronto Press.

Schryer, Frans J. 1990. *Ethnicity and Class Conflict in Rural Mexico*. Princeton: Princeton University Press.

Schryer, Frans J. 1998. *The Netherlandic Presence in Ontario: Pillars, Class and Dutch Ethnicity*. Waterloo: Wilfred Laurier Press.

Schryer, Frans J. 2001. "Multiple Hierarchies and the Duplex Nature of Groups." *Journal of the Royal Anthropological Institute* 7 (4): 705–21.

Schryer, Frans J. 2010a. "The Alto Balsas Nahuas: Transnational Indigeneity and Interactions in the World of Art and Crafts, the Politics of Resistance and the Global Labor Market." In *Indigenous Cosmopolitans: Transnational and Transcultural Indigeneity in the Twenty-First Century*, edited by Maximilian C. Forte, 97–125. New York: Peter Lang.

Schryer, Frans J. 2010b. "Globalization and *Indígenas*: The Alto Balsas Nahuas." In *Latin American Identities after 1980*, edited by Gordana Yovanovich and Amy Huras, 52–78. Waterloo: Wilfrid Laurier Press.

Schryer, Frans J. 2012. "Reflections on Multi-method Research: Developing an Ethnohistorical Survey of an Indigenous Community." *Revista de Investigación Social* 9 (15): 83–102.

Schryer, Frans J. 2014. *They Never Come Back: A Story of Undocumented Workers from Mexico*. Ithaca: Cornell University Press.

Shlossberg, Pavel. 2018. "Heritage Practices, Indigenismo, and Coloniality: Studying-Up into Racism in Contemporary Mexico." *Cultural Studies* 32 (3): 414–37.

Simpson, Eyler N. 1937. *The Ejido: Mexico's Way Out*. Chapel Hill: University of North Carolina Press.

Smith, Robert Courtney. 2006. *Mexican New York: Transnational Lives of New Immigrants*. Berkeley: University of California Press.

Stavenhagen, Rodolfo. 2007. *Promotion and Protection of All Human Rights, Civil, Political, Economic, Social and Cultural Rights, Including the Right to Development*. http://unsr.vtaulicorpuz.org/site/images/docs/annual/2007-annual-hrc-a-hrc-6-15-en.pdf.

Stephen, Lynn. 1991. *Zapotec Women*. Austin: University of Texas Press.

Stephen, Lynn. 2007. *Transborder Lives: Indigenous Oaxacans in Mexico, California, and Oregon*. Durham: Duke University Press.

Tiles, Mary. 1984. *Bachelard: Science and Objectivity*. Cambridge: Cambridge University Press.

Trnka, Radek, and Radmila Lorencová. 2016. *Quantum Anthropology: Man, Cultures and Groups in a Quantum Perspective*. Prague: Karolinum Press.

Vann, Elizabeth F. 1994–1995. "Quantum Ethnography: Anthropology in the Post-Einsteinian Era." *Lambda Alpha Journal*, nos. 25–26: 71–80.

Vasconcelos Calderón, José. 1948. *La Raza Cósmica: Misión de la Raza Iberoamericano (notas de viajes a America del Sur)*. Agencio Mundial de Libreria. 2nd ed. Buenos Aires: Espasa-Calpe. (The first edition was published in Barcelona in 1925.)

Velasco Ortiz, M. Laura. 2002. *El regreso de la comunidad: Migración indígena y agentes étnicos; Los mixtecos en la frontera México-Estados Unidos*. Mexico: El Colegio De Mexico.

Wagley, Charles. 1994. "On Social Race in the Americas." In *Race and Ethnicity in Latin America: Scholarly Debates from the 1950s to the 1990s*, edited by Jorge L. Domínguez, 13–27. New York: Routledge.

Wilson, Tamar Diana. 2017. "Sons of Peasants on the Beach: Venders in Cabo San Lucas, Mexico." In *Anthropological Consideration of Exchange, Vending, and Tourism*, edited by Donald C. Wood, 205–29. Bingley: Emerald.

Wilson, Tamar Diana, and Alba Eritrea Gámez. 2010. "A Consideration of Social and Human Capital among Beach and Marina Venders in Cabo San Lucas, Mexico." *Urban Anthropology and Studies of Cultural Systems and World Economic Development* 39 (4): 425–53.

Wimmer, Andreas. 2013. *Ethnic Boundary Making: Institutions, Power, Networks*. New York: Oxford University Press.

Wolf, Eric R. 1957. "Closed Corporate Peasant Communities in Mesoamerica and Central Java." *Southwestern Journal of Anthropology*, no. 13, 1–18.

Acknowledgments

I thank those whose cooperation enabled me to get the information I needed for writing this book. The people with whom I communicated, in one way or another, through interviews and during home visits, are too many to name. I am especially indebted to those whose hospitality enabled me to live in Ahuehuepan, which does not have hotels or restaurants. In Mexico I lived with several families: first with Ruben Ignacio and Santa Robles and then with Bonifacio Marcos, all of whom have since passed away. I also thank two couples for inviting me to stay with them: Toribio Pascual, with whom I had long conversations, and his wife, Ebdulia Enrique. Their daughter Jenny gave me rides to Ahuehuepan and put me in contact with people in Houston. I acknowledge Bonifacio's daughter, Magdalena, and Eucaria Delgado, the daughter-in-law of Ruben and Santa, who did the cooking in the houses where they lived. Juana Salvador, whose name came up in the preface, did more than looking after me when living in her house. She helped me with my research when she retired from teaching; I would not have been able to finish my census, nor obtain some of my information, were it not for my phone interviews with her up to the end of the fall of 2021. Her daughter Diana Adriana Cardoso and her partner Carmen Daniel Hernandez also helped me.

I want to express my gratitude for the couples who let me stay in their homes in the US: in Houston I lived with Valentina Muñiz and Fernando Gonzalez; in the Sacramento area, with Venancio Gómez and Joaquina Guzmán; and in Los Angeles, with Irma Marcos and Baltazar Natalio. They took off time to drive me around during visits with people from Ahuehuepan. During one of my stays, I did a long interview with Joaquina, who told me her life history. In Mexico I spent a lot of time in the homes of Basilio Gómez and Faustina Ignacio, including visits with Basilio's sister Margarita. Her brother Esteban helped with transcriptions in 2003, while Basilio helped me as a guide when I did readings in the town's territory, as did Faustina's brother, Roberto Ignacio; Roberto's son Antonio; Juan Gonzalez; Cenobio Díaz; Teodoro Isauro; Leobardo Ramírez; Rodolfo de la Luz; Alejo Cristobal; and Florentino Salvador and his wife, Primitiva Fabián. In my earlier stays in Ahuehuepan, Gregorio Pascual Muñoz provided me with valuable information. Some of the people so far mentioned are no longer with us.

When I started writing, I received valuable advice and constructive criticism. At the early stages of writing, I received both encouragement and advice from Clark Whitehorn. Other people gave me valuable critical feedback, including Ken Menzies and the University of Colorado's external readers. Flora Butler did detailed copyediting on an earlier draft, and Catherine Schryer supplied valuable feedback on the latest version of my book. Herman Schryer made professional copies of my maps, and Emily Schryer helped me with the statistical analysis of my census data.

Index

Page numbers followed by f indicate figures. Page numbers followed by t indicate tables.

Aakoontepeek (mountain), 26, 55
aalmah, 131; defined, 130
absent/absenteeism, 12, 123; landowners, 123
academic(s), 23, 31, 36; contrasting perspectives in academia, 43–44; of indigenous descent, 38; researchers, 177; writings of, 9
Acapulco de Juarez (city), 26, 27f, 52, 64, 65, 144
accidents, 89, 91; at home, 89; on the road, with vehicles, 22, 73, 85, 89, 91, 103; at work, 62, 163. *See also* collision
Adame (family), 97
administration, administrative, administrator(s), 32; business, 163; center (*cabecera*), 26, 51, 52; divisions, 52, 109; of justice, 110; Mexico's administration, 116; position, post(s), 26
adoption, 10; de facto/formal vs. informal, 100; of identity, 34
affair(s) (sexual), 90, 98; of unwed mother, 99
African: descent, 34; governments, 32
age classes, 10. *See also* Bourdieu
aggregation, large, 9. *See also* cluster; group
agribusiness: with a broader identity, 174; transnational, 174
Ahuehuepan (town), 24f; attachment and commitment to, 172; authorities of, 66, 86, 90, 111, 121, 132, 133, 145; census, household survey, 14, 167; changes in layering, 106–8; coping with stress and hardships, 88–93; dispute with Oapan, 61; economy of, 25, 34; family clusters with *riikos*, 107; geographical description of, 26, 117; governance, 109–13; history of, 51, 53, 55, 57, 58, 61–75, 116; identity with, 26, 176; impressions of, 21, 22, 25, 60; indigenous identity, 32, 44; kinship clusters, 102–6; land tenure, 121–24; language use in, 153, 155, 156, 159, 163; life in, 79–85, 91; locked-up houses, 83; lower remittances, 154; migration, 47, 92, 93, 137–140, 142–46, 151, 152, 165, 172; as the "new Taxco," 22; not affected by major events in other parts of Mexico, 60; perspectives of inhabitants, migrants, 4, 6, 178; professionals, 41, 42; public realm, 86; religious denominations in, 132; representative of, 9; stereotypes of, 22; those born in US, 125, 157, 158, 159; vehicles and consumer goods, 84; those living in Mexico City, 146–47; vendors from, 141, 149. *See also* Loomah (Guadulupe); Tlakaltech (San Agustin); Tlalpitsahko (San Miguel); Tlatsintlan (San Juan)
Ahuelicán (town), 20, 22, 23, 24f, 26, 28, 52, 53, 55, 66, 68, 74, 94, 103, 116, 123, 124, 132, 133, 178; abandoned, 53; breakaway church, 67;

195

dispute with Tetelcingo, 53; teacher from, 20; José Delgado from, 22
Alcaraz (family), 97, 107t; Cleotilde Alcaraz Martínez (born 1969), 26, 140; Gabino, 67
alcoholic beverages, 85, 92, 94; excessive drinking of, 85, 91
alcoholism, alcoholics, 84, 85, 91
Aldama (family), 96, 97; Bernardo, 81; Graciano, 91, 96; Rosa (born 1915), 59
Alejo1 (family), 97, 107t, 108, 139; Isidro, 63; Margaro (died in 1972), 108; Miguel, 61, 146
Alejo2 (family), 97; Juan, 92
Aliano (family), 4, 97, 107t, 114; Genaro, 14; Teresa, 143
All Saints (*Todos Santos*). *See* Day of the Dead
alternidad (regimen of otherness), 39
Alto Balsas (region), ix, xi, 4, 24f; craft production in, 11; failure of relocation in, 52; impact on globalization on, 3; *indigenas* in, 37, 44; inhabitants' limited autonomy, 58; landscape, 124; migrants, 41, 175; origins of name, 23; standard cost of living, 8, 92
amate(s) (painting), 19, 26, 65, 69, 88, 143, 144, 146, 162, 175; amate-style, 65; defined, 26
American, 46, 153, 154, 158; art dealers, 175; citizens, 43; as an identity, 156; native, 36, 39; offspring of Mexican migrants, 3, 28; students, xi. *See also* United States
Ameyaltepec (town), 22, 23, 24f, 25, 53, 55, 65, 66, 88, 139, 142, 178; compared to other towns, 22; craft vendors, 178; portrayal of, 44
amnesty (for undocumented migrants), 45; preamnesty era, 150
Amith, Jonathan (scholar), 5, 51, 53
Amway, selling food supplements for, 105
anthropologist(s), xii, 4, 6, 11, 37, 41, 43, 87, 174, 177; people's contact with, 38; working for national institutions, 11, 40
apellidos. *See* surnames
Apipilulco, 61
applied rationalism (theory), 4
archives, archival, x, xii, 12, 119, 172, 179; burning of, 73; data from, 118, 179; of Registro Agrario, 123
artist(ic), xii, 38; identity of, xii; Nahua, xii, talent, 175; views of, 127–8
assimilation; connection with transnationalism, xi; cultural, xi; of indigenous people, 34; positive versus negative, 173

Atenango del Río (city), 67, 68
Atlahko (place in Ahuehuepan), 53
Atlanta, 16, 143; migrants in, 144, 152
Ausencio (family), 97, 103–4, 107t, 108; Alicia Ausencio Martinez2, 104, 139; Emigdio, 61, 62, 104, 108; Eugenio Ausencio Alejo (born 1974), 153; Fortino, 104; Francisco Ausencio Barcenas, 104; Juan, 60, 104; as maternal surname, 112, 145; Roberto Ausencio Rios, 104; Rosa, 104; Santos, 142; Ubaldo, 139
authorities, 86; outside, 61; higher, 73, 111, 112; village/town, 86. *See also* Ahuehuepan: authorities
autonomy, 32; limited at local level, 108; municipal, 56; of Indian towns/republics, 52, 109; of people born in Milpa Alta, 38; of social fields, 8
Ayuntamierto (municipal town hall), 26. *See also* municipio
Aztec(s) (Meshicas), 35, 52, 65; calendar, 129; conquest/rule, 52; emphasis on Aztec ancestry, 38; empire, 35; "glorious" Aztec past, 34
Aztlan, 175

Bachelard, Gaston. *See* applied rationalism
Baja California (peninsula), 46, 47, 102, 138, 141, 142, 174
Bárcenas (family), 97; Bonifacio, 61, 93n1; Eulalia, 104; as maternal surname, 104
Bárcenas, Oscar (teacher from Tepecuacuilco who became municipal president), 68
Barra de Navidad (village), 143
barrios, 9, 10, 11, 114–15; outsiders mixing up their Spanish and Nahua names, 115. *See also* Ahuehuepan
Basilio1 (family), 97, 107t, 108; Bernal Basilio Salvador, 103, 162; Feliciano, 103; Francisca, 161; Loreto, 103; as maternal surname, 97
Basilio2 (family), 97
Becas para el Bienestar Benito Juárez (scholarship program), 116
Benemérita Universidad Autónoma de Puebla (BUAP), xiii
Bernal1 family, 97, 103–4; Galdino, 55, 62, 97, 103; Juan Marcario, 55; Julia, 95, 103; Santos Bernal de la Luz, 68, 104, 139
Bernal2 (family), 97
bilingual(ism), 37; education, 41; radio programs, 42; school, 68; teachers, 117. *See also* trilingualism

INDEX   197

binary opposition, 5, 7, 175. *See also* dichotomy
birth/born: American born, 3, 28, 32, 46; certificate, 68, 117. *See also individuals by name*
Blas (family), 97
Bohr, Neils (physicist), 4. *See also* complementarity
bomberos (bomb makers), 57
border (national/international), ix, xiv, 3, 145, 149, 171; arbitrary nature of, 175; border region, 145; border towns, 142; closure of, 45; creation of, 175; interdependence of people on both side of, 164; Mexico-US borderland, 33, 39, 64, 145, 175; opposite sides of, 175, 178; stricter border control, 74. *See also* border crossing; transborder
border crossing, 45, 46, 72, 74, 88, 99, 148–50, 172, 174, 178; cost of, 88, 150; going back a long time, 45; illegal (without documents), 28, 45, 47; increasing difficulty of, 177–78; increasing with new forms of globalization, 118; legal restrictions, 175. *See also* coyote
boundaries (border) of indigenous towns, 53, 54, 55; overlapping electoral and administrative, 116. *See also* administraton; indigenous: community
Bourdieu, Pierre (scholar), 4, 7, 133; concepts of age and sex classes, 10; and field, social and cultural capital, 9
Bracero, 46; Bracero Program for Mexican workers, 64
Bravo Valadés, Benigno (priest), 63, 64
bricklayer (*albañil*), 25, 62, 73, 80, 86, 92, 151, 165; assistants, 88; master, 55, 170
Brujeria, 88
BUAP. *See* Benemérita Universidad Autónoma de Puebla

Cabecera. See administration/administrative: center
Cabo San Lucas (city), 142. *See also* Los Cabos
Cacique (strong boss), 35; Nahua, 35
Calixto (family), 96, 97, 107*t*; Basilia Calixto Santiago (died 2015), 97; Dili Calixto Pascual (born 1994), 161; Esteban, 140, 141; as maternal surname, 95
camioneta. *See* vehicle: truck
campesino(s), 11, 31–32, 39, 119, 125, 126. *See also* peasant(s)
Canada, Canadian, x, 4, 15, 16, 71; at language institute, 144; first nations in, 41; Métis, 41;

students, xi. *See also* North American Free Trade Agreement (NAFTA)
Cancún (city in Yucatán Peninsula), 137, 144
capital, 25, 66, 69; accumulation of, 173; circuits of (intersecting with labor and communication), 174; educational, 170; relative distribution, 7; start-up, 88; economic, educational, family, human and social capital, 7. *See also* Bourdieu
Cardoso1 (family), 97
Cardoso2 or Cardoso-Salvador (family), 14; Daniel Cardoso Mendez, 14, 72, 88; Diana Adriana, 193
cargo system, 11, 110–11, 116; defined, 109–10; occupying important posts, 109. *See also* civil-religious hierarchy
casta, 35
Catalán (family), 97; Cesario, 61; Juan, 70, 145
Catholic(ism), Catholics. *See* Roman Catholicism
cattle, 21, 87, 88, 103, 110; branding, 67; cattle truck, 22, 104; displaced by farming, 53; gaining access to, 162; indication of wealth, 164, 180; loss of, 57, 104, 109; ownership, 25, 55, 87–88, 103, 104, 106, 124; pens (*corrales*), 125; ranchers (cattle producers, *vaqueros*), 52, 91, 110; relevance of ownership of, 165, 194; roaming freely, 124; sale of, 67, 164. *See also* oxen; rancho/ranchero
CCPC. *See* Closed Corporate Peasant Community
celador(*as*) (security guard[s]), 111, 117
census, xiv; agrarian, 12; data, 12, 71, 82, 99, 117, 118, 172, 180; information on talents, 170; Mexican, 37; population, 13, 14, 28. *See also* ethnohistorical census; survey
Central America, ix, 34
Chaantilowayan (former settlement in Ahuehuepan), 53
charismatic(s): Catholic, 70; Protestant, 128. *See also* religion
Chatinos, 46
Chicago, 16, 46; migrants in, 152
chikungunya (mosquito-related disease), 72
children (offspring): absence of parents, 99, 149; American-born, 3, 28, 97, 99, 115, 125, 146, 147, 151, 155, 157, 158, 159, 162, 163, 166, 177; beating of, 90; considered as illegitimate, 95; cost of raising, 157; death of, 60, 168; decline

198 INDEX

of power differences with parents, 99; of indigenous, 119; left in care of grandparents, 99; "lending" or "giving away" of, 100, 103; Mexican-born, 3, 28; of migrants, 21, 28, 114, 116, 143, 155–59, 179; not attending school, 67, 84; not talking back to parents, 99; of transborder families, 160–66; of unwed mothers, 99; US-born, 177; out of wedlock, 21; who speak only Nahuatl, 3; working as vendors, 105
Chilpancingo (district, town), 57, 63, 73, 116, 146
church (*tiopan*), 90, 94, 95, 101, 109, 111, 113, 128; activities and events, 105, 111; in another town, 92; *auxiliar* for, 111; breakaway church in Ahuelicán, 67, 132; Catholic Church in Ahuehuepan, 20, 26, 63, 70, 17, 70, 107, 175; joining another, 85; leaving offerings in, 128; not recognized by the Church, 110; restoration work on, 62; separation of church and state, 109; serving as sacristan, 149; serving it only, 112; yard, 111; wedding, 95. See also Roman Catholicism
Christianity, 129, 131; conversion to, 52. See also religion
citizen(ship), 9, 43, 154; of Ahuehuepan, 22, 111, 112, 113, 132, 154, 171, 176, 178; Mexican, 43, 117; national, 40; US/American, 3, 28, 43
civil registry, 12, 51, 60, 116, 117
civil-religious hierarchy, 23, 109–115; civil side, 110; not doing one's duty, 112; religious side, 110–11. See also barrios; cargo system
class (social or political), xiii, 4, 6, 7, 8, 10, 11, 169, 172, 181; class-based society, 36; conflict/struggle, 4; 10; differences, 5; dynamics, 34; formation, 11; middle class/layer, 56, 118, 164, 168, 169t, 180; polarization, 169; relation with ethnicity, xi, 30, 32, 34, 35, 36; shrinking of middle, 175. See also layer(ing)
clinic (health), 60, 73, 85, 112, 116; lack of access to, 88, 105. See also healthcare
Closed Corporate Peasant Community (CCPC), 23
cluster(s), xiii, 7, 10, 42, 43, 52, 104, 106, 108, 165, 175; ambiguity of, 10; barrio clusters, 11, 114; broad-based, 4, 10; conflation of cluster and layer, 10; defined, 9; discrepancies between material and symbolic sides, 10, 11; ethnic, 177; family, 108; fluctuations in, 97; identity, 35; indigenous, 114; inequality in, 11, 35, 103;

kinship-based, 11, 96, 97, 101, 102, 104, 106, 107t, 159, 161; new forms of clustering, 175, 177; overlapping, 9; with no *riiko* ancestors, 163; with *riikos* or *riiko* ancestors, 102–4, 108; sub-cluster, 9–10. See also group
Coahuila (state), 56, 146
cohort. See period
collision, 73, 91, 157, 158, 162. See also vehicle
Colonia El Progeso, 70. See also Tonalapa
Colonia Obrero (in Sonora), 140
colonial, colonialist, 41, 42, 145; control/model/rule, 36; era/period, 5, 52–53, 116, 144; nature of Western scholarship, 6
Comisaría (administrative office), 22, 61, 67, 73, 85, 110, 111, 113, 114, 121, 125, 140; top posts in, 67
Comisario(s) (commissar)/*juez* (judge), 20, 62, 85, 86, 91, 112, 116; associate costs, 109; *comunal*, 62; *ejidal*, 61; *municipal*, 62, 66, 67, 73, 108, 110, 111, 112, 115, 116, 142, 145n1; *suplente*, 91, 112
Comisariado (commission), 116
commerce, 11, 51, 58, 61, 147; small-scale, 56; success through kinship connections, 139. See also salt trade; wholesaler
community, 12, 14, 173; impoverishment of, 132; indigenous, 8, 44; Mayan, 153; one's own home, 12n2, 22; open, 53; research, 5; transnational, 173. See also Closed Corporate Peasant Community; *specific communities, villages, and towns by name*
Compadre, compadrazgo, 11, 37, 101, 180; *compadrazgo de medida*, 101; co-parent, 14, 101, 180; defined, 101. See also *compadre*; kinship (fictive); *madrina*; *padrino*
comparison(s), 35, 106; between men and women, 172; of cohorts (periods), 180; of different towns, 22; invidious, 22; of people working in Mexico and the US, 153; of migrant and US-born workers, 153; of posts, 111; of regions, 35; of relationship among variables, 5, 13
complementary/complementarity, 5n1, 6, 9, 11, 38, 160; facets of government, 118; variables, 5; views of insiders and outsiders, xi, 38. See also Bohr, Neils
confirmation (religious), 94, 101
conflict(s)/struggles, 10, 57; agrarian, 39, 40; class, 10; violent, 4. See also disputes
conjunto (musical group). See music

Consejo de Pueblos Nahuas del Alto Balsas (CPNAB), 23, 71. *See also* Díaz de Jesús, Marcelino
contact with people, 41, 63, 85, 158, 179, 193; with anthropologists, 38; author's, xii, 12, 179; level of (CNT2), 41, 180; loss of / no contact, 154, 164, 180; with one's hometown, 70; ongoing, 173–74; with the outside world, 116; with people left behind, 173; type of contact (CNT1), 179
contradictions, 44, 109, 141
conversion (to other religions), 52, 126, 132
cook(ing), 80, 111, 193; men never, 98; utensils, 55, 57
Cook, Scott (scholar), 43, 44
cooperation, 7, 124; network of, 101
Copalillo (town), 24f, 68, 71, 72, 139, 140
Cora(s) (an ethnic/indigenous group), 39
corn. *See* maize
Cosme (family), 97
coyote (human smuggler), 74, 148, 150, 158; deceiving people, 149; woman as, 147. *See also* border crossing: illegal (without documents)
CPNAB. *See* Consejo de Pueblos Nahuas del Alto Balsas
craft(s), 40, 46; boom, 13; connection of craft industry to political realm, 8; dependence on, 51; production, 43; vendor, 15, 25, 145, 146, 177, 178
Cuacoyula (town), 61, 67
Cuernavaca (town), 25, 65, 72, 145
cultural capital, 4, 7, 170–71, 172, 181; non-linear relationship with social mobility and layering, 181. *See also* capital
culture: as system of meaning, with no single meaning, 7; goal to create a single culture for the nation, 41; indigenous, 41; Nahua/ Nahuatl, 129; some scholars equate it with group, 7

dam (short-lived), 68. *See also* Tetelcingo Dam
day laborer, 26, 53, 55, 62, 170; *jornalero*, 31; *peon*, 25, 87, 178
Day of the Dead (Todos Santos), 28
dehydration, 150
De la Luz (family), 97; Alfonso, 142; Leonardo, 159; as maternal surname, 104; Rodolfo, 194
Delgado (family), 97; Gregorio, 104; José Delgado from Ahuelican, 22, 88

denomination(s) (religious), 8, 132; conversion to other, 127, 132; Evangelical, 175
Department of Indigenous Affairs (DAI), 40
deportation, 3, 88, 90, 92, 99, 158; delinquents, 72, 73, 91, 141, 158. *See also* migrants
diabetes, 85
Díaz, Encarnacion (Chon) (politician at state level), 56, 57–58
Díaz de Jesús, Marcelino (from Xalitla), 41, 61, 71. *See also* CPNAB
Díaz1 (family), 97, 139
Díaz2 (family), 97
dichotomy(ies): Mestizo/*Indígena*, 4; objective/ subjective, 4; white/non-white, 33
Dionecio (family), 97
discrimination: condemnation of, 34; different forms of, 6; against indigenous people, 33, 38; new forms of, 36
disputes, 109; family, 89, 101. *See also* conflict(s)/ struggles
Distrito Federal (DF), 146. *See also* Mexico City
doctor (medical): absence of, 85; in Ahuehuepan, 22, 73; paramedic seen as, 116
Doraville (city): migrants in, 152. *See also* Atlanta; Duluth; Lawrenceville
drug(s): cartels, 73; gangs, 8, 12
dualism. *See* dichomomy
Duluth (city), 3
duplex(ity) (approach, program, theory), xiii, 6–7, 9, 11, 44, 51, 101, 120, 125, 126, 177; definition, 4–5; perspective, 7, 22, 43, 125–26

Echeverria, Luís (Mexican president), 26, 40, 68
education, 39, 63, 138, 171, 177; bilingual, 4; Catholic education, 63; educational capital, 170; as field, 171; of indigenous people, 175; levels of, 42, 170, 175, 180; Mexico's system of, 14, 40, 105; public, 66, 72, 84, 102, 106, 116. *See also* school
ejido, 16, 61, 116, 121, 123, 132; extension of, 62
electric(al), electrician, electricity, 81, 82, 170; grid, 60; tools, 66, 79, 82. *See also* dam
elope(ment), 93–94, 156
elote (fresh ear of corn, corncob), 64, 82, 119, 120. *See also* maize (corn)
El Paso (city), 150
emic/etic distinction, 5, 6, 125; emic, 5, 6, 126; perspective, 5, 6, 125–26. *See also* dichotomy
emigration. *See* migration

Emiliano (forgotten maternal surname), 154
employ(ment), 150, 153; conditions of, 152; employee(s), 150, 153; employers denying they exploit migrants, 154; employing native-born Americans, 153; gainfully employed, 154; steady, 92. *See also* job
employer(s), 9, 151, 152; preference for workers of same background, 153; tapping into migrants' networks, 152
endogamy and exogamy. *See* marriage
English (language, speaking), x, 28, 41, 155–56; 177; exposure to, 152; learning, 148; minimal knowledge of, 157; speaking mixture of Spanish and English, 153; speaking more Spanish than English, 2; teacher of, 105; unable to speak, 99
ethnic(ity), 9, 11, 46; affiliation, 52; broad identity and consciousness, 52, 174; conflict between ethnic and religious cluster, 10; diversity of, 42; identity and its loss, 148; inequality (layering), 34, 35, 148, 175; linguistically defined, 46; relations to and coexistence with class, xi, 4, 8, 10, 11, 31, 32, 34, 35, 36, 43; stigmatization of, 96
ethnohistorical census (author's) and its findings, 2–13, 74, 81, 83, 88, 89, 117, 118, 120, 138, 145, 167–68, 176, 180, 193, 194; data from, 168, 172; as source of data, 179–80. *See also* census
evangelic(al) religion, 175

Fabian1 (family), 97; Amado, 137
Fabian2 (family), 97; Ponciano Fabián Mauricio, 146
Facebook: contact with people through, 16; as source of data/information, 158, 179; use of, 12
factions (rival/political/revolutionary), xiii, 57, 177; *curista*, 105; PRI faction, 73
family, 87; clusters, 97, 106, 107*f*; emphasis on family unity, 8; family capital as interval variable [FMCAP], 180–81; family social capital, 7; genealogy, 15; forgetting about, 99; formal relations between members, 99; intermarriage between, 106; larger, 104; as nominal variable (KINCAP2), 180; nuclear (as exception), 93; poor, 73, 108; proportion of those working in US, 108; rich, 94; upward mobility of, 75; variation in, 106. *See also individual families and relatives by name*

farmer(s), 25, 56, 123; cooperation with ranchers, 124; full-time, 125; moving to Palula, 53; poor, indigenous, 34, 55, 62, 116; Spanish, 52; subsistence, 133, 170; wealthy, prosperous, capitalist, 55, 125. *See also* peasant(ry), tenants
Felipe (family), 96, 97; Guadalupe, 41; as maternal surname, 161; Tomasa, 147
fertilizer, 74, 79; as essential, 120
festival. *See* fiesta
field(s) (social), xiii, 7–8, 11–12, 106, 147, 170, 171; as Bourdieu's concept, 4; defined, 10; diverse, 7; educational, 171; emergence of broader, 177; heritage, 5*n1*; interconnected/intertwined, 147; overlapping of, 8; both religious and political, 11, 109; subfields, 175, 177; transformation of political, 71; transnational, 175
fieldwork (anthropological), ix–xi, xii, 12, 13–16, 34, 47, 126–27, 132, 174; interviews, 172, 174; multi-sited, ix; reciprocity of, 15; writing fieldnotes, 16
firework (displays, explosion), 21, 95, 114, 132; as cause of death, 88, 89
fishing, 39; fishing economy, 140; village, 143
Florida (state), migrants in, 44, 152

Gamio, Manuel (1883–1960) (national and international leader), 36, 39, 40, 131
ganadero(s). *See* cattle (ranchers)
gañan(es) (farmer who guides team of oxen), 9
gang(s): activity, 73; criminal, 149; drug, 8, 112; of juveniles, 141, 157; ringleader, 73
gender(s), 79, 98; as a variable [SEX], 181; gender-based hierarchies, 8, 47, 111; new gender roles, 176
generation(s), generational, 36, 132, 153, 157, 165, 178; differences, 47; first, 67, 108; intergenerational mobility, 55, 103, 168; multi-, xiv; next, 103, 104, 133; numbers shown, 106–7*t*; one removed, 108; second, 164; after several, 178; third, 56, 97, 104, 126, 161; after three, 177; three or four removed, 108, 161
girls, 56, 67, 82, 129, 164; as cleaners and babysitters, 70; becoming homesick, 68; paid to prepare meals, 98; brought by boy to his parents' house, 93; girlfriend (*novia*); marrying her off, 94, 94–95; to "steal" (*se roba la muchacha*), 93. *See also ichpochtle*; women
GIS (Geographical Information System), 119; data from, 118

globalization, 11, 12, 177; earlier phase of, 11; fractal quality of, 177; global capitalism, 176; global context of, 177; global economy, 174; impact of, x, xi, 3, 5; latest forms of, 118
GMOP (geographical mobility), 181
Gómez, Febronia (an outsider), 54*n1*, 55, 63
Gómez1 (family), 58, 82, 97, 107*t*, 114; Basilio, 14, 128, 194; Esteban, 137, 144, 146; Margarita (1949–2018), 65, 80, 81, 88, 90, 91, 94, 95, 101, 113, 119, 128, 147, 159; Pablo, 160; Venancio Gómez Ignacio, 193
Gómez2 (family), 97
González (family), 107*t*; Eliseo, 123, 147; Fernando, 193; Juan, 194; Pablo, 147
gourd(s) (*guaje[s]*), 22, 65, 88, 136
governance, 35, 37, 86, 109–114, 170; broader (national), 115; complementary facets of, 118; overall decline in involvement, 118; own form of / local system of / town's, 26, 118. *See also* barrios; government; leader(ship)
government, 44, 57, 61, 64, 71, 74; African, 32; agencies, xi; American, 45; bureaucracy, 38; documents, xii, 123; force(s), 57; initiative, 42, 116; Mexico's, 39, 42, 117, 170; officials, x, 38, 42, 113; policy, 42; posts and jobs, 26, 38; programs, xiii, 38, 86, 116; state, 39, 59, 140; subsidies, 120; worker, 37
greetings, 80
group (social), xiii, 6, 10; broad-based as duplex entities, 4; ethnolinguistic, 46; identity, 44, 153; racialized, 6. *See also* cluster; aggregation
Guadalupe. *See Tonaantsin*
Guadalajara (city in Jalisco), 39, 138, 140, 146
guaje. *See* gourd(s)
Guanajuato (state), 145, 146
Guerrero (state), ix, x, xi, 5, 23, 25, 26, 34, 35, 40, 47, 54, 55, 56, 59, 73, 74, 86, 140, 142, 144, 145, 146, 177; creation of, 53; as a poor, left-behind Mexican state, 58, 65, 71
Guerrero, Francisco (priest), 63–64
Guzmán (family), 97; Joaquina, 193

Hagen, Jacqueline, 153
hardships, 21, 91–92; coping with, 88–89, 91, 92
healthcare, 14, 105, 106; low quality of, 85, 105, 171; workers in, 25, 41
Hellman, Judith, xii, 173
Hermosillo (City in Sonora), 146

Hernández, María Antonieta (teacher from Tepecuacuilco), 63
Hernández (family), 97
Hernandez, Carmen Daniel (an outsider married to someone from Ahuehuepan), 193
Hernández, Lorenzo (teacher originally from Xalitla), 66
Hidalgo (district in northern Guerrero), 54, 116
Hidalgo (state), x*n3*, xi, 34, 35, 47; wealthy cacique in, 35
high school. *See secundaria*
homesick (students away from home), 68
horse(s): owned in Ahuehuepan, 84; of Spanish conquerors, 35; soldiers on horseback, 57; *riikos* riding, 103; taming, 170; visitors arriving on, 79
house(s): big, better, luxurious (in Ahuehuepan), 9, 20, 22, 25, 108, 148, 161; burning to the ground, 60, 89; migrants building one in Mexico, 81, 106, 138; migrants in, 152; owning more than one house in Mexico, 82; in past, 55, 62, 64, 66, 80–82, 83, 103, 106, 108; renting, 144, 152; that have stores, 80, 164; thatched roofs prone to fire, 57
Hñähñu (once labeled as Otomí), 35. *See also* Indigenous (group)
Houston, Texas, 19, 89, 105, 139, 149, 158, 161, 162; author's trips to, x, 115, 157–8; Mayan community in, 153; migrants in, 152
Huejutla, Hidalgo (city, region): inter-ethnic inequalities and conflict in, 35
Huitzuco (town), 16, 24*f*, 56, 62, 67
human smuggler. *See* coyote
husband: abusive, 90; attending sewing school, 151; beaten up by in-law, 91; deported for repeated offenses, 9; disorderly conduct and not supportive, 86; ex-husband working for former father-in-law, 90; expenses for paying substitutes, 117; second husband, 161, 163; striking wife with machete, 90; a teacher like his wife, 68, 106; unfaithful, 22; well-off, 94; working in textile factories, 164

ichpochlamatsiin (old maid), 90
ichpochtle (girl, maiden), 100
identity, 28, 32, 35, 39, 179; altered social, 176; ambiguous, 39; American, 28, 156; with Aztlan, 175; change of, 174; collective, 174; complex nature of ethnic, 39; as Coras, 39;

group/cluster identity, 35, 153; hometown, 26, 153; indigenous, 31, 32, 33, 52; as Latinos, 177; loss of, 148; Mestizo, 34; of Mixtecs, 174; national, 34; peasant, 125; retention, 39; transnational, 174

Iglesias Mendoza, Francisco (retired lawyer from Tetelcingo), x, 26

Ignacio (family), 97, 107*t*; Antonio, 139; Faustina, 19; Julia (born 1951), 65; Roberto (born 1971), 60, 63, 64, 194; Ruben, 147, 193; Saul Ignacio Manuel (born 1986), 158

Iguala, xiii, 13, 24*f*, 60, 75, 113, 145, 161, 164; city, 13, 15, 37, 61, 62, 64, 66, 85, 105, 120, 148, 149, 165; district, 116; *municipio*, ix; valley, 51, 54, 55, 56, 67, 123

illness, sick(ness), disease, 35, 60, 72, 73, 130; fatal, 164; prolonged, 89. *See also chikungunya*; diabetes; measles

imperialism, xi

INAH. *See* National Institute of Anthropology and History

inconsistencies of intertwined dimensions of layering, 9; rarely consistent objective components of clustering, 9

Indio/Indian/*Indígena* versus Mestizo/non-indigenous, 31, 34, 36–37, 43, 175

Indianidad. See Indigeneity

Indian republics, 36; their limited autonomy, 52; versus Spanish republics, 36, 52

Indigena(s) (name for member[s] of a group), ix, xiii, 10, 11, 31, 32, 34, 35, 36, 37, 38, 39, 42, 177, 178; considered as inferior, 40; considered as poor and exploited, 31. *See also* Indigenous

Indigeneity/*indigenismo*, xiii, 30, 32, 38, 39–42, 43, 117; as a broader phenomenon, 44; contrasting perspectives on, 31; diverse sides of, 39; duplex nature of, 3, 44; global forms of, 33, 177; *neoindigenismo*, 43; and transnationalism, 175; versus *indianismo*, 42

Indigenous/indigenousness/*indígena*, xiii, 32, 33, 52; academics of indigenous descent, 38; broader meaning of, as identity, 41; claimed as an identity, 32; community/town, ix, 7, 8, 34, 40, 41, 43, 53, 54, 68; culture and way of life, 40, 41; Department of Indigenous Affairs, 40; eradication of indigenous identities, 34; group, 32; intellectuals, 31, 42; land (disentailment, restoration of), 52, 56; languages, 3, 31, 40; men, 35; Mexico's indigenous population, 44; nation, 34; politicians, 32; professionals, 5, 6, 42, 71, 129; region, xi, 116; with no single meaning, 32; Spanish-speakers presenting themselves as, 35; students, 28; spokesmen, 42; towns, 3, 36, 52, 109; versus non-indigenous, 7; women, 68. *See also* Hñähñu

Indigenous people, 32, 38, 40, 41, 44; assimilation of, 43; assumed inferiority of, 34; beliefs of, 127; children of, 117; complex and politicized meaning of discourse about, 32; declining numbers of, 40; demands, 43; discrimination against, 33; diversity of experience and identities of, 39; education of, 175; fewer rights of, 36; human rights of, 32; identity of, 32, 33; income of, 8, 34; institutions for, 32; migration of, ix, 44, 46–47; negative views of, 42; as newcomers, 39; organization for, 33, 47; participation in Mexican Revolution, 40; presence in US, 46; primary loyalty to own communities, 39; programs for, 140; racism directed against, 34; rights of, 32; with university degrees, 175

indio(s), 36; pejorative meanings of, 32; as racial category, 35; seen as casta, 35–36; seen as poor and ignorant, 8

inequality, 11, 25; between ethnic clusters, 35; different, dominant, and main forms of, 8; ethnic-racial, 33, 34; gender, 47; intra-ethnic, 35; mobilization against, 11; of native people, 35; new forms of, 12. *See also* layering

informant(s), 55; as collaborators and main informants, 180

INI. *See* National Indigenist Institute (INI)

insecticides, 79, 120

Institutionalized Revolutionary Party / Partido Revolucionario Institutional (PRI), 115

intermarriage. *See* marriage

internado. See school

international: conference(s), 40, 42; development, xi; International School of American Archaeology and Ethnology, 38. *See also* migration (international)

interval variables. *See* variables

interview(s), x, xii, 12, 16, 81, 137, 144*n1*, 149, 151; data from, 118, 172; long, 179; people interviewed once vs. many times, 180; phone, 16, 11*n1*; use of steno pad for, 15

Isauro (family), 97; Hermilo, 91; Teodoro, 194

Isidoro (family), 97; Alfredo, 138, 144
Isidro (family), 97
Ixcatla (town in Guerrero), 61

jail, jailed (locked up): in Ahuehuepan, 13, 64, 91, 132; in Chilpancingo (state capital), 66, 73; in the US, 159
Jaripeo (rodeo), 21, 114, 132
Jalisco (state), 39, 43, 143, 146
Jiménez González, Luz (linguistic informant), 38
job(s), 45, 46, 47, 62, 74, 84, 88, 106, 116, 148, 149, 150, 151, 152–54, 171; bricklayer, 73, 92; cleaner, 162; clerical, 105; in construction, 139, 146, 147; dead-end, 75, 169, 172; domestic, 47; good/decent/better, 74, 75, 87, 149, 163, 173; government, 38; as health worker, 85; insufficient, 75; job training, 151; lack of, 47; in landscaping, 151, 155; odd, 92; part-time, 157; physically demanding/stressful, 15; serving in restaurants/stores, 138, 143, 151; in teaching, 165; no training, 151; yard, 88. *See also* employment
jornalero. *See* day laborer
journalists, 8, 31, 154
juez. *See comisario*

Kammler, Henry (scholar), 8, 130, 133
Katy (city), migrants in, 152. *See also* Houston
Kearney, Michael, 125, 174. *See also* Nagengast, Caroline
kidnappings, 73
kinship, 92, 98, 101, 108, 114, 123, 139; connection with class, 102; diagrams, 13; fictitious, fictive, 11, 101; nomenclature, 100; solidarity, 101. *See also* cluster; couple; family; marriage; relatives
Kopaxokoihtik (former settlement in Auhuehuepan), 53

labor(er). *See* work(er)
Ladino, 32, 34, 40
lag effect, 9
land, 16, 25, 75, 103, 113, 118; abandoned, 124; appropriation of, 66; costs, 12; conflict/struggle/dispute over, 4, 39, 63, 66; disentailment, 54; encroachment of, 50, 66; forms of ownership, 23; grant, 53; and how changed, 124–25; inheritance of, 101; landless, 35; landscape / lay of the land, 20–21, 121; and Land Reform office, 66; loss of land, 54; not working the land, 74; polarization of ownership, 124; private property, 63, 116; reform, 16, 39, 41, 116, 169; rights to, 36, 54; sale of land, 63; the town/village's communal land and its legalization, 81, 116; use of, 120–21; working/cultivating the, 9, 12, 71, 74, 87, 88, 165. *See also* land tenure
land tenure: access to, 121–24; and access through kinship, 22, 103, 104, 123, 124, 162, 164, 165; ambiguous zone, 55, 121; communal fence, 71; communal ownership (*terrenos de común repartimiento*), 38, 39, 54; gaining access through *mercedes* or *títulos primordiales*, 52; landowners, 42, 52–53, 116; privatization of community land, 54; recipients, 116; reclassification of ownership, 43; (re)distribution of land, 61, 62, 116; rental of, 53, 67, 70, 139, 163; types of, 122–24. *See also ejido*; *pequeña propiedad*
landscape/lay of the land: changes in, 20–21, 41, 124–26
language(s), 5, 9, 32, 33, 35, 41, 46, 58, 156, 176; barrier, 6; being ashamed of parents' language, 156; indigenous, 3, 37; one's first, 46; institute, 144; loss of/ disappearance, 39, 40; maintenance/survival, 58, 178; native, 30, 117, 158; not speaking an indigenous/native, 42; pride in one's own, 44; unknown, 52; use, 25. *See also* bilingual; Cora; indigenous; Nahuatl; Spanish
Latinos, 177
Lawrenceville (city); migrants in, 152. *See also* Atlanta; Doraville; Duluth
layer(ing) (social hierarchy), 102, 147; changes over time, 106–8, 166, 168, 169*t*; correlations among, 171–72; defined, 8; discrepancies of intertwined dimensions, 9; duplex nature of, 9; economic, 168; educational, 8; educational level as form of, 170; along ethnic lines, 175; how layering has been examined, 8; intersecting axes of, 8; lack of generational continuity in, 56; at local level, 8; lowest/low middle, 118, 168, 169*t*; middle category, 164, 168; 169*t*; multifaceted nature with intertwined dimensions, 8, 9; new forms of, 11, 175, 177; not synonymous with clustering, 10–11; relationship with social mobility and cultural capital as non-linear variable, 181; shown by who holds

posts, 111; symbolic side of, 9; transformation of, 11–12; upper layer, 118, 169*t*; as variables [CLASS], 180; various forms of, 8, 9, 10, 111, 167, 171. *See also* class
Lazaro1 (family), 97, 107*t*, 137, 139; Luciano, 143
Lazaro2 (family), 97
leader(ship), leaders, 33, 56, 71, 73, 141, 167, 170–71; of band, 62; of CPNAB, 23; of *curista* faction, 105; intellectual, 40, 42; Mayan, 11; ringleader of a gang, 73; as variable [LDRS], 170, 171. *See also* Bernal, Juan Marcario; Bernal de La Luz, Santos; Calixto, Esteban; CPNAB; Díaz de Jesús, Marcelino; Estrada, Sabino; Gamio, Manuel; governance; music; Pascual, José Domingo
Leona Vicario. *See* school (state)
Leonides (family), 97
Leza, Christina (scholar), 33
licenciatura. *See* school(ing)
lifespan (shorter in Ahuehuepan), 85
Lincoln (city), 27*f*, 81, 133, 151, 156, 158, 159, 161–63
literacy, 171; basic, 170; lack of, 40, 99; as variable [LITC], 181
Loomah (Guadalupe) (barrio), 114. *See also* Ahuehuepan
López Caballeros, Paula (scholar), 33, 38
López (family), 97
Los Angeles, 14, 149; migrants in, 70, 94, 112, 131, 149, 150, 151, 152
Los Cabos, 142. *See also* Cabo San Lucas; San José de Cabo
lover(s) (*amante*), 90, 96, 98. *See also* mistresses
Lucas (forgotten maternal surname), 97

madrina (godmother), 101; *de medida*, 101. *See also compadrazgo; padrino*
maize (corn): corn cob, 82; corn dough, 65; cornfield, 21, 92; cornmeal (*masa/maseca* if packaged), 69; importance in Nahua cosmology, 126; toasted, 62. *See also elote*
man/men: courageous, 56; in dangerous occupations, 57, 59
Manuel (family), 57, 97, 108; Guillermo, 131
Marcos (as maternal surname only), 145
Marcos1 (family), 107*t*, 114
mariachis, 91
marriage/marital/married: breakup, 98; considered illegitimate, 95; endogamy, 114;

intermarriage, 61, 104, 105*f*, 106, 108; strategic, 103. *See also* couple
Martínez1 (family), 96, 97; Cristino Martínez Marcos, 142, 145; Juan Martínez Muñoz, 144
Martínez2 (family), 96, 97, 104, 107*t*; Abelino (Albino), 60; Ausencio, 104; Bernabe, 112; Bernardo, 66; Diego, 96; Flores, 60, 61; Florentino, 103; Fortino, 70; Graciano, 96; Heleodoro, 67, 111; Pedro Martínez Tomas (born 1948), 66, 120, 138, 146, 155; Salvador, 96; Vicario, 104
Martínez4 (family), 96, 97; Rodolfo, 137
Martínez Cobo, José (scholar), 32
Martínez Novo, Carmen (scholar), 33, 43
masa, *maseca*. *See* maize (corn)
masewaahle (country people), 38, 176; different than *indígena*, 176
mass (Catholic), 95, 128, 175. *See also* Roman Catholic
mass movement. *See* migration
Matamoros (city in Coahuila), 146
Matilde (family), 97
material(ism), 9; distribution of material wealth, 11; immaterial, 130; inexpensive, 81; interests, 10; raw materials, 125; reality, 4; versus symbolic/ideal, 5, 10
Maxela (town), 34*f*, 37, 53, 58, 66, 96, 103, 146
Mazatlan (city in Sinaloa), 66, 73, 90–91, 103–4, 137, 138, 139, 144, 160
Maya(ns), 35, 46; community, 153; leaders, 11; Mayan-speaking, 11
measles, 60
Melaque (also known as San Patricio) (town), 142, 132
men, 13, 21; with administrative positions, 26; as author's guides, 14; doing the paperwork, 72; indigenous, 35; learning woodworking and cattle branding, 67; older, 21; opinion of, 21–22; young, 21
Merced(es). *See* land tenure
Meshicas. *See* Aztecs
Mesquital (valley in Hidalgo), 35
mestizaje, 34. *See also* Mestizo
Mestizo, xiii, 10, 32, 34, 35, 36, 37, 38, 40, 42, 43, 44; as "bronze race," 37; as category, 34, 35, 36; Indo-Mestizos, 36; mestizo-izing, 39; versus *Indigena*, 31, 34, 35, 36–37, 38–39, 43. *See also Indio*

methods (research techniques), ix, xi; combination of diverse, ix, 4, 154, 177; ethnographic, ix; qualitative, 4; quantitative, 12; statistical, 167*n1*. *See also* research
Mexcalcingo (town in Guerrero), 61
Mexican Revolution, x*n3*, 13, 25, 36, 38, 45, 56; participation of indigenous people in, 40
Mexico (country), ix, x, xi, xii, 3, 10, 11, 12, 25, 26, 28, 31, 32, 33, 34, 37, 38, 53, 73, 84, 92, 96, 99, 119, 129, 133, 137, 144, 148, 151, 153, 154, 155, 156, 157, 163, 165, 167, 170, 171, 173, 174, 175, 176, 177, 178; considered to be racist, 37; constitution of, 109; creation of, 53; deterioration of economy in, 71; as empire, then republic, 53; formerly part of American Southwest, 45; free trade agreement (NAFTA), 71; and going once a year, 131; history of, 51–75; and "Indian problem," 40; interior of, 145, 146; international migration to, 44; layered along racial and ethnic lines, 8, 34; the Mexican state/government/centralized administration, 34, 39, 115, 116; multiculturalism in, 31, 33, 112; northern Mexico, 46, 139–142; oil boom in, 41; political elite, 42; political system of, 109, 115–17; and returning, 74, 95, 99, 100, 105, 137, 143, 148, 149, 159; spaces in, 42; staying in, 153, 162; racism as a tabooed topic in, 33; rural, xi, 6, 13, 31, 177; transformation of, 54, 62; wage gap with US, 46; what it is like to live in, 79–82, 139. *See also* Mexico City
Mexico City, x, 26, 35, 38, 62, 144, 146–47; march to, 71; massacre of students in, xi, 66; streets with Nahua names, 146. *See also* Distrito Federal; Mexico
Mezcala (town, region), 24*f*, 39, 52
Michoacan (state), 144
middle class. *See* class
midwife, 62
migrant(s), ix, xi, 5, 12*n1*, 23, 26, 39, 41, 45, 46, 47, 53, 70, 74, 80, 82, 83, 88, 92, 114, 117, 119, 126, 138, 139, 142, 143, 145, 147, 150, 151, 152, 153, 154, 156, 158, 159, 171, 173, 174, 175, 178; above age of forty, 133; in Atlanta area, 144, 152; in Chicago, 46, 152; crackdown on, 45; destination, 27*f*, 151, 152; documented, 173; deported, 88; external, 28; in Florida, 46, 152; former, 25, 73; from Guerrero, 140; indigenous, 46, 47; in Houston (and nearby Katy), 89, 105, 139, 149, 152, 153, 158, 159, 161, 162; internal, 16, 28, 71, 160; international, 3, 104, 160, 165, 171, 173; involvement in politics and social life, 173; locked-up houses of, 83; long-term, 177; in Los Angeles, 70, 94, 112, 131, 149, 150, 151; musical talents of, 175; Nahuatl-speaking, 175; not returning/sending remittances, 86, 92; offspring of, xiv, 3, 21, 114, 155–58, 164, 177; older, 153; perspectives of, 46; in Pisaflores, 34; in Sacramento, 152; in San Diego, 16, 152; in Seattle, 150, 152; symbolic connection with their parents' barrios, 114; recent, 177; return, 72, 91, 120, 140; social networks, 152; stereotypes of, 175; undocumented, x, xii, 3, 28, 45, 173; in Washington, 152; who speak language other than Spanish, 46; workers, 105
migration, emigration, 12, 28, 45, 46, 51, 69, 72, 74, 92, 93, 160, 171, 173, 177; altered patterns of, 3; consequences of, 99, 118; to the Iguala valley, 52; increase in external, 147; increase in out-migration, 124; of indigenous people, 44, 46–47; internal, 147; international, ix, xi, 3, 44, 45, 47, 71, 168; mass (en masse), 3, 28, 70, 118, 171, 172; migration to Mexico as a "revolving" door, 46; Mexican, from Mexico, xiii, 46; policy, 74; recent high rate of, 124; various forms of, 12, 26. *See also* deportation; migrants; relocation
Miguel (family), 97, 106
Milpa Alta (place), 38; considered as indigenous enclave, 38. *See also originarios*
Miracle, the Mexican (as period of rapid growth), 13, 62
miscegenation, 35; of indigenous people, 34; ongoing during colonial rule, 36
mistress(es), 21. *See also* lover
miscegenation (interracial), 35; of indigenous people, 34; ongoing during colonial rule, 36. *See also* marriage (inter); race
Mixtec(s) (indigenous group), 12, 34, 35, 46, 47; pan-Mixtec associations, 174
mobility (geographical), 166, 167, 171, 172, 181; association with layering (i.e. social mobility), 171; categories of, 167; different forms of, 171, 172; as spatial dimension (GMOB), 181
mobility (social), 166, 167; decline in, 169; intergenerational, 168; non-linear relationship with cultural capital and layering, 181; over time, 169*t*; patterns of, xiv; relation between

social and spatial, 171, 172, 176; transformation of, 25. *See also layering*
molendera(s), 103; defined, 9
Montaña region, 61, 67, 178
Molina Enríquez, Andres (scholar), 36
Morales (family), 97; Fructoso, 60, 62, 162; Hipolito, 145; as maternal surname, 60, 63, 65, 71, 74, 75, 84, 87, 99, 100, 102, 113, 116, 120, 121, 128, 137, 141, 142, 143, 149, 156, 161; Porfirio, 62; Reynulfo, 59
Morales, Juan Antonio (teacher, outsider), 63
Morelia (city in Michoacan), 146
movement of people, 3, 45, 55, 157, 175. *See also* migration (mass movement); relocation
movement (political, social), xi, 8, 23, 26, 56, 71, 176; guerrilla, 66
mozos (male servants), 103
mule trail(s), 26, 52, 121, 125
multiculturalism in Mexico, 31, 42, 43
municipio (municipal[ity], township), ix, 26, 52, 53; Manuel Salvador as *comisario of*, 62; limited autonomy, 56
Muñiz (family), 97; Antonio, 61; Valentina, 193
Muñoz (family), 97, 107*t*; as maternal surname, 108, 120, 144, 165; Porfirio (as *comisario comunal*), 57, 62
music(al), musician(s), 21, 40, 106, 111; band, 61, 175; ensemble, group (*conjunto*), 95, 165; instruments (trumpet, flute), 61, 164, 165, 170; loud, 20, 80; love of, 62, 158; part-time, 165; talents, 106, 175; transportation of, 111

NAFTA. *See* North American Free Trade Agreement
Nagengast, Caroline (scholar), 174. *See also* Kearney, Michael
Nahua(tl/s), 37; artists, xii; communit(ies) or town, 55, 101, 127; dignitaries, 52; Nahuas as cluster, 10, 44, 46, 52, 100, 109, 130, 131, 141; Nahua culture, 129; names, 115; other Nahua towns, 127; worldview/cosmology/cosmovision, 127, 130, 132–33
Nahuatl (language, Nahuatl-speaking), xi, 3, 4, 22, 32, 51, 71, 93, 99, 100, 117, 133, 153, 155, 161, 162, 163, 164, 177, 178; author's knowledge and use of, xi, xii, 13, 14, 28, 32, 37; minimal knowledge, 63; no longer wanting to speak, 7, 66; not able to speak, 22, 42, 155, 156, 157; preaching in, 63, 67; places where spoken, 68; punished for speaking, 63; singing national anthem, 117; speaking a mix of Nahuatl and Spanish, 153; spoken daily at home, 70, 142; understanding only, 164, 178
Natalio (family), 97, 107*t*; Baltazar, 193
National Indigenist Institute (INI), 39
National Institute of Anthropology and History (INAH), 38
native people. *See* Indigenous (people)
Nava (family), 97, 103, 104; Aurelio, 103, 104, 139; Gerardo, 142; Norberto Nava Roman, 104; Romualdo, 103
Nayarit (state), 111*n1*, 137, 138–39, 144, 146, 149, 163
Nazario (family), 97; Sergio, 112
neoliberalism, 42, 59
neologism, 7–12. *See also* cluster; field; layer(ing)
Netherlands (Holland), x, xi
New Spain, 53
Nicanor (family), 97
Nogales (city in Sonora), 146
nominal variables. *See* variables
norms (social), 80, 85, 93, 95, 98; diverse, 132; drinking, 85, 99; going against, 72, 90; local, 72; past, 81
North America(n), 101, 167, 174; continent, xiv, 3, 101; post-NAFTA era, 71–74
North American Free Trade Agreement, 13, 44, 71, 99, 147, 169, 172. *See also* Canada; Mexico; trade; US
nostalgia food, 173
novia. *See* girl(friend)
nutrition, malnutrition, 85

Oapan. *See* San Agustin Oapan
Oaxaca (state), 43, 47, 56, 125, 142, 143, 144, 174
Ocampo, Agripino (Pino) (teacher from Tecuescontitlan), 61
Ocampo (family), 97
Oceanside (city), migrants in, 152
occupation(s)/trade(s), 9, 55, 106, 119; background, 42; campesino as, 126; dangerous, 57; plurality/mix of, 125, 165
offspring. *See* children
opinion. *See* viewpoint
Oportunidades (government program), 116
oppression (political), xi
oral history, 12, 53, 176
ordinal variables. *See* variables

INDEX   207

originarios (identity), 38. *See also* Milpa Alta
Ortiz (family), 97; Blas, 60
Ostotipan. *See* San Agustin Ostotipan
Otomi. *See* Hñähñu
outsider(s), 10, 22, 35, 38, 51, 52, 54, 61, 94, 115, 117, 120, 123, 131–32; author's position as, xi; exclusion from, 167, 170; impression of, 22, 35; perspectives of, 6, 11, 37, 129; research of, 127
ox(en), 25; confiscated during Revolution, 57; to plow the land, 9, 67; renting, 123. *See also* cattle

padrino(s) (godfather, patron), 13, 101, 113, 128, 131, 145; *de medida*, 101. *See also compadrazgo*; *madrina*
paisanos (compatriots, buddies), 158
Palacios (family), 97
Palula (town), 24f, 53, 61; hacienda, 54; reconstruction of social and political structures of their town of origin (Oapan), 53
PAN. *See* Partido Acción Nacional
party, parties (political), 71, 72, 118, 172; alternating, 73; multi-party democracy, 59, 115; one-party system, 115; party affiliation, 73; ruling party, xiii, 72. *See also* Partido Acción Nacional (PAN); Partido de la Revolución Democrática (PRD); Partido Revolucionario Institucional (PRI)
Partido de la Revolución Democrática (Party of the Democratic Revolution) (PRD), 71
(El) Partido Acción Nacional (PAN) (National Action Party), 72
Partido Revolutionario Institutional (PRI) (Institutionalized Revolutionary Party), 60, 61, 115. *See also* party (political)
Pascual (family), 64, 67, 96, 97, 104, 105–6, 107t, 165; Agripino, 105; Alejandro, 105, 165; Cirilo (died 2020), 67, 105, 144; Eduardo, 105; Francisco, 64, 105; Fulgencia, 96, 104; Gregorio Pascual Muñoz, 64, 105, 112, 194; Jenny, 193; Jose (Ponciano) Domingo, 105, 119, 146, 165; as maternal name, 161; Maximina, 105; Noe, 105; Pedro (born ~1905), 165; Roberto, 144; Salustia, 105; Toribio Pascual Muñoz, 14, 26, 56, 64, 67, 68, 104, 105, 108, 112, 115, 120, 165, 193; as vendors, 105, 165
peasant(ry), peasants, 35, 58, 119, 125, 126; community, 125; defined, 125–26; the duplex nature of, 125–26; fate of, 125; federation, 60;

indigenous, 42. *See also campesino(s)*; Closed Corporate Peasant Community
Pedro (family), 97; Felix, 80
Pentecostal (congregation), 175. *See also* religion
pequeñas propiedades, 123. *See also propiedad*
perspective(s), 4, 5, 35, 51, 127, 166; contradictory/inconsistent/opposing, 6, 7, 43, 46; contrasting, 6, 22, 31, 43, 101; discrepancies, 6; diverse/different, 6, 8, 10, 44, 127–28, 166, 173–75; going beyond emic and etic, 6–7; holistic, 4; of local people, 51; of migrants, 46; non-Western people, 6; one-sided, 6; of outsider observer(s), xi, 44; realist, 4. *See also* duplexity; emic/etic
peon. *See* day laborer
period(s) or cohort(s), 13, 26, 36, 52, 53, 55, 58, 59, 60, 62, 70, 71, 74, 90, 112, 117, 124, 162, 167, 168, 169t, 169, 171, 180; NAFTA period, 99; pre-revolutionary, 55, 118
physics, 5; quantum, 7
Pilcaya (town in Guerrero), 146
police(men), 13, 110, 112, 110, 112, 113; complex, 8; harassment, 65
political: affiliation, 118; clashes, 73; decline in involvement, 118; dichotomous variable [POL2], 181; elite, 42; field, 71, 109; goals, 33; influence, 25, 26; mobilization, 11; movement, 56; as a nominal variable [POL1], 180; orientation, 154; parties, 72, 118; posts, x, 11, 171; project, 34; prominence, 60; rival factions, 177; situation to be held in account, 15; spaces, 42; status quo, 66; system (consolidation/ securing of), 59, 60; unrest, 56
politics, 14, 37, 62, 102; declining involvement, 118; involvement in, xi, 173; involvement of migrants in, 173; local level, xi; national, 118; of recognition, 43; state politics, 51
post(s), 112, 113; in *comisaría*, 67; comparisons of, 111; expectations, 111; at federal level, 26; government, 26, 38; influential, 26; occupants paid an honorarium, 109; occupying important posts, 109; leaders holding, 117–18; level of prestige of and commitment to, 111; local (not part of cargo system), 117; more important, 111; more onerous, 110; political, x, 11, 171; public, 66, 111, 170; religious, 110, 113; term of office, 111; as variable (PSTS), 117, 164; variations in level of prestige, 111. *See* government

preparatoria (high school, preparatory). *See* school(ing)
PRI. *See* Partido Revolucionario Institutional
priest(s), xi, 57, 63, 64, 94, 95, 101, 105, 110, 132, 165; in jail, 63–64. *See also* Bravo, Benigno; Guerrero, Francisco; Pascual, Eduardo
primaria (elementary school): including attendance at, xiii, 28, 68, 151, 163; not going to *primaria*, 157. *See also* school(ing)
professional(s), x, xii, 38, 41, 104; 115, 159, 165, 177; class status of, 5; indigenous/native, 5, 6, 42, 71, 129; speaking on behalf of indigenous people, 41
plow(ing), 8, 9, 25, 67, 106, 121, 124, 127; plow animal, 170
public affairs/domain/realm, xii, 26, 86, 110
Purépecha(s), 35, 46
Procampo, Progresa, Progresa (government programs), 116
propiedad (private property): *de Pedro Santiago*, 55, 121, 122; larger, 121, 124. *See also pequeñas propiedades*
Protestant, 132; charismatic, 128. *See also* religion
pseudonyms, xii
Pueblos Nahuas del Alto Balsas, Consejo de (CPNAB), political leaders of, 23, 23, 71
Puerto Peñasco (city in Sonora), 25, 26, 112, 138, 140, 141, 142, 162, 163
Puerto Vallarta (city in Jalisco), 83, 114, 137, 139, 142, 143
Puerto Escondido (town in Oaxaca), 87

quantitative vs. qualitative, 4; data, 15, 16; quantification, 172; research techniques, 12; study, 4
Quetzala de Progreso (town in Guerrero), 61

race/racism, 6, 33–34; "bronze race," 37; categories, 35; "cosmic race," 34; "Indian race," 39; layering, 8; mixture, 34, 36; "racial discourse of *mestizaje*," 34; racial/ethnic inequalities, 33, 34, 42; "racial geography," 33; racialized groups, 6; racialized violence, 33; racially divided labor force, 174; racial privileges, 43; racism against indigenous people, 33, 34, 43
Ramírez Castañeda, Isabel (archeologist), 38
Ramírez (family), 97, 107t, 108; Carmelo Ramírez Felipe, 162; Leobardo, 194; Rosalba, 142

Ramón (family), 97, 139
rancho, ranchero(s), 4, 55, 122; Spanish-speaking, 4. *See also* cattle
rape, 57, 95
rebellion, 56. *See also* resistance
reciprocity: of anthropological fieldwork, 15; of economy of indigenous community, 44; as a form of moral symbolism, 132
reemplazo (replacement/substitute), working as, 139. *See also* substitute
refugees, 34, 44, 45
regidor, 110. *See also comisaría*
Registro Agrario (Office of Land Reform Records), 12, 123
relatives, x, 96, 152, 163; close, 100, 112, 138, 150, 153; disputes among, 101; as network for babysitting, 157; sending money to, 92. *See also* family; kinship
religion, religious, 37, 130, 131; as cluster in conflict with ethnic cluster, 10; conversion, 85, 132; in conflict in some towns, 22, 63, 67; diverse perspective on, 127; as field, 8, 9, 11, 170, 175. *See also* charismatic; Christianity; conversion; evangelical; Roman Catholic; Pentecostal; Protestant
relocation, 3, 52, 71; cost of, 160. *See also* migration
remittances, 12, 46, 71, 80, 82, 86, 120, 162, 164; decline in, 146
rent(al): accommodations, 68, 81, 138, 142, 143, 144, 145, 152, 153; of land, 54, 55, 56, 58, 67, 70, 75, 116, 123, 138, 139, 163; of plow animals, 9, 25, 106, 123; pumps for irrigation, 75; "renting oneself out" (*se alguilan*), 88; "renting" someone to make one's meals (*la alquila*), 98; a stall (to sell), 142; vehicles, 22
research, ix, x, xi; archival, x, xii, 119, 172; ethical dilemmas, xii; ethnographic, ix; grants, 14; limitations, 16; multi-sited, ix, 12; need for institutional affiliation, xii; project, ix, x*n*3, 16; techniques (diverse), ix, 4, 177; trajectory and logistic, 13–15; use of tape-recorder, 126. *See also* emic/etic; fieldwork; informants; methods (quantitative and qualitative); variables
residence: postmarital, 95; principal, 103; status, 174
resistance, 42; "nucleus of resistance," 38. *See also* rebellion

revolution. *See* Mexican Revolution
Reynosa (city in Tamaulipas), 146
riiko(s), 25, 55–56, 60–61, 66, 87, 14, 106, 160, 162, 168, 169, 171, 176; claiming to be poor, 88; clusters with, 102–4; decline in number of, 108; defined, 9; people descended from, 106, 107*t*, 168, 177; pre-revolutionary, 168; as a minority within the family clusters to which they belong, 104. *See also* class; layering
Rios (family), 97, 114; as maternal surname, 104
rodeo. *See jaripeo*
Rodríguez1, 97, 107*t*, 108; Alfonso, 113
Rodríguez2, 97
Rojas (family), 97, 108*t*, 161
Román (family), 97; Juana, 103; as maternal surname, 104
Roman Catholic(ism), Catholics, 10, 70, 101, 132, 177; charismatic movement, 70; Catholic education, 63; replacing Latin with Spanish, 67; resemblance to Nahua religion, 131. *See also* church (Catholic)
Rufino (family), 97
rural, rurality, xi, 6, 13, 37, 40, 47, 67, 177; American rural destinations, 47, 68; indigenous communities in, 35; proletariat, 125; research in, 31; Rural Development Office in Tepecuacuilco, 13

Sabana Grande (small town in Guerrero), 67
Sacramento, 139, 149, 151, 152, 162; advantages of, 162; author's stay in, 14, 193; indígenas in, 37; migrants in, 151, 152
sacristan (*sacristán*), 110, 111, 149
saint(s), *santos*, 6, 63, 67, 101, 128, 129, 130; capricious, 12; cult of, 127, 131–32; with dominion over water, 130; favorite, 92; interaction with, 92; merciful but moody, 132; patron, 113; powerful, 101; rich, 128; turning one's back on, 67
salesmen (travelling), 42
salt trade, 60–61, 62; forbidden, then renewed, 61. *See also* commerce; trade
Salvador (family), 14, 97, 103, 106, 107*t*, 108, 114; Faustino, 112; Florentino, 194; Juana Salvador Morales, 14, 65, 67, 71, 74, 75, 84, 87, 89, 94, 99–101, 106, 113, 116, 120, 121, 128, 137, 141–43, 149, 156, 161, 179, 193; Manuel, 62, 103; Marcelo, 103, 104, 112; as maternal surname, 162; Petra, 104; Santos, 103, 139; Wenceslao, 80

San Agustin Oapan (town), 22, 23, 24*f*, 37, 53, 61, 63, 65, 66, 102, 121, 123, 128, 133, 139; and with Ahuehuepan, 63; as collection point for tribute, 52; dispute with Tetelcingo, 54; as former seat of parish, 67
San Agustin Ostotipan (town), 24*f*, 26
San Blas (town), 67, 137, 138, 139
San Diego (town and area), 150, 152; migrants in, 152
Sandstrom, Alan and Pamela, 12, 130*n*1, 132, 133
San Felipe (city in Baja California), 138, 142
San Francisco del Rincón (Guanajuato), 146
San Francisco Zumatlán (town), 24*f*, 138, 146*n*3
San José de Cabo (city), 142. *See also* Los Cabos
San Juan Tetelcingo, x, 22, 23, 33, 52, 53, 55, 102, 140, 141, 143, 144, 165; with Ahuelicán, 53, 54; dispute with Oapan, 54. *See also* Tetelcingo dam
San Lucas / Saint Luke the Evangelist, 14, 128, 131, 133
San Marcos (town in California), 70, 137, 152; author's stay in, 137; migrants in, 152
San Marcos Oacacingo (town in Guerrero), 24*f*, 53
San Miguel de Allende (city in Guanajuato), 145
San Miguel Tecuicuipan (town), 58, 63, 71, 133
San Patricio. *See* Melaque
Santiago (family), 97, 108; as maternal surname, 97; Pedro Santiago Margaro, 55–56, 66, 97, 108, 121, 122, 123, 161. *See also* land tenure
school(s), schooling, 7, 8, 11, 13, 21, 24, 40, 41, 43, 57, 58, 63, 66, 67–68, 79, 84, 90, 99, 106, 110, 113, 116, 117, 129, 133, 143, 146, 155, 156, 157, 158, 159, 161, 162, 163, 164, 170, 170*n*2, 171, 181; bilingual, 28, 68; closing of, 64, 72, 116; curriculum, 129; dropping / not finishing / quitting schooling, 68, 84, 161, 173; director, 104; inspector, 22; *internado*, 67, 88; International School of American Archaeology and Ethnology (precursor of School of Anthropology and History), 38; introduction of, 61, 116; *licenciatura*/*preparatoria*, 163–64; middle school, 156; not attending, 67, 92, 128, 130, 161; one-room, 61; private school, 64, 151; publicly funded, 63; relationship to layering and to schooling, 172; state school(s), 16, 116; sewing, 151; upgrading, 105; technical, 67, 161. *See also* education; *primaria*; *secundaria*

schoolteachers. *See* teacher
Seattle (city in Washington state), 16; migrants in, 152
Sebastian (family), 97; Miguel, 164; Pascual Sebastian Antonio, 164
secundaria (secondary school, high school), 74, 91, 157, 171, 177; graduates from, 144, 150; *telesecundaria*, 72. *See also* school, education
sempoalxoochitl (flowers), 128. *See also* Day of the Dead
separation (of couples), 90, 98, 99, 161, 162. *See also* marriage: breakup
settlements, 51, 52; network of, 174; nucleated, 52. *See also specific places by name*
Sex: as variable for gender [SEX], 170, 181; -classes, 10; of siblings (imbalanced), 97
sexist, sexism, 6; attitudes, 68; comments, 21
sexual: connotation of riddles, 129; division of labor, 98; orientation, 8
sibling(s) (i.e. brother and sister), 99; close ties with, 22; exchange, 97, 98*f*; half, 100, 163; imbalance in sex of, 97; Nahua words for, 100; opposite sex of step-, 97; US-born, 28
sick(ness). *See* illness
Sinaloa (state), 139
Smith, Robert Courtney, 173, 174
social space: multidimensional, 7, 175; of postmodernism, 147; transnational, 47
Spanish, 35; adoption of Spanish changing social identity, 153; conquest/rule, xiii, 22, 51–53; knowing no Spanish, 137; learning Spanish in Mexico City, 63; loanwords, 130; outsiders adopting a Spanish name, 152; perfecting author's, xi, 28; single Spanish-speaking nation as goal, 38; Spanish-speaking Ladino elite, 41; Spanish-speaking town(s), 8, 34; speaking a mish-mash of Spanish and English or Nahuatl and Spanish, 153; speaking more Nahuatl than Spanish, 38; speaking more Spanish than English, 3; surnames (*apellidos*), 96; teacher speaking only, 63
Schryer, Frans: background, x–xi; relationship to people, x; as outsider, xi
Simmel George (scholar), 4
social scientist(s), 43, 177
social space, 174; multidimensional, 175; transnational, 47
Sonora (state), 140, 146, 162, 163

spatial, 147; dimensions, 181; dispersal, 176; mobility, 171; of social interaction, 5
sport(s): fishing, 140; team(s), 158
state, separation of church and, 105, 109. *See also* government (state)
statistics, statistical analysis. *See* research techniques
store(s), 25, 64, 85, 87, 88, 103, 139, 144; bought, 65, 102; closure of, 75; in people's homes, 80, 164; jobs in, 138; looted, 58; that sell clothes, 103; variety, 144
struggles. *See* conflict(s)
sujetos (subordinate towns), 52
suplente. See comisario
surnames (*apellidos*), 104; forgotten maternal surnames, 97; having same maternal and paternal, xiii, 97; local, xii; losing paternal surname, 47; maternal, xii*n4*, 47; origin of, 96–97; paternal, xii*n4*; surnames of children reversed, 97; Spanish, 96; spelling of, xiii; stigmatized, 96; that did not survive, 97; of unwed mother, 96; without Santiago as, 108; women not assigned, 96
survey(s), 12, 89, 126; author's findings (data), 93, 98, 99, 106, 123; household, 12, 14; statistical analysis of, 172. *See also* census
susto (fright), 130

talents, 7, 170; artistic, 175; diverse, 164; musical, 106, 175; no special, 106; special (TALT2), 172
tamales, 79. *See also* tortillas
Tamaulipas (state), 144, 145, 146
Tampico (city), 16, 26, 89, 98, 137, 143, 144, 144*n1*, 145
Taxco, 25, 26, 65, 145
teachers, xii, 11, 14, 20, 21, 22, 40, 41, 44, 63, 66, 68, 73, 84, 85, 87, 88, 91, 104, 106, 115, 156, 165; bilingual, 117; of English, 105; government-appointed, 44; of Nahuatl, 14; outside, 166; teachers' college, 73
Tecuiciapan. *See* San Miguel Tecuiciapan
Tekiloomah (land), 63
Telcel, 163
tenant(s), 53, 55, 56, 61, 63. *See also* rent
Tenochtitlan (now Mexico City), 35, 146
Tepecua(cuilco) (town), 24*f*, 63, 105
Tepeyewaahle (mountain), 113
Tepic (city in Nayarit), 146

terrenos de común repartimiento. See land
Tetelcingo (town). *See* San Juan Tetelcingo
Tetelcingo dam, x, xi, 8, 23, 33; cancellation of construction of, 33; movement to stop construction of, 26, 71, 176
Texas, x, 83, 139, 149, 151, 152, 165, 178. *See also* Houston
Ticuani (town), 173–74
tio ("uncle"), broader meaning of the word, 100
tiopan. See church
títulos primordiales. See land tenure
Tlakaltech/San Agustin (barrio), 114, 181. *See also* Ahuehuepan
tlakpaikniiwtle (stepsibling), 100
tlakpamontle (husband of stepdaughter), 100
Tlapa de Comonfort (government center), 40
Tlalpitsahko/San Miguel (barrio), 114. *See also* Ahuehuepan
tlamachilistle, 130, 131
Tlatsintlan/San Juan (barrio), 114. *See also* Ahuehuepan
Tlaxcala (state), 25, 46
Todos Santos. See Day of the Dead
Tomás (family), 97; as maternal surname, 102, 138, 148, 155; Santiago, 57; Victor, 54, 87, 138
Tonaantsin (our Lady/*Virgen* of Guadalupe), 128, 131
Tonalapa (del Sur), 24f, 37, 61, 62, 70, 145. *See also* Colonia El Progeso
toonal, 130, 131. *See also aalmah; yoohloh*
Toribio, as family, 96
tortillas, 9, 57, 59, 65, 79, 80, 108, 114, 119, 156. *See also* tamales
tourists, tourism, decline in, 39, 46, 65, 92, 138, 139, 140, 141, 143, 144, 145, 163, 177; tourist season, 140
town(s). *See specific communities or villages by name*
trade (employment). *See* occupation
trade/trader (*viajero*), 103, 104; deficits, 68; itinerant, 61. *See also* commerce; NAFTA; salt trade; wholesaler
traditional practices, 3
transborder: communities, 173; families, 161–66. *See also* border
transnational(ism), xiv, 3, 173, 174, 175; agribusiness, 174; communities, 174; connection with assimilation, 173; corporations/organizations, 42, 174; different perspectives on, 173–75; and

indigeneity, 175; life, 173; social field, 175; and social space, 47; vs. national, 175; weak forms of, 174
transportation: of bodies of people who died in the US, 145n2; of musicians, 111; of nostalgia food, 173
trilingualism, 157. *See also* bilingual(ism)
Trique(s), 46
truck. *See* vehicle

UNAM (National Autonomous University of Mexico), x, xii
union (labor), xiii, 60
United States (US, USA), 45, 71, 116, 133, 175, 176, 178, 179; aspiring to work in, 88; comparisons with Mexico, 157; deported from, 72; people who died in, 145n2; those who have never been in, 82; US-born children, 177; working in, 89, 139, 144, 149–153. *See also* North American Free Trade Agreement (NAFTA)
university (*universidad*), xi, xiii, 14, 38, 170; indigenous people with degrees, 175; programs, 42; undergraduate students, ix; University of Minnesota, 41. *See also* Benemérita Universidad; education; school; UNAM

vaqueros. See cattle ranchers
variables, 118, 167, 170; comparison of, 13; complementary, 5; dichotomous, 181; mutually reinforcing, 10; nominal, interval, and ordinal, 180–81. *See also* research (techniques)
vehicle(s), 13, 25, 73, 79, 84, 85, 89, 106, 112; car, 157; four-wheel drive, 124; losing though theft, 73; truck (*camioneta*/pickup), 84, 91, 108, 145, 164. *See also* accident; cattle: truck; collision
vendor(s), vending, ix, 10, 13, 25, 26, 46, 65, 66, 67, 68, 69, 72, 73, 75, 79, 82, 83, 87, 89, 90, 94, 104, 105, 112, 125, 126, 132, 137, 138, 139, 140, 141, 143, 144–45, 146, 149, 160, 162, 165, 171, 178; artisan-vendors, 10, 69; beach, 7, 11, 126, 147, 160; craft, 15, 25, 177; full-time, 66; street, 25; who have never been, 83; who stopped growing maize, 119; working the land, 87, 88. *See also* commerce; trade/trader
viajero. See trade/trader
Vicente Guerrero (name of school). *See* school(ing) (bilingual)
view(point), opinion, 22, 60, 111, 154, 180

village(s). *See specific communities or towns by name*
Villalba (as maternal surname), 68
Villalba1 (family), 97, 106, 107t, 114
Villalba2 (family), xiii; José, 60
Virgen de Guadalupe. See Tonaantsin

wedding (*boda*), 21, 91, 95, 153, 153–54, 158; cost of, 95, 150; described, 95–96
Weei Aatlahko (place in Ahuehuepan), 124
wholesaler, 25, 66, 68, 72, 103, 104, 108, 142, 145, 147, 165, 170, 171. *See also* commerce; trade
wife, 22, 61, 66, 73, 81, 83, 88, 89, 90, 94, 100, 105, 111, 112, 120, 129, 139, 143, 149, 151, 162, 163, 164, 193; being left behind, 129, 140, 142, 144; first, 104, 128; hit/whipped, 90; her husband living with her parents, 93; obeying mother-in-law, 96; taken by force by another man, 58; from another town, then returning, 89; wife's land, 22, 123, 162. *See also* woman
woman/women: archeologist, 38; being ignored in *comisaría*, 86; being told her place is in the kitchen, 21; coyote, 148; car registered in her name, 84; doing work on posts assigned to husbands, 117; giving up on a husband, 99; holding religious posts, 113, 170; indigenous, 68; looking after sick mother, 63; as maids, 64; more likely to marry man from another barrio, 114; as only member of school committee, 113; promoting idea of kinder, 67; property claimed, 66; rarely leaving abusive husband, 90; no stigma on drinking, 85; strong-willed, 86; struck with machete by husband, 90; suffering consequences of separation, 90; with a rich husband, 212; working in the fields, 68, 90, 102. *See also* girls; wife
work(er), labor(er): in agriculture, 45, 47, 62, 63, 64, 71, 74, 87, 88, 99; in American city, 25, 26, 34, 46, 47, 70, 88, 89, 139, 144, 148, 149–53; in assembly plants (*maquiladores*), 39; capitalist division, 174; as clerical, 146; on commission, 88; comparison of workers, 153; conditions, 153; in construction projects, 146; control over allocation of, 153; as day laborer/maids/helpers/hired hands/*peon*/servant, 26, 65, 74, 87, 94; exerting pressure on co-workers, 46; de facto guest worker program, 45; in government bureaucracy, 38; with gunpowder, 57; in health care sector, 61, 105; in kitchens, 74; migrant, 25, 26, 46, 92, 105; never working the land, 74; on one's own, 87; part-time, 75; permit, 149; in restaurants, 75, 149; on road projects, 88; as sales clerk, 143; as security guard, 142; service sector, 26; sexual division, 98; as tenant, 61; undocumented, without a permit, 45, 149, 157, 177; in variety stores, 144; as vendor, 89; volunteer, 92; in yards, 88. *See also* job(s)
world view, cosmovision, 12, 131, 133, 178; adoption of new, 133; different, 12, 130, 133; emergence of alternative, 133; Nahua, 127, 130, 132; rupturing of, 133; traditional, 7, 133; transformation of, 3, 133, 177
worship(per), worshipping, 86, 131, 141, 175. *See also* religion

Xalitla (town), xiii, 13, 22, 24f, 64, 66, 67, 68, 74, 132; free clinic in, 85; people from or moving to, 26, 58; professionals from, 71; technical school in, 161

yoohloh, 130, 131. *See also aalmah; toonal*
young couples, 94, 148, 164, 193; going back and forth across border, 21, 143
young men (brothers, nephews, sons) 21, 74, 89, 91, 95, 164; abusive, 90; deported, 141, 157–78; dying in US, 150; going back and forth across border, 74, 143, 163; not married, 113, 143; literacy of, 84; as suitor(s), 11, 93. *See also* men
young people, 21, 25, 28, 72, 74, 80, 92, 129, 155, 156, 176; aspiring to cross border, 88; dying in US, 163; going back and forth to US, 159; not giving up hope, 150; not growing maize, 84; not speaking Nahuatl, 157
young women (daughters, sisters), 74, 101, 120, 142; and their stories, 156
Yucatán peninsula, 47, 137, 144. *See also* Cancun
yunta (yoke), 9, 121. *See also* oxen

Zacatecas (state and city), 2, 173
Zapotecs, 46
Zitlala (township in Guerrero), 68

www.ingramcontent.com/pod-product-compliance
Lightning Source LLC
Chambersburg PA
CBHW020028040426
42333CB00039B/569